D0913930

APR 03 200

APR 2 8 2005

JAN 0 2 2007

Leroy Ostransky is Professor of Music and Composer-in-Residence at the University of Puget Sound. He has published over fifty musical compositions, and his UNDERSTANDING JAZZ and THE ANATOMY OF JAZZ are standard texts in the field. He was chosen by *People Magazine* as one of America's twelve outstanding university professors.

Leroy Ostransky

JAZZ CITY

THE IMPACT OF OUR CITIES ON THE DEVELOPMENT OF JAZZ

A SPECTRUM BOOK

Prentice-Hall, Inc., *Englewood Cliffs, New Jersey 07632*

Library of Congress Cataloging in Publication Data

Ostransky, Leroy.
   Jazz city.

   (A Spectrum Book)
   Bibliography: p.
   Discography: p.
   Includes index.
      1. Jazz music—United States.   2. Cities and towns—
United States.   I. Title.
ML3561.J3084   785.4′2′0973   78-18492
ISBN 0-13-509380-5
ISBN 0-13-509372-4 pbk.

A Spectrum Book

10   9   8   7   6   5   4   3   2   1

Printed in the United States of America

Prentice-Hall International, Inc., *London*
Prentice-Hall of Australia Pty. Limited, *Sydney*
Prentice-Hall of Canada, Ltd., *Toronto*
Prentice-Hall of India Private Limited, *New Delhi*
Prentice-Hall of Japan, Inc., *Tokyo*
Prentice-Hall of Southeast Asia Pte. Ltd., *Singapore*
Whitehall Books Limited, *Wellington, New Zealand*

For Natalie

CONTENTS

Chapter 10

PREFACE

The history of jazz may be studied through the characteristic styles of its major periods, the development of significant jazz performers, "white" jazz versus "black" jazz, or through the development of regional styles—jazz as played in New Orleans, say, or in New York. Jazz may be studied in other ways, of course: the influence of politics on jazz, the effects of slavery, Prohibition, the effects of other economic and social conditions, as well as the influence of radio, records, the movies, the popular press, and so on.

This book is not a study of the technical aspects of early jazz; these have already been extensively surveyed in *The Anatomy of Jazz* and in Gunther Schuller's seminal study *Early Jazz*. It is rather an introduction to those nontechnical aspects of jazz as they developed in New Orleans, Chicago, Kansas City, and New York. That these cities each in its time was America's major jazz center is a certainty. *Why* these cities provided incredibly fertile ground for the development of jazz and other cities did not is less certain. The point I am trying to make is that jazz is a phenomenon that is intricately bound to the history of America and intimately connected with the lives of large groups of Americans.

In the past, a number of jazz historians have staked their claim to the major jazz cities, and jazz history owes a debt to such men as Al Rose and Martin Williams for their work on New Orleans; Richard Hadlock and John Steiner for their work on Chicago; Ross Russell and Frank Driggs for their work on Kansas City; and

Samuel B. Charters and Leonard Kunstadt for their work on New York. My own work differs from the work of these men in at least one significant way: I have tried to keep the jazz and nonjazz aspects clearly separated. The early history of cities, for example, is often important in showing the spirit in which a particular city was formed. This is not to say that such a spirit is necessarily a "jazz" spirit; it may be a "frontier" spirit, or one of laissez-faire, or simply one of great lawlessness. My aim is to show what each city—or at least its "jazz district"—was like at its beginning, during its slow or rapid development, and what each city was like when it experienced its earliest jazz stirrings. It is my hope that readers will see the sections dealing with each city's nonjazz history as necessary background and introduction to those sections dealing with the men and circumstances of jazz.

Jazz can happen anywhere. For jazz to flourish, however, special conditions are required, and these conditions are taken up one at a time in the chapters on the respective cities. It will be worthwhile to remember that New Orleans, Chicago, Kansas City, and New York were in their time America's major transport cities, and transport cities have a special set of characteristics. Jazz did not develop in a vacuum. As a unique American phenomenon, it grew according to its surrounding conditions, environment, and spirit. A special combination of historical events and conditions—social, political, economic, military—*permitted* jazz to flourish in four great jazz centers.

I trust the reader will recognize how these nonjazz activities contributed not only to the general atmosphere of the cities, but to the rise of jazz, and—above all—to recognize that the rise of these activities and the simultaneous rise of jazz were not a coincidence.

ACKNOWLEDGMENTS

I wish to thank W. Desmond Taylor, Director of the Library at the University of Puget Sound, for his helpful suggestions, special interest, and cooperation; Daniel Bischel, public services librarian, for his help with the New Orleans books; Raimund E. Matthis, technical services librarian, for his effort in locating hard-to-come-by out of print material; Bradley F. Millard, reference librarian, for his supply of government references; and Raymond Serebrin, assistant reference librarian, for his help with the New York items.

I wish to express my appreciation to Margaret Wilson for her help in typing early chapters, and to Robin Stovall for her part in compiling the bibliography.

I am indebted to Shifra Stein of the Kansas City Star for her cooperation and the news clippings she sent to me. I also wish to thank Ken Wiley for listening to me at great length, and for making a number of suggestions leading to a closer look at several New Orleans items.

Finally, I wish to thank Lester Baskin for his comments and encouragement after reading the first draft of the Chicago chapters.

I wish to express acknowledgment and thanks to the publishers and authors who have granted permission to use the following:

Excerpts from *A History of Jazz in America*, by Barry Ulanov. Copyright 1950, 1951, 1952 by Barry Ulanov. Reprinted by permission of The Viking Press Inc.

Scattered excerpts are reprinted with permission of Macmillan Publishing Co., Inc. from *Jazz Panorama*, by Martin Williams (editor). © Jazz Review, Inc., 1962.

Excerpts from *Big Bill of Chicago*, by Lloyd Wendt and Herman Kogan are used by permission of The Bobbs-Merrill Company, Inc. Copyright 1953 by The Bobbs-Merrill Company, Inc.

EARLY NEW ORLEANS: THE MOST WICKED CITY

1

In its early years, jazz required the hands of black men, so to speak, to make it grow. In the nineteenth century, many black musicians practiced their trade in "sporting houses," honky-tonks, gambling joints, dance halls, and other regions where the devil worked; there, the money came easier than from "screwin' " cotton, and excitement and pleasure were in the air. New Orleans was exceptional in this regard; it was the most exciting and wicked city in the South, perhaps in the world—one nineteenth-century wit called Shanghai the New Orleans of the Orient. In its time, the Crescent City had lifted her skirts for Spaniards, Frenchmen, Irishmen, Germans, Italians, and Americans, as well as black and white desperadoes, black and white hustlers, and the ambiguous caste who called themselves Creoles of color.

The spirit of New Orleans in the eighteenth and nineteenth centuries grew in part out of the vast sums of money and goods readily available to corrupt political leaders and the growing New Orleans underworld—an underworld drawn from all continents. The New Orleans spirit was one of permissiveness and noninterference: anything goes. It tolerated with impartiality small-time hustlers and high crimes, self-serving royal governors and fifty-cent whores. New Orleans has been called the cradle of jazz—an apt if not felicitous expression. It is our intention to record briefly whatever seems pertinent to the birth of jazz, for a broader understanding of the nature of jazz. To this end, we expect to move about freely in the centuries of the prehistory of jazz, discussing the origins of people and places and the beginnings of what we will call the jazz spirit. We will show direct jazz connections with the past when we can, and indirect ones only when the digression promises to be illuminating. It seems appropriate to begin with the Mississippi Bubble, an eighteenth-century confidence game offering Louisiana (New Orleans especially) as the bait—a seriocomical venture that helped to establish New Orleans's early *esprit* and rake-hell qualities.

In 1717 John Law, a Scotsman with powerful French connections, persuaded the government of France to grant him the right to sell shares of stock in the French-owned swamps of Louisiana. A profit-sharing scheme was agreed upon, and Law formed his Company of the West. Shortly after (perhaps as an ingratiating gesture) he suggested to the French regent Louis Philippe, the duc d'Orléans, the establishment of a city to be called Nouvelle-Orléans. The duke accepted Law's suggestion, and a year later French workers and soldiers began clearing the site for what would soon be the most important city in the French colony.

When the explorer La Salle came down the Mississippi from Canada to the Gulf of Mexico in 1682, he had claimed the entire valley in the name of Louis XIV and named it Louisiana in his honor. The sieur d'Iberville, a French-Canadian officer in the king's navy, was then charged with creating a French settlement in the lower Mississippi valley. Later, Iberville and his younger brother the sieur de Bienville, with four shiploads of soldiers, colonists, and supplies, entered the mouth of the Mississippi from the Gulf of Mexico and established Old Biloxi. Eventually the settlement was moved to Mobile Bay, and Bienville became its leader—lieutenant of the king in Louisiana and governor of the colony.

After ten years of hardship, famine, benign neglect, and apparent royal indifference to the colony's plight, Bienville learned that the king had given exclusive control of Louisiana's commercial activities to Antoine Crozat, a French merchant with apparently unlimited backing and wealth. Bienville also learned that Crozat had replaced him with a new colonial governor, Antoine de la Mothe Cadillac (who earlier had founded Detroit). It then took five years of little profit and greater loss, of constant bickering over questionable investments and a futile search for gold, silver, and pearls, before Crozat was ready to give up his monopoly and his royal franchise and return the control of the colony to the duke's newest, trusted admirers, John Law and company. Crozat gave Cadillac his notice and John Law returned Bienville to his old post with the new title of commandant-general.

Law now held the sole right to work the province for the next twenty-five years, and he promised all those who would buy stock in his Company of the West the privilege of owning land abounding in gold and silver and waters crowded with pearl-bearing oysters. All that was needed were good men and women to colonize this new and glorious land and in no time become rich beyond their Old World dreams. Law promised a grand new adventure in a land of inexhaustible treasure, and the response to his promotional material (considering how few facts there were to act upon) was bizarre. Frenchmen waited their turn, money in hand, begging Law to take their money and make them rich. At the outset, investors and speculators abounded, but not many were anxious to leave France for the colony. The government pitched in by rounding up the dregs of French society and forcibly shipping them to Louisiana. As shipload after shipload of Parisian undesirables arrived in port, Bienville was appalled, and finally frightened. He notified the regent that he could not defend New Orleans (the regent's namesake, we may recall) with "a band of deserters, smugglers and scoundrels, who are all ready not only to abandon you but also to turn against you." Shortly thereafter, the regent decreed that criminals would no longer be shipped to the colony. Meanwhile, John Law's agents and aggressive salesmen had turned to Germany, where they were able to persuade a considerable number of Germans to leave their ancestral homes for a life on the Mississippi (estimates range from 10,000 by German historians down to 2,600 by French historians).[1]

Whatever their true number, the newly arrived immigrants did not find gold, silver, and pearls. What they did find were swamps, "miasma," heavy fogs, dampness everywhere, alternating extremes of heat and cold, and limitless swarms of mosquitoes. And waiting on shore to greet the newcomers were likely to be honest settlers, disaffected soldiers, stoic Indian squaws, and a ripe assortment of former inmates of French hospitals, prisons, and brothels. (In 1721, the Company of the West found it necessary to deliver to Louisiana a bevy of prostitutes from La Salpêtrière, a house of correction in Paris.) In short, the ingredients were being gathered in for the development of the New World's most wicked city.

The construction of the original city of New Orleans, as approved by the Company of the West, was a rather modest undertaking. Adrien de Pauger, assistant engineer to the colony, laid out eleven blocks along a 4,000-foot crescent on the Mississippi, then went back 1,800 feet from the river to lay out six blocks, and divided the whole into roughly 300-foot squares. Deep ditches, usually water-filled and disease-breeding, surrounded the squares. Bienville, however, saw the new city, the new Orléans, as being a noble achievement, and he named a number of the city's streets accordingly: Bourbon, Conti, Chartres, Orléans, Royale, Toulouse, Ste. Ann, St. Philippe, and, of course, St. Louis; and the street with the governor's mansion, where he would live, he called, forthrightly, Bienville.

The population in 1721 included 145 men, 65 women, 38 children, 39 white servants, 172 black slaves, and 21 Indian slaves, for a total count of 480.[2] Another head count, a year later, showed "72 civilians, 44 soldiers, 11 officers, 22 ship captains and sailors, 28 European laborers, 177 Negro slaves, and 22 Indians. Sixty-five of the civilians, officers and ship captains were married, and there were 38 children."[3] An official count taken in 1726 showed a population of 880, of which 65 were servants and 129 slaves; the census also included the names and addresses of New Orleans inhabitants: Chesseau the *cannonier* on St. Philippe Street, for example; and Michel Brosset the surgeon on Bourbon Street; and the aristocratic François Philippe de Marigny de Mandeville, his wife, and two children on Chartres Street.

It took John Law's twenty-five-year royal franchise (starting in 1717) about three years to run its course. The "Mississippi Bubble" (as it came to be known) burst in December 1720, with a report heard in France, Germany, and England. By now it was clearly established that Louisiana's plethora of frogs, snakes, and alligators was not an acceptable substitute for gold, silver, and pearls, and

John Law and his Company of the West were deposed by the government. Bienville, however, was permitted to carry on with his attempts to lift New Orleans out of the surrounding swamps and marshes.

In the spring of 1743, when he took what was to be his permanent leave of the colony, Bienville was replaced by Pierre Rigaut, the marquis de Vaudreuil, a nobleman who would have made a suitable governor of Storyville, New Orleans's red-light district of the late 1890s. Bienville handed over to the marquis a community already resembling a city: about 2,000 inhabitants, including 300 soldiers and 300 Negroes (presumably free men of color as well as slaves). The marquis showed his adaptive qualities from the start. Relatively unconcerned with such prosaic city problems as housing, employment, and proper governance, he reigned with lavish governmental show and splendor. With the urging of his wife, the marchioness, and the support of the aristocratic officers with whom he had surrounded himself, he created a sort of Versailles in the swamp. Velvet, lace, and gold braid were the order of the day; *bals de masque* could be turned into state occasions; and pomp became at least as important as the city's sanitation problem. New Orleans had become, in W. J. Cash's phrase, "a pageant of dandies and coxcombs."[4]

The marquis as dandy, however, is not the fully realized characterization. His velvet glove covered an iron fist, and he governed New Orleans in a manner that would affect its social spirit through the nineteenth century. He was responsible for an era of dishonesty, debauchery, rampant nepotism, and straightforward thievery. He encouraged drunkenness among his troops (the city's only licensed liquor shop was his), and he and the marchioness held virtual control over the sale of medicine and drugs to the sick. The marquis's permissiveness and his tolerance for immorality of every sort became common knowledge, and the city grew to be irresistibly attractive to those of base motives. Historian Herbert Asbury summed it up when he said:

The thieves, vagabonds, and prostitutes who had been sent to the New World by the Mississippi Company and the French government still formed, if not a majority, at least a large and disturbing minority of Louisiana's inhabitants.[5]

With the onset in Europe of the Seven Years' War (1756–63), gloom descended on Louisiana and its capital city. The end of the conflict, and the resulting Treaty of Paris, showed Great Britain as the world's chief colonial power—a position come by at great cost, in colonies, to France. In North America, France was left only with the Louisiana Territory, and Frenchmen in New Orleans did not as yet know the half of it. Three months before the treaty was signed, Louis XV had secretly presented his Bourbon cousin, King Charles III of Spain, with all of Louisiana, including the island containing New Orleans—something New Orleanians did not learn until about twenty months after the fact. They were also unaware that for another seven years of tangled arrangements, the people of New Orleans would be ruled by French governors while the province itself would be owned by Spain. The new Spanish regime took over with a vengeance in 1769. As an intimation of what French patriots who resisted the new regime could expect, the new commander, Don Alexander O'Reilly, an Irish mercenary, had five French leaders taken out to the parade ground, lined up before a firing squad, and shot.

On the positive side, O'Reilly (with the aid of a Spanish nobleman who had accompanied him to New Orleans) initiated a small building boom that was to give the French-style city its first Spanish look. It was not until the great fire of 1787, however, and the rebuilding that followed, that New Orleans began to take on its special Spanish cast.

The typical early New Orleans house, James Marston Fitch tells us in his "Creole Architecture," had been a free-standing structure, with a steeply pitched roof extending beyond the walls to form galleries, with dormers used to ventilate the attic during the long, hot, humid summers. For the Spanish, the basic single-family dwelling "took the form of the centripetal, inward-turning, blind-walled hollow square of the Mediterranean basin," and a secluded patio provided "the necessary environment for the gynaeceum of Classic antiquity or the seraglio of the Arabs, with all its physical and psychological implications for protection from the hostile, outside world."[6]

By the end of the eighteenth century (and after disastrous fires in 1787 and 1794), the Franco-Spanish synthesis, the New Orleans look, was quite firmly established. New Orleans houses adjoined each other along the street front with shops occupying the ground floor, while a *porte-cochère* gave entry to a hidden rear courtyard. "Continuous galleries or balconies," Fitch wrote, "shielded both patio and street walls against sun and blowing rain, as well as providing all rooms with access to light, air and outlook."[7] Despite attempts to neutralize the pervasive New Orleans heat and dampness, the horror of the encompassing swamps, with their disease-breeding insect life, made these architectural attempts at control seem futile. Yellow fever controlled the population growth. "In the last decade of the 18th century," Hodding Carter wrote, "New Orleans was free of yellow fever only in 1792. No precise records of yellow fever deaths were kept until 1817, when 80 were listed. . . . A high mark was reached in 1858 with 4,845, and in 1867, 3,107 bodies were carried away in the yellow fever carts."[8]

Still the immigrants came: French, German, Spanish, Italian, Irish, and, from eastern Canada, late in the eighteenth century, the Acadians. Throughout Louisiana's early history the immigrants continued to arrive. Those who arrived willingly—the majority—came, surely, with hope. Of the undesirables, some came willingly (or at least uncaring) and some came only with coercion. Still, even for the meanest and least adventurous of these, there was held out some glimmer of hope for gainful employment and perhaps even upward social mobility. Only the black slaves arrived both unwillingly and without hope. They came sick at heart, often sick in body, and expecting the worst. They were seldom disappointed.

From the beginning, slaves came to the colony directly from Africa on the slave ships of the major slave-trading nations—Spain, France, England, and Holland—or with a delay en route by way of the West Indies, and later by slave trading among the states. In any case, for over two centuries it made little difference to African slaves who transported them or where they were going. The death rate aboard slave ships was so high that simply arriving in the New World alive could be regarded as a superhuman achievement. (The *Brookes*, a 320-ton British slave-trading ship of the eighteenth century built to carry 451 souls—a horror not to be believed—was reported to have carried 609 slaves across the Middle Passage, the slave-trade route from Africa to the Americas, in addition to the crew, supplies, and provisions.) Slaves were commonly chained together hand and foot and stacked below decks like cordwood. The strangling crush resulted in the spread of sickness and disease, the chills, fever, and nausea of smallpox, and frequent wounds and self-maiming brought about by fighting the chains and shackles.[9]

The story of slavery in Louisiana is tied to African slavery, and slavery in Africa was probably as old as man in Africa. It was not until the end of the fourteenth century, however, that black slavery began in Europe. The Portuguese were among the first to see the commercial advantages of slave trading, and the Spanish were not far behind. After the French secured control of the Mississippi Valley in the seventeenth century, slaves became an essential part of the New World economic system and its reliance on cheap labor.

The earliest instance of slaves on the American mainland dates from 1619, when a Dutch ship deposited twenty blacks in Jamestown, Virginia. By the end of the century England dominated the world slave trade, and had established African posts to which ships delivered cargoes of cloth, foodstuffs, and cheap-jack jewelry which factors, or slave traders, then tried to exchange for slaves. The most conservative estimates indicate that nearly 3 million African slaves were taken in the seventeenth century, 7 million in the eighteenth century, and 4 million in the nineteenth century. These numbers, John Hope Franklin said, "are themselves a testimonial to the fabulous profits that must have been realized in such a sordid business, to the ruthlessness with which the traders must have prosecuted it, and to the tremendous demands being made by New World settlers for laborers."[10]

We may begin by asking: Who were the slaves? Who were these blacks taken from their African land and sold into a nightmare of servitude? What sort of beings were they? Southerners often asked: Are they indeed human? Slaveholders and ante-bellum white southerners, in the main, had their own answers to these questions, their own views, special attitudes, and sentiments concerning the black man. George Washington Cable, who was born in New Orleans in 1844 and whose parents owned slaves, asked the question, "What are these sentiments?" and answered:

> Foremost among them stands the idea that he is of necessity an alien. He was brought to our shores a naked, brutish, unclean, captive, pagan savage, to be and remain a kind of connecting link between man and the beasts of burden. . . . The occasional mingling of his blood with that of the white man worked no change in the sentiments. . . . Generations of American nativity made no difference; his children and children's children were born in sight of our door, yet the old notion held fast.[11]

Although it is not likely that "the old notion" can be changed by argument, we should summarize (for the record, at least) some aspects of the reality of the black man's world before he was loaded onto ships and carried away. The notion, for example, that blacks prefer to be footloose and fancy free, with no ties to family—a popular view for centuries—has no basis in fact, and certainly not before they were brought to America. African blacks considered themselves, first, to be a part of their immediate and local family; and, second, a part of all families with whom they had ancestors in common, including those families in distant places. Family relations were of the utmost importance. Franklin tells us that "nothing is more impressive in the social institutions of Africa than the cohesive influence of the family. The immediate family, the clan, and the tribe undergird every aspect of life."[12]

The relationship between daily work and religion was a complicated one. Magic and rituals helped to relate those things that could be seen to those that couldn't. Thus, the burying of the dead carried special significance. The funeral symbolized at once a departure from this life and the taking up of another, and a proper burial required the most conscientious and ritualistic preparation. The funerals of African natives were elaborate ceremonies, with much expression of regard for the dead. Commenting on this common practice, Franklin tells us that:

> the funeral was the climax of life, and costly and extensive rituals were sacred obligations of the survivors. . . . The grave was not completely closed until every member of the family had had an opportunity to present offerings and to participate in some rite incident to the interment. Nothing more clearly demonstrates the cohesiveness of the African family than the ceremonies and customs which were practiced on the occasion of the death and burial of a member.[13]

It is not difficult to see the parallels between the spirit of the African funeral and that of the traditional black New Orleans funeral. Black funerals have been a favorite subject ever since jazz historians discovered New Orleans: the solemn procession of friends, relatives, and lodge members, the picture of curious young men and boys moving along the sidewalk paralleling the line of march (the "second line"), the final dirge at the open graveside, the interment, the tears and moans of loved ones, and now the return to the living as the marching bandsmen strike up a little jazz on the way home, improvising on "Oh, Didn't He Ramble?" or one of the favorite songs of the deceased, after which the bereaved family join together, with food and drink, to honor the dead.

Black funeral processions making their way through the narrow New Orleans streets to the accompaniment of music by black bandsmen could not have taken place before the Civil War. Black Codes, sets of local regulations and ordinances created to restrict the movement of blacks, to prevent them from organizing themselves, and in general to keep blacks "in their place" would have made the funeral procession and the music illegal. (Mississippi Black Codes prohibited slaves from playing drums or blowing horns.) The Emancipation Proclamation gave blacks a new life. Unaccustomed to freedom, however, and not certain what they were "free" to do, they tested the various local Black Codes. Warily, they tried sporting a white handkerchief, say, and when they found they were no longer whipped, branded, or jailed for it, they tried gathering in small groups on streetcorners; later, they formed clubs, societies, and marching bands.

Many of the former slave's attitudes (after Emancipation and particularly after he migrated to the cities) came about as a reaction to the local Black Codes that had previously controlled his life. In New Orleans, the *Code Noir* established in 1724 by Bienville was based on an earlier code used by the French government to control the activities of slaves in their island colonies. (As time went on, other New Orleans governors set up new codes, each adapting the previous code to current use.) The Bienville Code included fifty-four articles (Gayarré's *History of Louisiana*, volume 1, 3rd edition [New York: AMS Press, 1972], includes the entire code), and it may be worthwhile here to summarize its main points.

Several articles prohibited the practice of every religion except Roman Catholicism (masters were required to provide slaves with proper religious instruction); other articles provided that no slave could carry a heavy stick or anything else resembling a weapon; there was to be no gathering of slaves unless a white person was present; a slave—like a horse or a cow—was to be considered movable property; a slave who struck his master or a member of his master's family was to be put to death; death was also the penalty for stealing something important—a horse, say; whipping and branding (with the *fleur-de-lis*) were the punishments for stealing items of lesser importance—food, say, or shoes; the master, however, was forbidden to use shackles on his slave. Still other articles explained when and how a slave could be freed (manumitted) and set out the rights of manumitted slaves (the same as those of free-born persons of color).

The Black Codes were intended, of course, to control the slave's desire for freedom. The Codes were also intended to control, and perhaps dispel, the southerner's incessantly nagging fear of miscegenation and, to this end, the New Orleans Code included a number of telling prohibitions: marriages between the races were forbidden, and clergymen were forbidden to sanction such marriages; no whites, manumitted slaves, or free-born men of color could hold female slaves as concubines (this would become the most flouted of the articles dealing with sexual relations between the races); and if, by chance, a master and his female slave *did* engage in illicit sexual intercourse (and if, presumably, the action was later discovered), the slave could never qualify for freedom; moreover, if there were issue from the union, the child would become a ward of the government; however, if a free black (presumably male) had illicit sexual intercourse with a slave he personally owned (in New Orleans in 1830 "749 free Negroes owned slaves"[14]), he was permitted to marry her, after which she would enjoy the same rights as other free persons of color. To sum up the various punishments for breaking the laws of the Code, there were whipping, branding, and death for the slave; and, for the master, cash fines.

The southerner's concern with miscegenation had its foundation in fact. The distinguished anthropologist Melville J. Herskovits, in *The American Negro*, summed it up when he said, "A maxim which is never challenged in fact—since the fact is self-evident—is that two human groups never meet but they mingle their blood."[15] The mixing of blood in New Orleans was as old as New Orleans itself, and conflicts over this question developed not only between New Orleans blacks and whites but, late in the nineteenth century, in the jazz context of Storyville days, between "uptown" black musicians and "downtown" black musicians. This conflict (to be discussed at some length in Chapter 2) centered around those blacks of light complexion who thought of themselves not as blacks but as Creoles. Their definition of *Creole*—the issue resulting from sexual union between early French or Spanish settlers and female slaves—distressed nineteenth-century white New Orleanians. The black use of the word *Creole* bewildered and embarrassed them because they had their own narrow, exclusive meaning for *Creole*. Blacks, as they saw it, could not be Creoles— blacks were black; true Creoles were white, the offspring of early *white* settlers, male and female. Furthermore, according to New Orleans's Black Code, children resulting from racial interbreeding became government wards. The facts, however, do not support this view. While there may have been instances of the government's taking racially mixed children, such comfort was, on the whole, wishful thinking.

The controversy over who was and who wasn't Creole grew out of the writings of George Washington Cable who, as mentioned earlier, was born in New Orleans in 1844. Cable was a Confederate soldier in the Civil War; he had trained to be an engineer, and later wrote articles for the *New Orleans Picayune*. His literary works include a history called *The Creoles of Louisiana*, *Old Creole Days* (a collection of short stories), and a novel, *The Grandissimes*.

Mark Twain, with whom Cable frequently shared the lecture platform, called Cable "the South's finest literary genius." In the author of *The Grandissimes*, Twain said, "the South has found a masterly delineator of its interior life and its history."[16] W. J. Cash, in his *Mind of the South*, reminds us of the impact of Cable's work. *The Grandissimes*, he wrote, "was so predominantly a piece of sentimental glorification that it goes mainly unread nowadays, yet had so many flashes of untrammeled insight, so many sudden lapses into realism, that his countrymen actually denounced it as a libel."[17] And Joy J. Jackson, in her *New Orleans in the Gilded Age*, observes that "Cable indeed is the key to the entire literary image of New Orleans. . . . He sparked the one literary and historical argument of the generation—over the identity of the Creoles."[18]

As a young man, Cable collected songs and folk tales from the French-speaking blacks in the *Vieux Carré*, the old French Quarter. He took notes on the inhabitants and their curious English and pidgin French, source material for the characters and language in his short stories and novels. Jackson wrote:

> One of the richest veins of local color was the segment of local society who called themselves "colored Creoles." . . . What white Creoles found startling in Cable's stories was his presentation of such colored Creoles as protagonists. . . . They were depicted as complex human beings with emotions and sensitivities which had heretofore been reserved for white heroes and heroines. His indiscriminate use of the word "Creole" to cover the colored Creoles as well as the white French-speaking New Orleanians was the sorest point of all to local whites of French-Spanish background. Grace King, who although not a Creole was one of their major defenders and spokesmen, observed that Cable did not understand the Creole.[19]

Grace King's position on the identity of Creoles was a straightforward one, and among aristocratic whites was well met indeed. The first sentence of her *Creole Families of New Orleans* tells us:

> The old Creole families of New Orleans date from the foundation of the city, and even before that—from the settlement of Mobile, Dauphin Island and Biloxi, their good old names figuring in the lists of military, naval and civil officers who followed Iberville to the discovery of the Mississippi and remained with Bienville to hold on to the French possession of it.[20]

In citing a late-eighteenth-century manuscript history of New Orleans, King offers a compendium of "Creole" characteristics, of which the following is a fair sample:

Creoles are defined to be the children of Europeans born in the colony. They in general measure about five feet, six inches, in height; they are all well shaped and of agreeable figure; they are lively, alert, and agile. . . . They are endowed with a natural disposition for all sciences, arts and exercises that amuse society. They excel in dancing, fencing, hunting, and in horsemanship. . . . They are good fathers, good mothers, good friends, and good kinsmen. The women besides having the qualities above enumerated are agreeable in figure and seldom deformed. They make good mothers and are devoted to their husbands and children.[21]

The word *Creole* is derived etymologically from the French *créole*, Spanish *criollo*, and Portuguese *crioulo*: a Negro (slave) born in his master's house. Perhaps the most extensive early research on the variety of the uses of *Creole* is to be found in Rousseve's *The Negro in Louisiana*. He cites passages from a variety of printed sources from the late eighteenth century to the twentieth century, which include such phrases as "*Ce nègre libre, créole de Cavaillon*"; "*J'aime le Créole de couleur*"; "the songs of the black creoles of Louisiana"; "*nègre créole*" (in a Jamaican slave's baptismal record of 1779); "*Créoles de couleur*"; and "*gens de couleur libres*"—all phrases linking the concepts of black and Creole. (In New Orleans archives, from early times up to the middle of the nineteenth century, slaves were simply designated as *nègres*.) "These '*Créoles de couleur*' or '*gens de couleur libres*,' " Rousseve writes, "played an important role in Louisiana, and are mentioned very early in the history of the colony. From the beginning a hot-blooded, self-assertive class, militant and proud, theirs was a firm and persevering belief that they were in every respect the equals of their Caucasian fellow-citizens."[22] (By the time of the Civil War, New Orleans *créoles de couleur* paid tax on property worth about $15 million.)

New Orleans free men and women of color who spoke French, or Creole (and most of them did), referred to themselves as *créoles de couleur*. (Those readers especially interested in the sound of the Creole language—Negro-French, or Gombo French as it is sometimes called—may wish to hear Kid Ory sing his "Creole Song" on *Tailgate! Kid Ory's Creole Jazz Band*, Good Time Jazz; or Lizzie Miles's Creole rendition of "Won't You Come Home, Bill Bailey?" on *The History of Jazz, Vol. 1*, Capitol.) As a final note, we need to mention that free persons of color were also frequently described by the degree of their color: *griffe* meant three-quarters black; *mulatto*, one-half black; *quadroon*, one-quarter black; and *octoroon*, one-eighth black. New Orleanians—the city was the largest slave-trading center in the South—when referring to slaves from Louisiana who spoke French or Creole and who were on the block for sale or trade or auction, called them "Creole Negroes."[23]

The colored Creoles with the richest opportunity for upward social mobility in early-nineteenth-century New Orleans were the female quadroons. And the arena in which they competed for what might be the good life (or, at any rate, a better life than they had known) were the *bals de Cordon Bleu*, commonly called "quadroon balls." The earliest balls were open to all—white, free black, mixed, male and female. The first true quadroon ball was held in 1805, when Auguste Tessier, a professional actor and dancer, advertised "a plan to give two balls a week for the free women of color at which all colored men would be excluded." Black male musicians, however, were permitted to supply the dance music, as they did at a good many of the quadroon balls. The quadroon balls were so sensationally successful that only a few years later the Winter Tivoli Ballroom held quadroon balls every Wednesday and Saturday nights, while the Union Ballroom held its balls every Tuesday and Friday nights. Interest in the balls was so lively and participation so keen that, before long, quadroon balls took place regularly, at least six nights a week, in as many as eight different ballrooms, many of which were just around the corner from each other in the French Quarter.[24]

White New Orleans gentlemen with an eye for the ladies, given the choice of attending all-white balls or quadroon balls, invariably chose the latter. The white balls may have had their "flirtation walk," but most of the quadroon balls emphasized the excitement of promiscuous sexual indulgence, and what took place in one ballroom, at least, was characterized, perhaps exaggeratedly, as "the saturnalia of the depraved portion of our population."[25] Pagan considerations not altogether aside, the quadroon balls were in fact arenas of competitive prostitution, with the white New Orleans gentlemen—the magnates of municipal, state, and federal governments, army officers, members of the learned professions, "in short, the white male aristocracy in everything save the ecclesiastical desk"—as the rich prizes.[26] These white gentlemen, in turn—the local Black Code notwithstanding—apparently found the quadroons irresistible.

At the ball, after a gentleman had spied the girl of his choice, a courtship followed, after which the girl's mother brought up the matter of money, both for her daughter and for herself; other arrangements included an agreement to set up housekeeping, and to take care of any children that might result from the union. Mothers and daughters both looked upon this *placée* (or *plaçage*) as a form of marriage, despite the fact that many suitors were already married. After the agreement was satisfactorily completed, the girl was installed in a house, usually one of a long row of small cottages in what is now Rampart Street, and frequently lived out her years there, providing her man with children and other amenities of married life. The *plaçage*, as a system, extended from the late eighteenth century to about 1850, after which it declined rapidly, ending with the onset of the Civil War. Some saw the system as one of common-law marriages between black and white, while others preferred to look upon it as a form of prostitution.

Where there is easy prostitution, the spirit of crime and corruption is generally not far behind. In New Orleans, from the early nineteenth century onward, the elements necessary to the development of an environment in which jazz could readily take root were already clearly evident. Easy prostitution means easy money, and easy money attracts both criminals and corrupt men in positions of power; easy money also gives rise to those establishments that thrive on easy money: bordellos, gambling joints, saloons, cabarets, and dance halls, to name only a few. And it was in the atmosphere and ambience of places catering to the illicit fancies of their pleasure-seeking clientele that the popular music antecedent to jazz, which showed some early jazz characteristics, was encouraged to grow, and flourished.

The New Orleans dance hall was a convenient place for prostitutes to solicit potential customers. The band's exhilarating music, the soft shuffle of shoes on wood, the murmur of the lonely crowd—all combined to create an air of aloneness and intimacy; physical contacts were easily and, in the course of the dance, naturally accomplished; and assignations could be arranged on the dance floor or after the ball was over. For would-be prostitutes, unable to compete with dance-hall professionals, night spots and lowlife boarding houses stood ready, with less waiting time and faster turnovers. From here it was but a step up to joining the professionals in the city's more or less permanently located sporting houses. In 1857, the New Orleans City Council, in an attempt to control the spread of prostitution across the city, passed an ordinance that required prostitutes to be licensed and taxed. Mrs. Emma Pickett, an established madam, paid for her license and then sued to recover her money; the courts eventually upheld her position, and the City Council's ordinance was found to be unconstitutional. New Orleans whores celebrated their victory by parading jubilantly through the French Quarter, some of them nude.[27]

In New Orleans there was seldom a shortage of customers for illicit sex. The riverfront alone, with its sailors, flatboatmen, dock workers, and warehousemen, provided the sporting-house girls with all the business they could handle; in addition, the city's young bachelors and old men about town seemed always ready for a night out. In discussing the city's easy marks, Reinders notes the colorful presence, during the New Orleans winter season, of "wealthy upriver planters, of gawking Hoosiers and rube Texans, of Southern planters and cracker farmers, of Californians long on gold and short on experience, and of mystified immigrants."[28]

And then there were those patrons for whom crime was a way of life. New Orleans bred criminals as easily as its swamps bred mosquitoes: hustlers, con men, gamblers, forgers, and counterfeiters multiplied steadily. The waterfront was a haven for river pirates and crooked warehousemen, as well as buyers and receivers of stolen goods; young toughs, hoodlums, and petty racketeers roamed the wharves during the day while burglars, pimps, and pickpockets worked the city at night. New Orleans was not only the most wide-open city in the Southwest, but it seemed to enjoy its reputation for being the most wicked city, perhaps, in all America. It was certainly America's most lawless city, and in this regard held a special attraction for America's immigrants, floaters, vagabonds, desperadoes, and whores.[29]

Where, we may ask, was the law? Who, if anyone, was responsible for the control of crime in New Orleans? The simple answer, of course, should be the police. But the police were relatively few, and even those policemen who were honest and competent were helpless. In 1857, the New Orleans police force included less than 400 policemen to protect the lives and property of some 170,000 citizens.[30] Most police officers at mid-century did not wear uniforms (in 1855 they were issued blue coats with brass buttons) and worked on foot, patrolling their beats for $45 a month, frequently not even receiving their pay on time. If the city of New Orleans could not pay its policemen regularly, others—prostitutes, gamblers, and an assortment of criminals and their political protectors—could and did. Nevertheless, between 1857 and 1858, the police made over 25,000 arrests, thus proving to the rest of the world that "New Orleans had one of the highest crime rates in the United States."[31] The arrests, of course, were mostly for such minor infractions as drunkenness, disturbing the peace, and soliciting. Just the same, the numbers of arrests were impressive and gave those out-of-town adventurers who might be interested in settling in New Orleans the correct impression that crime in New Orleans was something more than a cottage industry.

NINETEENTH-CENTURY NEW ORLEANS: PLAGUES, CREOLES, AND STORYVILLE

2

In 1800 Spain *secretly* retroceded Louisiana to France. Although Napoleon Bonaparte promised he would never turn away from Louisiana, it took him three years to realize there was no immediate advantage in owning a remote colony of discontented whites and potentially dangerous blacks, and in 1803 he sold the territory to Thomas Jefferson, and New Orleans became part of the American frontier. The Louisiana Purchase eventually brought a flood of immigrants to New Orleans, and by mid-century the city's population was an interesting, if ill-balanced, mixture of French, Spanish, German, Irish, and Italian immigrants, American adventurers, free men of color, and slaves.

New Orleans in the early nineteenth century was a raw frontier city; it lacked proper sanitation facilities, and pernicious odors drifted throughout its unpaved streets. Buildings were constructed primarily to provide shelter—a sense of style (they were Spanish or French provincial) meant little to early settlers. During the 1830s, however, new buildings began to reflect the taste of a number of first-rate architects, particularly James Gallier and the Dakin brothers, all of New York.

Gallier and Charles Dakin came to New Orleans in 1834 and set up a partnership in an office on Canal Street. Almost at once they were commissioned to design row houses on North Rampart Street to be called "Three Sisters." Arthur Scully, Jr., the architectural historian, describes the structure:

> It extended from the corner of Bienville toward Iberville Street, in the French Quarter. The "Sisters" were frame, two stories high, with four Corinthian columns. . . . They were originally conceived as fine residences, but because of the commercialization of Rampart Street over the years and the growth of a small red-light district one block to the rear [the incipient Storyville], they declined.[1]

The work of Gallier and Dakin was much in demand. Newly rich Americans, who needed houses to define the social positions to which they aspired, happily exchanged their sprawling Spanish residences of stucco-covered brick for the lofty pillars and columns of Gallier-Dakin (and ancient Greece) and the decorative wrought-iron lacework and cast-iron balconies that eventually characterized much of the city's architecture. In addition to building houses, Gallier and Dakin built stores, business buildings, the Arcade Baths—a public bath house with a Corinthian-columned exterior characteristic of the Greek Revival—and the St. Charles Hotel. The hotel, once the grandest and most impressive in the United States (at its peak it employed 170 servants to wait on 502 guests), became the business and social center of the American sector of the city. The early development of New Orleans had taken place mainly in the *Vieux Carré*, bounded on its west side by Canal Street; later, when developers started work on the swampland just above Canal Street, the city began to expand in that direction, and it was here, in a section called the Faubourg Ste. Marie, that solvent Americans came to live.

In 1835 James Dakin, Charles's older brother, arrived in New Orleans and, like the firm of Gallier and Dakin, found himself in much demand. (He was soon to be referred to as "D'Aquin.") He moved into a boarding house in the French Quarter, bought himself a slave called Tishy, and was soon building stately houses on the "proper" side of Canal Street. Before long his Doric porticoes and Ionian and Corinthian columns could be seen on structures all over the old and new districts. With his death in 1852, at the age of forty-six, the era of the early Greek Revival in New Orleans architecture came to an end.

Gallier and the Dakins designed their Greek-inspired structures for the New Orleans rich. There was nothing Greek, however, about the houses of the middle and lower classes. Middle-class houses were usually two-story frame cottages; the lower classes, including the free blacks, lived in rundown tenements of wood or brick or in rows of rotting shanties—filthy, rat-ridden hothouses for disease. Summer or winter, the streets of the city were a horror to behold. New Orleans, as Gerald M. Capers reminds us, was "the dirtiest city in the country. Dead animals, garbage of all kinds, and even 'night soil' were dumped on its mostly unpaved streets, which intermittent subtropical rains turned into quagmires and even lakes."[2]

It is no wonder that New Orleans at mid-century had the highest death rate in the country; more than 50,000 died of yellow fever between 1840 and 1860. In the epidemic of 1853, which started in the shanties along the waterfront and then spread uptown, 12,000 people died. The city's helpless physicians, appalled at the number of fever victims, sought vainly for either cause or cure. Some things were easy to see: "They were quick to observe that the open sewer gutters and uncovered cisterns gave rise to 'myriads of mosquitoes,' and that the filthy, unpaved streets, shallow-ground privies, swampy yards, and slums of New Orleans invited plagues."[3] When the epidemic had run its course, a number of these same physicians pleaded with the city for underground sewers, paved streets, strong sanitary laws, destruction of the tenements, and quarantine of suspected vessels in the port. But nothing was done. The results of the epidemic, however, made it easier for the city to raise money for the provision and maintenance of a number of new orphan asylums.[4]

If May to October was a season of dread, November to April was nonetheless New Orleans's social season. Epidemics and plagues notwithstanding, New Orleans's ebullient social life went on—for six months of the year, in any case. The two centers of social life for whites were the St. Charles Hotel and the St. Louis Hotel. Here visitors and their families, together with businessmen and politicians, would gather in lobbies, meeting rooms, barrooms, and guest rooms to debate, connive, or simply make small talk. (As a special attraction, in each of the hotels' high-ceilinged rotundas New Orleanians and their visitors could watch or participate in the daily slave auctions.)

For those who preferred eating to talking, first-rate restaurants such as Victor's and Moreau's offered local seafood delicacies and the special New Orleans stews *gumbo* and *jambalaya*. Drink could be found nearly everywhere. Gentlemen, for example, could drink (and, if they wished, play billiards) in the privacy of the Boston Club, say, or the Pelican; middle-class drinkers could settle at the Pickwick, the Orleans, the Gaiety, the Hiawatha, or the Louisiana—social clubs where drinking and gambling were high on the evening's agenda. For the working classes, black and white, there was an assortment of public drinking houses: saloons, cabarets, gin mills, taverns, and even grocery stores whose specialty was selling liquor, illegally, to slaves; and for the large German population, there were the beer gardens. In 1854, according to an estimate by the City Council, there were over 2,000 places in New Orleans where just about anyone could buy liquor (slaves, of course, were permitted only in the grocery stores).[5]

New Orleanians and visitors to the city also enjoyed attending bare-knuckle prizefights, horse races, and the city's red-light districts. Their most active participation, however, was in the hijinks associated with Mardi Gras ("fat Tuesday"), a celebration of Shrove Tuesday initiated by a group of young men in 1857 that eventually included a parade of bands, extravagant floats, and grotesquely masked figures parading through the city streets as thousands of sidewalk merrymakers cheered them along their way to City Hall, all of this followed by unrestrained dancing and drinking in the streets.

Parades and band music, pomp and circumstance, were already a New Orleans tradition. Every occasion—birthdays, holidays, public events—called for a celebration, and parades and display became commonplace. As early as 1806, the city turned out to celebrate the Fourth of July with a parade. Henry Kmen tells us of these early parades, and one of the hazards of participation:

> By the end of 1814, there were enough bands to fill the streets with martial airs as New Orleans prepared to do battle with the British. And of course each clash of arms in that campaign would provide further anniversaries on which to parade, especially December 23 and January 8. It was during a parade on the latter date in 1821 that James Audubon was relieved of his purse by a pickpocket.[6]

Parades were social events that were free—and open to black and white alike. The free blacks of New Orleans enjoyed much the same social life as lower-class whites. The fact that whites and free blacks lived in close proximity, without residential segregation, provided the blacks with a broader social life.

Slaves, too, were provided with a social life of sorts. In New Orleans they were less restricted than slaves in the countryside, and received better food and shelter and a greater degree of freedom. While many served as domestics, others were skilled workers trained in carpentry, masonry, baking, and other useful work of the kind masters could hire out to other white employers. Because the skills of these slave artisans were in great demand, masters treated them as valuable property. John W. Blassingame relates:

> Sometimes the slaves were even allowed to hold balls in their masters' homes. Lavishly dressed, the bondsmen frequently ate cakes, fruits, and candies and drank freely of wines and liquors at dances, where they performed the bamboula and polka to drums and violins played by slave musicians. . . . Sunday was a holiday for the slaves; they gambled, got drunk, watched cock fights, gathered in restaurants and barbershops, or congregated in Congo Square to sing and dance.[7]

The Civil War, of course, altered the city's social life.

In January 1861, Louisiana joined those southern states which had already seceded from the Union; three months later, Confederate commander Pierre G. T. Beauregard ordered the firing on Fort Sumter, and the war was officially started. New Orleans became the center of military activity for the state; troops were recruited there and then transferred to other parts of the South. The black population of New Orleans at the time included about 13,000 slaves and 11,000 free persons of color, and there is little question that many—the slaves particularly—were reluctant to embrace the principles and spirit of the Confederate cause. Others, however, the free men of color, especially those who were themselves slaveholders, appeared to be ready to die for the Confederacy—if the Confederacy would let them.

Any apparent black enthusiasm for the Confederate cause was extinguished when the Union army and navy—the navy under Admiral David G. Farragut and the army under General Benjamin F. Butler—took New Orleans on April 28, 1862. A few days later Butler became the city's military governor backed by 18,000 troops, none of whom had previously seen action. Starting on a distinct note of disrespect, crowds of New Orleanians jeered the new arrivals and sent up cheers for the Confederate General Beauregard and President Jefferson Davis. When Butler commandeered the St. Charles Hotel as his headquarters, people called him "Picayune" (i.e., cheap—a picayune was a coin worth 6¼ cents), and when he later initiated rigorous and punitive measures against propertyholders and impudent women, they called him "Butler the Beast."

Butler's most famous order was issued about two weeks after the occupation had begun. Defiant New Orleans women had taken to wearing Confederate flags on their bosoms, and upon meeting Union soldiers anywhere jeered at them and treated them as if they were carriers of a dread disease. Butler's reaction to these taunts, jibes, and insults was General Order No. 28:

> As the officers and soldiers of the United States have been subject to repeated insults from the women (calling themselves ladies) of New Orleans, in return for the most scrupulous noninterference and courtesy on our part, it is ordered that hereafter when any female shall, by word, gesture, or movement, insult or show contempt for any officer or soldier of the United States, she shall be regarded and held liable to be treated as a woman of the town plying her avocation.[8]

"A woman of the town plying her avocation" had a clear meaning for soldiers stationed away from home, and many of them interpreted Butler's order to mean that *all* New Orleans women were fair game. The city was outraged. It was not as if there were a shortage of prostitutes. The New Orleans underworld looked upon the Union troops occupying the city as customers in a wonderfully booming tourist industry—in a two-year period, the Military Division estimated a loss of "from 50,000 to 100,000 days of service from its men as a result of venereal disease."[9]

Butler ruled New Orleans for eight months, from May to December 1862, the federal government recalling him on January 1, 1863. A few weeks later, Lincoln proclaimed that "all persons held as slaves within any State, or designated part of the State, the people whereof shall be in rebellion against the United States, shall be then, thenceforward, and forever free."

After four years of bloody conflict and senseless death, in April 1865 Lee surrendered to Grant at Appomattox. For slaves, Lincoln's proclamation and the war's end meant they would be "forever free." Thousands of former slaves, no longer bound to the agricultural life, came to New Orleans to test their new-found freedom. They found not only freedom but an atmosphere of permissiveness that encouraged abandon. Transients, river men, and black migrants—numbers of men without wives and families— found easy employment, ready cash, open gambling, and a host of confidence men and women with an eye for the main chance, an environment especially conducive to sexual immorality and crime.

The districts into which the black migrants moved (the First, Second, and Fourth districts) were also the favorite temporary residences of sailors, fishermen, and river men. These neighborhoods also sheltered the largest number of prostitutes and experienced the highest crime rate in the city. To white southerners in general, the loose morals evident in black neighborhoods (added to what they believed was the former slave's disdain for anything resembling a permanent job) were, in their view, unequivocal proof that blacks did not comprehend the true meaning of "freedom" and at the very least were wanton and irresponsible. "Having a good time" seemed to be the goal, and now the former slave's exuberance, and what seemed like his often uninhibited conduct, was more than most white gentlemen could tolerate. While poor whites had found it easy and convenient to hate blacks, white gentlemen had believed they were above an emotion so intense as hatred—that is, hatred toward blacks. But as they observed the actions of the now-free blacks, they were deeply disturbed. Simple distaste turned to distrust, apprehensiveness, and finally to an apparently inextinguishable hatred. Commenting on this postwar development, W. J. Cash observed that, with few exceptions;

> the most superior men . . . seeing their late slave strutting about full of grotesque assertions, cheap whiskey, and lying dreams, feeling his elbow in their ribs, hearing his guffaw in high places, came increasingly to feel toward him very much as any cracker felt; fell increasingly under the sway of the same hunger to have their hands on him, and ease the intolerable agony of anger and fear and shaken pride in his screams.[10]

The "intolerable agony" of the white gentlemen may have been eased somewhat by the Knights of the White Camellia—a secret order along the lines of the Ku Klux Klan—founded in 1867, with headquarters in New Orleans.

Some of the bitterness arose when whites learned that not all those they had thought to be white were actually white. New Orleans whites and blacks had been mixing for such a long time that it was often difficult, if not impossible (particularly in the case of light-skinned blacks) to tell who was white and who was pretending to be white—"passing." An easy solution to the problem, some thought, was to make "passing" illegal, and to this end, the Louisiana Legislative Code No. 111 specified that anyone with any black ancestry, however remote, would be considered black.

Blacks whose blackness could be seen were, of course, not affected by the Code's new specification. Those heavily affected were the Creoles of color—light-skinned mulattoes, quadroons, octoroons—who had been passing for white. Among them were respected physicians, dentists, lawyers, businessmen, and fashionable women who suddenly found themselves designated as black and could now expect to receive the same treatment from whites as the blackest emancipated slave. The Code simply gave the age-old prejudice legal sanction; it also brought to the fore the prejudice of "light" blacks against "dark" blacks, and the schism that developed between these lights and darks subsequently had a significant effect upon the development of jazz.

There were many reasons for this class division. Creole blacks who before the Civil War had had educational and social advantages bestowed upon them by white fathers, went on to become important members of the black community after the war. Moreover, a number of Creole blacks had themselves been slaveholders, and thus considered themselves superior to former slaves.

There were other differences: Creole blacks thought of themselves essentially as French, while blacks saw themselves as Afro-American; Creole blacks spoke and read French, while blacks spoke English and read little. The differences in language, particularly, separated the Gombo-French-speaking Creoles of the *Vieux Carré* from the blacks in the uptown sector, but Blassingame notes "that as the popularity of the French language declined in the 1870s, the cultural barriers to social intercourse between the two groups decreased."[11] Still, as late as the 1900s the difference persisted, as is evident in a childhood scene recalled by the New Orleans jazz musician Lee Collins as he wandered about the downtown streets. "There you'd see the Creole housewives out shopping in the early morning," he said, "with their baskets on their arms and bidding each other the time of day in French. They all preferred speaking French to English. Tonti, Laharpe, North Derbigny, Dumaine, St. Ann, and many other Downtown streets—that was Creoleville."[12]

For Creoles of color, the regulation making all those with black ancestry equally black was an economic nightmare. Whites would no longer do business with them nor patronize their shops. The boycott, although not formally organized, was nonetheless strong and pervasive.

Many Creoles for whom music (and poetry and fashion and manners) had been part of their early social training, and who had studied musical instruments as one more step on the aristocratic road to cultural enlightenment, were economically the hardest hit. Generally unfit, physically and psychologically, for the kind of work New Orleans had theretofore reserved for blacks, they discovered that they could earn extra money by hiring out as musicians. (Census figures of the time showing occupations of free Negro males do not list "musicians" in any substantial number simply because few considered music as the field in which they earned their living; music, for many of them, was more than a hobby but something less than an occupation.) "Every Creole man in New Orleans," Lee Collins said, "even if he was a musician, learned some kind of trade. Some were plasterers, and a great many of them were cigarmakers. For musicians, of course," Collins added proudly, "this would only be a second trade."[13]

From the start, the *Vieux Carré* musicians—the downtown musicians—found work easily: they often knew those whites responsible for hiring musicians, they had a relatively high caliber of musicianship, and, of course, they looked "right." And looking "right" in this self-imposed class division counted heavily. George ("Pops") Foster, who was born on a plantation near New Orleans in 1892 and later became a first-rate jazz bassist, had considerable experience with the circumstance of looking "right." In his autobiography he recalls:

> The worst Jim Crow [i.e., racial discrimination] around New Orleans was what the colored did to themselves. . . . The lighter you were the better they thought you were. . . . There was a colored church in town that had seating by color. The lightest ones down in front and darker and darker as you went back. . . . They're the most mixed-up race of people you ever saw. You get every color in the Negro race, the skin is different, the eyes, the hair is different color and kinky or not so kinky.[14]

Recalling the good feeling and rapport that existed between the "colored musicians in New Orleans" Foster discussed his cousin, the trombonist Dave Perkins. "The whites had a musicians' union," Foster remembered, "and my cousin Dave Perkins was president of it. They didn't know he was colored. . . . He played with all the white bands."[15] Now, Pops Foster was almost eighty when he related that recollection, and perhaps he believed it himself. What is likely to be closer to the truth, however, may be seen in jazz historian Samuel B. Charters's directory of early New Orleans musicians in his *Jazz: New Orleans, 1885–1957* where, under the heading for Perkins we read:

> Many of the lighter-skinned Negro musicians played with either white or colored bands; although it was pretty generally known that they were colored. Perkins was probably the best known of these musicians. He had a Union card in both locals, and in his younger days played with the Toca Brass Band or with Jack Laine's Reliance Brass Band, both white bands.[16]

For the dark-skinned blacks, breaking into the city's musical life outside the neighborhoods in which they lived was not an easy task, certainly not at the outset. On the whole, they knew only a hand-to-mouth existence and were, besides, musically illiterate. What they did have—those with aspirations to break out of their seemingly narrow musical existence—were persistence, drive, ambition, vigor and a deep understanding of the kind of music that "spoke" to other blacks, that is, dark-skinned blacks like themselves. The best jobs, however, and the most frequent, required practiced, literate musicians. The competition for jobs between Creoles and uptown blacks grew keen, and, as Charters put it, "There was no love lost between the two groups of musicians. . . . The uptown musicians reacted, finally, by identifying themselves with their uptown audience."[17] Later, as we shall see in Chapter 3, uptown and downtown musicians discovered each other's strengths, and the resulting synthesis helped bring about the first authentic jazz style, what come to be called the New Orleans style.

A considerable part of the musical synthesis took place in Storyville, the red-light district officially established in 1898 by the city government. Named after Sidney Story, the alderman who proposed the ordinance, Storyville was known to New Orleans blacks as "the District." The "establishment" of Storyville was merely official acknowledgment of its activities and an attempt to cope with the vice and crime that had flourished in New Orleans from its earliest days.

In the decade before the street boundaries of Storyville were set, the city between the Mississippi River and Lake Pontchartrain abounded in tough bars, bawdy dance halls, concert-saloons (where customers could drink while watching prostitutes dance the cancan), and the ubiquitous "cribs" and "sporting houses." The "houses" could be found in streets just off the riverfront—the Gallatin Street district, for example; scattered throughout the *Vieux Carré*—on Burgundy, St. Louis, Conti, Bienville, and Customhouse Streets; and in the American section—on Franklin and Gasquet Streets.[18] (Gasquet was two blocks *outside* the boundary later set for Storyville, thus showing the intention of the ordinance to delimit where prostitution could be practiced.)

Storyville, with its aura of easy women and illegal activities accompanied by hot jazz in smoke-filled rooms, has long been a favorite topic in jazz literature. The amount of attention that has been devoted to Storyville throughout the years is, I believe, commensurate with its significance in the history of prostitution in America. Its significance in the history of jazz, however, has been magnified and somewhat embellished. Early writers on jazz tended to play down or ignore jazz in New Orleans as a whole; this tendency was particularly evident in the work of those writing in the late 1930s on New Orleans jazz and of those who were promoting the New Orleans, or Dixieland, revival of the 1940s. Their enthusiasm and romantic effusiveness frequently left limp readers with the impression that Storyville was not so much a district in New Orleans as another name for New Orleans. It is important to remember that there was considerable jazz-related activity in New Orleans *outside* the Storyville district, activity to which the music in Storyville must be related if we are to fully understand how jazz grew.

The results of the most exhaustive research on Storyville are found in Al Rose's *Storyville, New Orleans*, the definitive history of the district. When Rose began his research in his native city, there were several good reasons, as he put it, "why nobody had ever written a history of the area":

> The Storyville researcher can spare himself the trouble of seeking to consult the photo files of the New Orleans daily papers (the *Times-Picayune, et al.*), since they have maintained no such files for the period under consideration. Investigation of the New Orleans plat books, birth records, death certificates, police records, etc., in the appropriate municipal offices will prove to be almost as fruitless: the records, insofar as they concern Storyville and the people connected with it directly or indirectly, have been vandalized.[19]

Storyville was in the past a place of whorehouses, and jazz has frequently been characterized as "whorehouse" music. While no one questions that a number of sporting houses hired musicians to play for the girls and their clientele, the claims for this music as jazz, or its forerunner, are greatly exaggerated. The Storyville passing scene, and its folklore of madams, saloonkeepers, celebrated bawds, and its rough, naughty night places, deserves to be summarized if only to show the basic stuff myths are made of. Storyville was unique among the nation's red-light districts. Unlike other big-city areas where prostitution was tolerated by officials but illegal, prostitution in Storyville was "legal." The spread of prostitution and the disruption of the tranquillity of various neighborhoods in the city had been, for its law-abiding citizens, a matter of anxiety and concern. Prostitution existed, of course, and that could not be changed, but perhaps where it was practiced could be controlled and contained. To this end, citizens urged the city fathers to act. The resulting ordinance was a masterpiece of the legal mind at work: the establishment of a district where prostitution could be practiced, under rules prescribed by the city government, without saying that what was taking place was legal; outside the district, prostitution would be illegal, but within the district, well, it was neither illegal nor legal. The fact remains that no one within the district limits was ever arrested for prostitution.[20]

The ordinance proposed by Sidney Story created a nearly rectangular district of about thirty-eight blocks (there were alleys dividing some of them). The district was bounded on the river side by North Basin Street and on toward the lake were Franklin, Liberty, Marais, and Villere Streets, with North Robertson Street the outer limit; from the south side of Customhouse Street (later called Iberville), the district encompassed Bienville and Conti Streets, with the north side of St. Louis Street as its outermost edge. A year after its inauguration, Storyville took on all the characteristics of a flourishing industry.

Lulu White was the district's best-known madam, and her Mahogany Hall its best-known house, with those establishments operated by the Countess Willie Piazza, Emma Johnson, Gypsy Shafer, and Josie Arlington nearly as famous. Black customers were not permitted in any of these upper-crust mansions, and black and white prostitutes could not, by ordinance, operate in the same house; two houses, however (Lulu White's and the Countess Willie Piazza's) specialized in octoroon women. The New Orleans songwriter Spencer Williams recalls what the houses looked like to an impressionable black boy:

> Those places were really something to see—those sportin' houses. They had the *most* beautiful parlors, with cut glass, and draperies, and rugs, and expensive furniture. They were just like millionaires' houses.[21]

Williams's description grew out of a young boy's Basin Street fantasy. The reality of Basin Street was the saloon on the corner—Tom Anderson's, the gateway to Storyville. Tom Anderson was the white boss of Storyville and its unofficial mayor. He opened his saloon in 1901, and there he dispensed liquor and political favors and on occasion recommended the right houses to the right people.

The ceiling of his saloon was lit by a hundred electric bulbs, and all who came to visit the "mayor's" place of business were awestruck. In 1904 he was elected to the Louisiana State Legislature and his saloon became a pocket version of City Hall. He later joined forces with Josie Arlington (who kept a house just a few doors down) and changed the name of his saloon to Arlington's Annex. Miss Arlington's advertisements for her house appeared in the *Blue Book*, a basic directory to the best sporting houses in Storyville published by Anderson and available for 25 cents a copy in the saloon and, presumably, wherever books were sold. In addition to his Storyville interests—financial, political, and sexual—Tom Anderson was political boss of the Fourth Ward and president of an oil-refining company; for sixteen years he divided his time between Storyville and the state capital in Baton Rouge, where he was a member of the Legislature's Ways and Means Committee. (Later we will meet his counterparts in Chicago, Kansas City, and New York.)

Anderson's saloon was a combination bar, beer hall, and gambling joint—together with Josie Arlington's house, it was a Storyville supermarket. In addition, he provided his customers with music. Sidney Bechet, who was born in New Orleans and grew up there, recalled something about the music he heard coming from Anderson's saloon: "Sometimes you'd hear accordion, guitar, mandolin, sometimes bass, maybe a violin; other times you'd hear someone singing there. It wasn't a whorehouse but you'd hear *whorehouse* music there."[22] Of course, the business of Storyville was whorehouses, and it is no surprise that musicians of the Storyville era made distinctions. They generally associated whorehouses with the kind of ragtime and popular music played by such solo piano players as Jelly Roll Morton and Tony Jackson, who apparently were great favorites in the Countess Willie Piazza's establishment.

Not all madams could afford musicians. For those who couldn't there was the mechanical piano player—the pianola. Lulu White could afford both. Spencer Williams, who considered himself Lulu White's adopted son, remembered, "I'd go to sleep to the sound of the mechanical piano playing ragtime tunes, and when I woke up, in the morning, it would still be playing."[23] The pianola was also used to spell the regular pianist in his long night's musical journey; and while customers preferred the live piano player to the mechanical one, showing their appreciation by buying him champagne and giving him generous tips, the piano player still needed an occasional intermission. And at that moment, Williams tells us: "When the piano player would get tired, there would be a player piano that you put a quarter in and we'd make money then too. These houses hired nothing but the best, but only piano players, and maybe a girl to sing. And there was no loud playin' either. It was sweet, just like a hotel."[24]

On a given night during Storyville's twenty-year history, the saloons, cabarets, dance halls, and sporting houses together employed about fifty musicians. The highest paid were the piano-playing "professors," whose take depended almost entirely on tips from patrons; if their stories are credible, the professors some weeks earned as much as a thousand dollars. Leaders of the best-known bands, men like Joe Oliver, Kid Ory, and Freddie Keppard, sometimes earned as much as seventy-five dollars a week (if the tips were heavy), while the players in their bands averaged between thirty and fifty dollars a week. Pops Foster, who played bass in and around Storyville, has still another version of the money paid to Storyville musicians: "We made a dollar and a half a night, or nine dollars a week playing the District. We were the best paid band in the District."[25] Storyville had two large dance halls: the Tuxedo, on North Franklin between Bienville and Iberville Streets, and the 101 Ranch across the street. These halls (as well as a number of smaller places) regularly employed small ensembles or dance "orchestras." Rose estimates that the total number of musicians who worked in Storyville during its twenty-year life was no more than two hundred.[26]

Still, the myths persist. A representative sampling of the legends and old jazzmen's tales would show that every New Orleans musician, black and white alike, grew up with the musical sounds of Storyville in his ears, played all the important spots, and personally knew all the major figures. New Orleans jazzmen as they grew older were prone to exaggerate. Lee Collins, for example, tells how he met Danny Barker who, at sixteen, was known as "the ukelele king." Collins says he asked Barker if he had ever played banjo, and when he said he hadn't, Collins bought him one. "In a few months," Collins says, "he was one of the best banjo players in New Orleans."[27] Similarly, Jelly Roll Morton, who by his own admission invented jazz and implied that he was the greatest piano player in Storyville, may have been a less significant luminary than he imagined himself to be. He was seen in a somewhat dimmer light by Pops Foster, who said, "I never played with Jelly Roll Morton around New Orleans. . . . sometimes I used to let him take me to some of the whorehouses with him. He'd take me in, talk big, and show me some of his chicks. . . . Jelly worked mostly at Lulu White's place, and back then was just another piano player who worked the District."[28]

The legends grew. In a 1939 essay, "New Orleans Music," William Russell and Stephen Smith reported on the old 28 Club ("a colorful part of Storyville life") and on the extraordinary number of black pianists who knew only the blues:

> . . . if anyone sat down at the piano in the 28 Club, he knew he'd better not play anything else but the blues. In these dives they dragged out the blues with a slow beat and fierce intensity. *Apparently there were hundreds of Negroes who could sit down and play and sing the low-down blues.* They made up the words to fit their mood and the occasion, but invariably pianists knew only one tune. If someone yelled, "Play somethin' else!", he played the same blues a little faster, and the entire tonk, satisfied, shook in a quicker tempo.[29] (My italics.)

And in still another flight of fancy, Herbert Asbury reported on the "real" creators of jazz. After discussing brothels that employed small "orchestras" and itinerant groups who played in the street and saloons, Asbury says, "One of the most popular of these combinations—though not for dancing—was a company of boys, from twelve to fifteen years old, who called themselves the Spasm Band. They were the real creators of jazz, and the Spasm Band was the original jazz band."[30] Rudi Blesh, whose *Shining Trumpets* was one of the early significant books on jazz, perpetuates Asbury's fancy: "New bands sprung up overnight and the folk academy of the second line and the children's groups called 'spasm bands,' with their toy and homemade instruments, blossomed. Fine bands and great players emerged."[31]

Jelly Roll Morton's "invention" of jazz, the "hundreds" of Negro piano players who played and sang the blues, the teenage Spasm Band who were the "real creators" of jazz, and other tall tales are all part of the Storyville folklore, the engaging but faulty remembrances of things past. It will be our purpose in the following pages to sketch in the facts of black musical life in New Orleans from its beginnings to the closing of Storyville during World War I; to show aspects of its African ancestry; the influences of minstrelsy, the dance, and ragtime; to survey the New Orleans musicians and the bands, black and white, in and out of Storyville; and to map the long road, the synthesis that resulted in the first jazz style—what Sidney Bechet meant when he summed up over a hundred years of waiting, of musical evolution. "All that waiting," he said, "all that time when the song was far-off music, waiting music, suffering music; and all at once it was there, it had arrived. It was joy music now."[32]

NEW ORLEANS JAZZ: THE EARLIEST STIRRINGS

3

T he early city of New Orleans was fortified on one side by a rampart—which later became Rampart Street—that marked one boundary of what came to be called the *Vieux Carré*, or the French Quarter. The northwest side of the old city was bounded by Canal Street; the far side of Canal Street had not yet been developed, and when Americans began to settle in this "uptown" district during the 1830s, Canal Street became the dividing line between the French Quarter and the American Quarter—in John Smith Kendall's phrase, "the frontier between Creole New Orleans and American New Orleans."[1] This division created, in effect, two dissimilar cities, and when we read descriptions of life in nineteenth-century New Orleans, we should know whether the views are those of a "French" observer or an "American" one; and before we discuss the development of the city's musical life, it may be worthwhile to assess the importance of these views, even briefly.

George Washington Cable's literary works presented poor Creole blacks as a colorful, romantic people. John Smith Kendall, who also roamed the French Quarter as a young man, preferred the company of those socially prominent Creoles who were, or had been, rich. Kendall was born in Mississippi in 1874; after attending New Orleans's Tulane University he became a reporter for the *New Orleans Daily Picayune*, where he remained until 1914, after which he joined the Tulane faculty as an instructor in Spanish. In 1922 he wrote his three-volume *History of New Orleans*. In his reminiscence, "The French Quarter Sixty Years Ago," published in 1951 when Kendall was seventy-seven, he tells us that the social life of the Quarter was dominated by "a few old aristocratic families" (he mentioned eighteen by name) who "dwelt in stately mansions."[2] The young Creoles enjoyed "merrymaking of a simple-hearted, unpretentious sort"—masquerade balls called "domino parties," neighborhood parties, family get-togethers, occasional balls and dances at the French Opera House, and, always, the Carnival. The Opera House and the Cathedral of St. Louis, together, were the heart of social life in the *Vieux Carré*.

In summing up, Kendall shows that his memories of the delights of the French Quarter characterized, for him, the rest of the city. After stating that "the French Quarter of New Orleans was never more charming than it was in the last two decades of the century," he continued:

> Nor there only, *but throughout the city.* A spirit of gaiety, of grace, of hospitality, of kindness prevailed that probably did not exist at an earlier date, or at least did not exist in a notable degree, and certainly does not exist now. I think it can be said that the 1880s and 1890s were the years when New Orleans was most genuinely New Orleans.[3] (My italics.)

Who can really say when "New Orleans was most genuinely New Orleans?" Let us take gambling, for example, an activity which Joy Jackson reports "could be found almost everywhere, from the notorious Negro barrelhouses at the foot of Canal Street, where frequent fights and stabbings took place, to the plush exclusive gambling casinos on Royal Street." The *Daily Picayune's* society column reported that although fashionable ladies could be seen playing cards for money, they were nonetheless "against gambling and gamblers"[4]—perhaps because they knew that gambling was illegal. Furthermore, it was common knowledge that gamblers paid the city $150 a month to operate a keno game and $100 a month for faro, and "since the law did not allow licensing," Jackson observes, "this was not a legal arrangement." In any case, the city's take eventually averaged about $20,000 a year, and the money was used to build and maintain a new poorhouse, which (as Jackson says unsmilingly) "was desperately needed."[5] Surely, respectable New Orleanians knew where the revenue came from and must have been aware of the poorhouse and its inmates.

The poor, at times, seemed to overrun the city, particularly those who were both poor and young. Jackson gives us a fair idea of their pastimes: "Juvenile delinquents stoned streetcars, snatched purses, wrecked grocery stores, broke gas lights, carried off park benches, and stole merchandise from the levees and local lumberyards."[6] At the same time, the working classes seethed, and clashes between strikers and strikebreakers often resulted in deaths. Ships were set afire; streetcars were brought to a halt; and violence was the order of the day as the police force, absurdly undermanned, stood by helplessly. Prostitutes ranged the city. In the 1890s, one New Orleans law tried to prevent them from patronizing cabarets and mixing with the customers. Another law, passed in 1895, forbade houses of prostitution outside the area bounded by Poydras, Claiborne, and St. Louis Streets and the river. Storyville and "legal" prostitution were foreshadowed by these ordinances.

Near the neighborhood just mentioned, amid the city's stately mansions, stood the French Opera House, the bastion of the old city's Creole culture, a symbol of the sophisticated European society, particularly Gallic, of which they happened to be American representatives. The structure itself, in which the music performed was unequivocally European, was a visible and welcome reminder of their Old World affiliations. In 1813, John Davis had built a theater in the *Vieux Carré* to present plays, ballet, and opera; four years later, after a fire, the Théâtre d'Orleans was rebuilt. Because opera was its specialty, it came to be called the French Opera House, and New Orleans became "the only city in the United States enjoying regular seasons of opera under a permanent local management."[7] There were special sections for the elite, the bourgeoisie, and nearly everyone else who could afford a ticket. Through the winter season New Orleans society filled the Opera House nightly to hear the works of such fashionable French composers as Auber, Boieldieu, Herold, and Méhul, as well as new operas by the Italian favorites Donizetti and Rossini. New Orleans and its taste for opera became so well known wherever opera was performed that by the late 1820s the New Orleans Opera was touring Philadelphia and New York, and a Parisian opera company arrived to give performances in New Orleans.[8]

Along with opera, the French Quarter also showed a taste for the light classical pieces of Louis Moreau Gottschalk, the first American pianist and composer to gain an international reputation. Gottschalk was born in New Orleans in 1829 and trained in Paris, and although Chopin admired his piano playing, his greatest admiration came from young ladies overcome by such sentimental salon pieces as "The Dying Poet" and "The Last Hope." Among his works that reflect the years he spent in New Orleans are a *chanson nègre* called "Le Bananier," a *ballade créole* called "La Savanne," and a popular dance called "Bamboula," a black dance we will discuss later in this chapter.

The most popular music, however, the social music of the majority of white New Orleanians, came from black or white ensembles playing for dances, picnics, outings, and parades in and around the city. The best-known resort areas were on the shores of Lake Pontchartrain: Gretna, West End, Milneburg, and the Old Spanish Fort. Early New Orleans jazzmen remember those places well. Clarinetist Sidney Bechet, for example, tells us he played for "some picnic out at Milneburg Lake."[9] And Louis Armstrong, recalling his youthful days in New Orleans, said, "One day we went to play at a white folks' picnic at Spanish Fort near West End. There were picnics there every Sunday for which string orchestras were hired or occasionally a brass band. When all the bands were busy we used to be called on."[10]

Black musicians took work where they could find it. Those who played in brass marching bands frequently donned their parade uniforms to play for society dances "at the New Orleans Club, the Louisiana Restaurant, perhaps doing a Saturday afternoon tea dance with Papa Celestine and his band."[11] Tulane University students regularly hired bands for their social occasions, and trumpeter Lee Collins remembers playing a job for "a white fraternity house,"[12] while trumpeter Joe Oliver was called on to play junior proms at Tulane.[13]

White bands playing at white social functions were the order of the day, but black bands playing for white functions were not unusual. But whether the band was black or white, the music they performed during this period was not jazz; it was popular dance music. By contrast, when blacks played for blacks, their performances were an amalgamation of musical sounds and styles seldom heard by most whites, and which some had *never* heard. For the source of this special mixture in black music, peculiar to New Orleans, we must turn to the history of black music in general.

African music consists of many different rhythms and rhythmic patterns, together with many different meters, all combined and played *simultaneously*. The rhythms of African music are not immediately apparent to most Western ears (what those with an African rhythmic sense hear as *separate* sounds, coming at incredible speed one *after* another, in "cross-rhythms," Westerners often hear as sounding at the same instant), and these rhythms may be, in fact, the most complicated of any in the world.[14]

Technically, African music is based on three important principles: a regular, steady beat or pulse; improvised melodies and rhythms played one against the other in the manner described earlier; and the call-and-response—a format basic to African music. The leader's part—the call—is generally new each time he takes his turn; the chorus's turn—the response—usually consists of the repetition of one or two ideas supportive of the leader's musical or spoken remarks, as, for example, in the relation between a southern fundamentalist preacher and his congregation.

Dancing has always played an important role in African music, and for white observers in New Orleans the dances in the Place Congo, or Congo Square (now Beauregard), provided a Sunday afternoon's entertainment. For slaves, however, the dance was a religious and spiritual activity. New Orleans was predominantly Catholic, and dancing was not forbidden—influences from the evangelical Protestant religions were not as marked in New Orleans as they were in Virginia, say, or Georgia. There was some Protestant influence, of course; slave trading among the states brought Protestant-trained slaves and their hymns to Louisiana. On the other hand, the trading would have reopened for many the cult and ritual of West African voodoo, celebrations of which, while generally forbidden in the Protestant South, were freely permitted in Catholic New Orleans during the Sunday dances in Congo Square. The Square, as George W. Cable remembered it, was at one end of Orleans Street, near where the rampart once enclosed the Spanish city, "outside the rear gate," with "the poisonous wilderness on three sides." On a Sunday afternoon in 1886 he saw two drums large and small laid along the ground with the players astride them, who "beat them on the head madly with fingers, fists, and feet." The smaller drum was called the *bamboula*, so named because it was made from bamboo over which was stretched an animal skin. (Edward Larocque Tinker tells us that "the word is composed of *bambou* plus *la*, the definitive article 'the,' which in Creole often follows the noun. *Bamboula* is also the name of the dance performed to the music of the drums."[15])

Cable describes the *bamboula*, a lively dance for couples, as "the furious Bamboula"; the *counjaille*, or *coonjai*, as a group dance with "thigh-beating and breast-patting and chanting and swinging and writhing"; and the *calinda* as "a kind of fandango, . . . a sort of vehement cotillion."[16] Cable saw a gourd, triangles, jew's-harps, an animal jawbone whose teeth were scraped with a key, a plucked reed instrument with a single vibrating string, a four-stringed banjo, and a sort of three-reeded panpipe. And he heard the sound of black voices—"that long-drawn human cry of tremendous volume, richness, and resound, to which no instrument within their reach could make the faintest approach."[17]

W. E. B. DuBois, in his *Souls of Black Folk* (1903), thinking back on the times of slavery, put it simply: "They that walked in darkness sang songs in the olden days—Sorrow Songs—for they were weary at heart."[18] Frederick Douglass, who had himself been a slave, provides an additional insight. "Slaves sing most," he said, "when they are most unhappy. The songs of the slave represent the sorrows of his heart; and he is relieved by them, only as an aching heart is relieved by tears."[19]

The end of the legal slave trade in 1808 lessened somewhat the easy flow of slaves to America and therefore lessened the flow of African musical influences. During the nineteenth century, musical influences came from the slaves' American environment. For example, religious instruction of slaves by whites often included the teaching of standard "white" hymns. Singing of the Old Testament's (and the master's) Promised Land later became not so much a cry for religious and spiritual sustenance as a disguised cry for secular freedom. As Sablosky put it, "The melodies, no longer so often sung in company of the whites, wandered in the direction of the Negro's own musical inheritance."[20] Country slaves, during and after the Civil War, brought the sounds of plantation music—the shouts, hollers, and field hands' songs—to the ears of New Orleans blacks. In turn, the new arrivals heard the songs of black river men—stevedores "screwin' " cotton on the levees and black boatmen working the river steamers as they moved in and out of New Orleans. In addition, in the postwar period black men worked on the railroads, in lumber camps, and on chain gangs, and always there were the songs. The longer blacks lived in America, the less African their music became. Eventually white musicians, taken with certain rhythmic and harmonic devices in black music, imitated them, after which blacks, in their turn, and for social reasons, imitated the imitators. The minstrel show is a case in point.

Although some blacks participated in minstrel shows before the Civil War, the overwhelming majority of performers were white. After the war, however, black troupes (often in blackface, in imitation of their white counterparts) created their own minstrel shows. The shows included comedians, singers, dancers, and bands to accompany them. Minstrel bandsmen earned their money. They played for a daytime parade, followed by a short concert in the town square before the evening performance; another outdoor concert to attract a crowd just before the show began; and then they played for the show itself. The band usually sat on the stage on a platform behind the performers, where they switched when necessary from their band instruments to such stage instruments as tambourines, guitars, banjos, and fiddles.

The standard minstrel show ran about an hour and forty-five minutes, and was in three-part form. Part one began with a loud, rhythmically exciting opening, with singing and dancing to a tune, perhaps like "Dixie." Performers in blackface and outlandish costumes sat in a semicircle, facing the audience, with an interlocutor in the center, in whiteface, who would bandy jokes with the men at each end of the semicircle, Mr. Bones and Mr. Tambo, the "end men"; specialty songs and a mock lecture on a current subject would often close part one. Part two, the olio, included a potpourri of solo ballads, comic songs, and dances. A grand finale constituted part three, and frequently ended with a "walk-around." In the 1890s, this walk-around became the cakewalk—a highly stylized prancing and strutting that Nathan Irvin Huggins suggests "parodied the *quadrille d'honneur* of white society's grand balls."[21] Blesh believes this cakewalk music later "emerged as ragtime," because in the 1890s "compositions which had been published earlier were reappearing, rescored in syncopation and labeled 'ragtime.' "[22] We will return to this question in a moment.

From the 1830s to the turn of the century, New Orleans was visited regularly by minstrel shows and their bands. Oscar Henry, a New Orleans jazzman born in 1888, claimed that as a boy he "heard and saw every band that come to the city of New Orleans" but, he emphasized, "those bands we heard and second-lined to, was minstrel bands. Like Primrose and West; Primrose and Dockstader. The Dirtz Dixie Minstrels—R. G. Fields, Lew Dockstader."[23] The bands Henry heard played marching band music, and this music, particularly in its structure and instrumentation, was to have a strong influence on the development of the New Orleans style. Before the traditional jazz ensemble came into being, however, New Orleans musicians played in a variety of musical ensembles. A slave ensemble, for example, performing for a plantation party just outside New Orleans, included two violins, flute, triangle, and tambourine. In the city itself, however, as early as the 1830s, the free blacks of New Orleans organized a Negro Philharmonic Society of over a hundred members, with an orchestra conducted by black violinist Constantin Debarque. From several sources we learn of the twenty-five-to-thirty-piece Ida Club Symphony Orchestra—a Creole orchestra of the 1870s; and the Lyre Club Symphony Orchestra, organized by John Robichaux in 1897, which included the Tio family, Alphonse Picou, and George Baquet.[24]

The groups playing in and out of Storyville in the late 1890s were a mixed lot, instrumentally speaking. The "25" Club had a trio which included the accordion player Henry Peyton; later, Tom Anderson's saloon had a trio led by the mandolin player Tom Brown. In 1906 bassist Pops Foster, who started out as a cellist, played with a string trio called the Roseals Orchestra. And as late as 1913 the redoubtable Robichaux put together an orchestra of "some of the finest musicians in the city" to play for a grand ball— an orchestra that included ten strings, three woodwinds, five brass, and percussion.[25] The symphonic groups played light classical pieces, overtures, operatic medleys, ballroom dances of various kinds, and arrangements of popular songs. The small ensembles played mostly popular dance music.

Music in New Orleans, as many oldtime New Orleans jazzmen have pointed out, was to be heard everywhere—uptown, downtown, the French Quarter, Storyville, and the city's resort areas. Small marching bands playing for parades, funerals, wakes, and picnics were commonplace. Fraternal halls, church halls, and neighborhood dance halls were all available for parties and dances, and their weeknight functions were a regular part of New Orleans musicians' employment. Storyville of course had its own places where music was heard, and an area just outside Storyville, around Iberville and Burgundy Streets in the French Quarter, sometimes referred to as the Tango Belt, also included many places that regularly offered their customers music and dancing. In addition, the various downtown hotels offered bands and dancing, as did the seemingly endless cafés, cabarets, and honky-tonks scattered about the city.

With music constantly in the air, as it were, it is not surprising that, for many lower-class black children, learning to play an instrument was of the greatest urgency. Local musicians were frequently seen as cult heroes who spent their days in attractive idleness while others worked, and their nights making music in glamorous and exciting surroundings. They were admired, envied, and imitated. Being a musician was something a boy could aspire to, but first, he had to learn to play an instrument.

Before the Civil War, Creole children received traditional European musical training from the men connected with the several New Orleans symphonies and opera orchestras of the time; among the best-known teachers in New Orleans were Debarque, Gabici, and Thomas Martin.[26] After the war, this type of instruction continued. Isadore Barbarin, for example, a New Orleans–born brassman with the Onward Brass Band during the 1880s and '90s, received his training from Charles Shaw, who played bassoon in the French Opera House orchestra. Later, with money rather scarce, students took lessons from local teachers, or from whoever was willing and close at hand. Theogene Baquet was such a teacher. He was a cornet player, leader of the Excelsior Brass Band in the 1880s, and a neighborhood music teacher. He was also the father of George Baquet, later an important clarinetist, and no doubt instructed his son. George Baquet later gave clarinet lessons to one of New Orleans's most important clarinetists, Sidney Bechet, who in turn taught another important clarinetist, Albert Nicholas. Lessons, however, were frequently something less than formal. Describing a characteristic way in which musical information was passed on, Bechet said, "I'd been kind of giving lessons to Albert Nicholas—they wasn't lessons exactly either; it was just that Albert was younger than me, and afternoons we'd sit together on the back steps and we'd play along together and I'd kind of advise him."[27]

Frequently the memories of early years are hazy, and since so few records were kept, most of what we know about the musicians' early training is hearsay. Tony Jackson, perhaps the best-known pianist working in Storyville, was apparently self-taught, first on organ and then piano. Jelly Roll Morton, born in 1885, was supposed to have had guitar lessons at age six and piano several years later, but probably, like Tony Jackson, Morton was essentially self-taught, picking up pointers by listening to and observing other piano players. Kid Ory was another self-taught musician, starting on banjo and eventually switching to trombone. Even when information is firsthand, it is generally laconic. Alphonse Picou, who started on guitar at fourteen and then switched to clarinet, recalled what he had been doing in 1895. "I had been taking lessons before that. I took lessons for about eighteen months. My teacher's name was Mr. Morand. He was a Creole."[28]

To be able to say that one had studied with any of the city's jazz masters was almost as good as actually having had the lessons. All cornet players sought connections with Joe Oliver; even Louis Armstrong, who received his earliest instruction in cornet from a Mr. Davis, who led the band at the Colored Waifs' Home for Boys, tells us he received his own first cornet from Joe Oliver—"a beat-up old cornet of his which he had blown for years"—along with some words of encouragement and later some lessons.[29] Lee Collins, who also played cornet and whose father and grandfather both played cornet, claims to have followed Joe Oliver during a street parade during which he played a bit on Oliver's very own cornet.[30]

Information on the training of white New Orleans musicians is equally meager. Paul Mares, a New Orleans–born trumpet player with the influential New Orleans Rhythm Kings, was self-taught and supposedly unable to read music. (It may be useful to remember that in certain early jazz circles there was some cachet in being known as a nonreader.) Leon Rappolo, clarinetist with the same group, was born in Lutcher, outside New Orleans, started on violin, and probably had some clarinet lessons, but was otherwise self-taught. George Brunies, the trombonist, however, came from a decidedly musical family. His parents were both musical, his four brothers played several brass instruments, and he no doubt received an early and sound musical foundation. On the other hand, Nick LaRocca, cornetist with the Original Dixieland Jazz Band, tells us he borrowed his father's cornet and experimented with making sounds, writing down the valve numbers as a means of memorizing the songs. After a year of this, "he dispensed with the habit of writing down the numbers,"[31] formed various local groups, listened to the sounds emanating from hot spots he was too young to enter, practiced diligently, and eventually the jazz came.

Despite the efforts of writers and performers to show that someone or other "invented" jazz, there is little to be gained by designating any individual or group of players as having been the first to play jazz. A more useful and provocative exercise than trying to hunt down the first jazzman is found in Rose and Souchon's *New Orleans Jazz: A Family Album*—a valuable collection of pictures and directories of jazz in New Orleans from the late nineteenth century to 1917—in which they classify the many New Orleans ensembles into eleven jazz bands, three Dixieland bands, twenty-two dance orchestras, two ragtime bands, thirteen brass bands, and a number of novelty orchestras and string bands. In their system, jazz bands improvise their music; Dixieland bands read their music, as well as improvise; dance orchestras read; novelty orchestras play mainly on homemade instruments; and ragtime bands, string bands, vaudeville bands, and brass bands are what their names imply.[32]

The summary of early New Orleans brass bands I have made shows the St. Joseph Brass Band under Claiborne Williams, the Imperial Band under Manuel Perez, and the Excelsior Band, probably under John Robichaux, all of the 1880s. In the 1890s we know of the Peerless, Indian, Columbus, Diamond Stone, Onward, Adam Olivier's, and Excelsior brass bands. In the 1900s the Olympia Band was led by Freddie Keppard; the Eagle Band included Sidney Bechet; and Bill Johnson's Original Creole Band employed Keppard briefly. From 1905 to 1912 the Superior Band had Bunk Johnson, and the Magnolia Band had Joe Oliver. And an important white band of the period, Papa Laine's Reliance Brass Band, included Nick LaRocca, later the leader of the Original Dixieland Jazz Band.

Among early New Orleans cornetists, Buddy Bolden was considered the uptown king and Manuel Perez the downtown king. When Bolden was confined to a mental institution in 1907, Freddie Keppard took his place—although Chris Kelly had *his* supporters. When Kelly left New Orleans around 1913, some maintained that the crown had passed to Joe Oliver. There is no question, however, that the first "king," Buddy Bolden, and his six-piece Ragtime Band of 1893, had a significant influence on the development of early jazz. The band specialized in improvising the blues (the characteristic New Orleans blues were 8-, 12-, or 16-bar verses based on the several traditional primary blues harmonies), and Wallace Collins, who was born in New Orleans in 1858 and had played with Bolden, claimed Bolden's band also played rags. He described Bolden's method:

> To "rag" a tune . . . he'd take one note and put two or three to it. He began to teach them—not by the music—just by the head. After he'd get it down right, he'd teach the others their part.
>
> They had lots of band fellows who could play like that after Bolden gave 'em the idea.[33]

The meaning of "ragtime" when it refers to a piano style is crystal-clear in contrast to the ambiguity that later arose when it was applied to music played on other instruments. Before we attempt to clarify these later confusions, it will be useful to discuss, briefly, ragtime unadorned, as it were. Ragtime (as piano music) is a style developed by blacks between 1890 and 1910, and was the first black music to become commercially successful. The rhythmic foundation of ragtime was that of the two-step, that is, the rhythm of a Sousa march. The piano player's left hand provided a steady, bouncing, regular rhythmic pattern against the right hand's off-the-beat syncopated rhythms. In *The Art of Ragtime*, one of the best books on the subject, William J. Schafer and Johannes Riedel write: "Basically it is a formation, an organization of folk melodies and musical techniques into a brief and fairly simple quadrille-like structure, written down and designed to be played *as written* on the piano. It is formational music, as distinct from improvisational music."[34] (Authors' italics.)

The term *rag* had been used to designate a black folk tune; later, a number of these brief rags would be strung together in the short forms generally found in marches and in such dances as the quadrille, polka, jig, and the minstrel cakewalk.

The best known of the ragtime composers was Scott Joplin, who was born in Texas in 1868 and came to St. Louis when he was seventeen, where he took a job in the city's red-light district playing piano in the Silver Dollar saloon. After ten years of touring the Midwest, he finally made his home in Sedalia, Missouri, where he continued to study music theory at a local college for blacks, to compose, and to play nights at the Maple Leaf Club. In 1898, the publication of his "Maple Leaf Rag" made Joplin the most famous ragtime composer of the time. Other ragtime composers—Tom Turpin, who owned a café in St. Louis, and James Scott, who later settled in Kansas City—came under Joplin's influence and went on to become prominent on their own.

Musicians were as much taken with the sound and spirit of this syncopated piano music as were ordinary people. And when musicians recognized the popularity of ragtime, instrumental (i.e., ensemble) imitations of ragtime piano music soon followed. Generally speaking, the rhythm instruments provided the left hand's regular rhythmic pulse, while the melody instruments imitated the right hand's function as best they could. A great deal of adaptation was necessary, of course, because composed ragtime pieces are essentially pianistic in conception, with musical ideas, figures, and ornaments that lie easily in the experienced performer's hands. We now know that part of the adapting process—that is, transferring the music from the piano to the cornet or clarinet or trombone—is what Bolden and others were engaged in when they "ragged" a tune. Schafer and Riedel sum up the evolution of classic ragtime this way:

In schematic form, it can be said that classic ragtime derived from traditions of minstrel music, through the popular rage for "coon songs" in the 1890s, through a similar fad for march-cakewalk music for dancing in the late nineties, on to classic ragtime as formulated by Scott Joplin and his peers in Missouri from 1900 to 1910, through popular adaptations of piano ragtime as instrumental music and in song forms, on to late adaptations of ragtime as dance music (the foxtrot and variants) from 1910 to 1920.[35]

It is essential to keep in mind that ragtime—the piano music—is not jazz. Piano ragtime is composed music, and jazz is a manner of performing music in which an attempt at creative improvisation is the essential ingredient. There are times, however, when ragtime, the written music, is made the *basis* for a jazz improvisation, in which case the totality may properly be called jazz. Among New Orleans musicians and later commentators, the words *rag* and *ragtime* had various meanings. Jelly Roll Morton, for example, considered jazz, ragtime, and the blues to be three distinctly separate categories of music.[36] Pops Foster suggests still another category, "sweet music":

> From about 1900 on there were three types of bands around New Orleans. You had bands that played ragtime, ones that played sweet music, and the ones that played nothin' but blues.[37]

Lee Collins, recalling his father's cornet playing (probably around 1907 to 1910), said his father did not play jazz—"it was called 'ragtime' in those days."[38] In St. Louis in the 1890s, ragtime piano was called "jig piano," and bands imitating the ragtime rhythms were called "jig bands."[39]

The greatest mixup of terms, however, is to be found in H. O. Brunn's *The Story of the Original Dixieland Jazz Band*; in that book's table of "Ragtime Bands Prominent in New Orleans Before the Chicago Exodus," Braun's Military Band and Emile Tosso's Concert Band are both curiously classified as ragtime bands. Blesh, in his *Shining Trumpets*, believed that white bands were called ragtime bands "simply because all jazz and hot piano music were originally called ragtime in New Orleans."[40] In any case, ragtime was an important influence on early jazz, and twenty years after "Maple Leaf Rag" was published, rags were in the library of nearly every band calling itself a jazz band.

By the late nineteenth century, the marching band had become directly responsible for the makeup of the traditional New Orleans ensemble—usually three melody instruments and a variety of rhythm instruments—and the way in which the instruments functioned. The cornet (later replaced by the trumpet) carried the lead, staying rather close to the original melodic line, while the clarinet improvised elaborate embellishments above the cornet, as the trombone, below, punched out tones defining the agreed-upon harmonies; rhythm was provided by piano, drums, banjo or guitar, and bass fiddle or tuba, depending on whether the performance was indoors or outdoors. The players, of course, came from assorted musical backgrounds which, when brought together, resulted in the first authentic jazz style—a synthesis of the music of slaves, free blacks, Creoles, and later modifications by whites; or, to put it another way, a synthesis of Afro-American and Anglo-European music. Gunther Schuller puts it this way: "The only generalization we can permit ourselves is that the music that became known as jazz existed for many years as a multi-faceted music whose character depended largely on geographical disposition and the social and racial constitution of its audience."[41] Still, for Schuller, the African influence is overwhelming. "The sonority of real jazz," he writes in his *Early Jazz*, "is traceable directly to African singing and indirectly to African speech and language." Nor is this all. He believes his analytic study "shows that *every* musical element—rhythm, harmony, melody, timbre, and the basic forms of jazz—is essentially African in background and derivation."[42] (Schuller's italics.)

That early jazzmen were influenced by African music is of course unquestionable. However, as I wrote in *The Anatomy of Jazz*:

Starting with a background of West African culture, for about two centuries they had heard and made music at Saturday night dances, weddings, baptisms, candy stews, corn shuckings, evening gatherings, picnics, parties, and funerals; they knew work songs, love songs, devil songs, jigs, quadrilles, and stomps. They had heard the folk tunes of Scotland, Ireland, and England, the art songs of Italy and Spain, the melodies of French operatic arias, and the bright tunes of minstrel shows. The heat of plantation religion brought them the spirituals based on the simple harmonies and ardent spirit of the evangelical hymn. And above all they knew the blues. Add to these ragtime . . . and all the ingredients are gathered in.[43]

Early jazz, whenever it started, had its foundation in both religious and secular, both notated and improvised music. It flourished in New Orleans between the 1890s and the First World War. During that time a number of New Orleans musicians left New Orleans for brief visits elsewhere, taking the New Orleans style with them and returning to New Orleans with musical information from, say, Chicago or St. Louis. For example, around 1904, New Orleans touring groups employing musicians included Bush's Ragtime Opera Company, Ducournan Bros. Colored Southern Minstrel Company, the New Orleans Minstrels, and the New Orleans Troubadours. In 1908 Freddie Keppard, the first leader of the Olympia Orchestra, organized what may have been the first tour by a New Orleans band.[44] In 1913 his Original Creole Band—trumpet, clarinet, trombone, and rhythm—had vaudeville bookings from New York to Los Angeles. A year later the band played in Chicago, and then a year after that in New York; and the exotic New Orleans style was heard, firsthand, in large urban areas outside New Orleans.

Representative examples of musicians on the go include Eddie Atkins, a trombone player with Keppard in the Olympia Orchestra, who played in Chicago in 1915 and upon his return to New Orleans played with the Tuxedo and Onward Brass Bands. A year later he was playing in a band with Joe Oliver, who was himself soon to leave New Orleans for Chicago.[45] The musicians with the greatest mobility, however, were the solo piano players, the "professors," men like Jelly Roll Morton and Tony Jackson, who enjoyed touring a number of the country's principal red-light districts. "Everywhere," Blesh noted, "the tight-knit clan was meeting—at Tom Turpin's Rosebud Cafe in St. Louis, at the Frenchman's in New Orleans, at Johnny Seymour's Bar in Chicago, at the Maple Leaf Club in Sedalia, in Louisville, Nashville, Little Rock, Indianapolis, and El Reno in the old Oklahoma Territory."[46]

The lives of jazzmen were to be transformed by the First World War. In August 1917, four months after the United States entered the war, Secretary of the Navy Josephus Daniels declared that open prostitution was to be banned within five miles of any naval installation, and New Orleans (with its nearby naval base) came under this ban. New Orleanians with Storyville interests were unhappy with Daniels's order. Discussions followed between a representative of the navy and, among others, saloonkeeper Tom Anderson, with the navy standing firm. The city fathers appealed to Washington, but again to no avail. After weeks of impatient negotiation, Secretary Daniels said to the mayor, "You close the red-light district or the armed forces will."[47] Two weeks later the City Council passed an ordinance disestablishing Storyville, and on November 12, 1917, Storyville went out of business.

We shall now consider the development of the art of jazz as it was influenced by the effects of the First World War: the collapse of Storyville, the labor shortage in war industries in large northern and western manufacturing cities, and the great migration of blacks to these cities, particularly Chicago, where we will once again meet a number of important New Orleans jazzmen.

CHICAGO: THE MAKING OF A TRANSPORT CITY

4

For many years, particularly in popular writing, the history of jazz was oversimplified. This sketchy chronology says that jazz was born in New Orleans, "the cradle of jazz," then went "up the river" to Chicago and, from there, all over the world. Neat, in three parts, and easy to remember. There is, of course, some truth in this general statement, but it is not very useful. We now know that the growth and development of social music in New Orleans (of the sort that led to jazz) had its counterparts in other cities as well—Memphis, St. Louis, Oklahoma City. New Orleans was not unique; red-light districts throughout the country produced similar music. It was in New Orleans, however, that this special kind of music not only grew but flourished—accumulating along the way musicians, a repertoire, and a characteristic musical style—in sufficient variety and abundance to enable the historian to trace influences, analyze developments, make comparisons, draw inferences, and speak with confidence of a New Orleans style. We study the music of New Orleans (instead of Dallas, for example) for the same reasons historians focus on Bach as the principal representative of eighteenth-century baroque style, instead of Handel, say, or Telemann. New Orleans was the exemplar of the jazz city.

When musicians left New Orleans before the First World War, they did not all migrate to Chicago, nor were the musicians coming into Chicago all from New Orleans. However, sufficiently large numbers of New Orleans musicians went to Chicago to strongly influence the rise of jazz in Chicago. Although jazz and the makings of jazz could be heard in other cities, in the years just before and after the war Chicago became its focal point. As Marshall Stearns put it: "Sometime before 1920, the hypothetical peak of jazz intensity shifted from New Orleans to Chicago."[1] The period during which the shift occurred, when the New Orleans style came together with music in Chicago, can be made somewhat narrower. Oldtime Chicago musicians, according to John Steiner, who talked to a number of them, "remember no jazz hornmen or anything like Dixieland jazz in Chicago before 1911."[2]

It is important to remember that the majority of New Orleans musicians were not especially affected by the closing of Storyville, because Storyville had not been, for them, a major source of employment. Those who had worked in Storyville regularly, however, had to look for work elsewhere. In fact, Storyville as a lowlife center had been diminishing for some time before it was closed, and for as much as a decade before the closing, musicians were leaving New Orleans for work in other cities. Pops Foster, who played with the Magnolia Band, recalls:

> A lot of musicians left New Orleans before the District closed. Laurence Duhé was one of the first to leave about 1907. Bill Johnson went to Los Angeles and another Johnson, Nookie Johnson, I think, went to L.A. too. Sugar Johnny left early and went to Chicago. Manuel Perez and Arnold Metoyer went up. Freddie Keppard left about 1909. They left because there were more places to work or they just wanted to travel some.[3]

Because of Chicago's location as a water and rail transportation center, and the consequent gathering of transients with money to spend and a short time in which to spend it, Chicago attracted musicians—particularly piano players—from all around the country. When they got there, in the early 1900s, they discovered that visiting "professors" had already introduced the city to ragtime as early as the Chicago World's Fair of 1893. Men like Tony Jackson who came to Chicago around 1906 and Jelly Roll Morton who came about two years later continued to build on the early ragtime foundations with their performances at such Chicago hotspots as Pony Morris's, the Everleigh Club, Dago and Russell's, and the Elite. There was no movement afoot, as such; there was only the appropriate environment. It was through the efforts of Jackson, Morton, and others, that, as Eileen Southern put it, "Chicago became the center of ragtime playing that St. Louis had been a decade earlier."[4]

As we mentioned earlier, New Orleans was an important jumping-off place for traveling shows of all kinds; for many of these shows, Chicago was a principal stop on their itinerary, and tours frequently ended in Chicago. The city was a usual stop for shows playing the TOBA circuit (Theater Owners Booking Association, which produced shows for black audiences), as well as the Orpheum circuit. Between 1912 and 1918, for example, Bill Johnson's Original Creole Band, a New Orleans group playing the Orpheum circuit, is known to have worked at a number of Chicago places. Other New Orleans musicians came to Chicago, especially if they had been offered employment as a group. One such instance occurred when George Filhe, a New Orleans trombonist who had come to Chicago in 1913, persuaded Charlie Elgar, a New Orleans musician-turned-booking-agent, to import an entire band from New Orleans to play at Chicago's well-known Arsonia Cafe. Elgar notified friends in New Orleans, and a band arrived en masse, including Manuel Perez on trumpet, Lorenzo Tio on clarinet (replaced by Alphonse Picou a year later), Eddie Atkins on tuba, Frank Haynie on piano, and Louis Cottrell on drums.[5]

It was a common practice of New Orleans musicians in Chicago to urge other New Orleans musicians to join them. From John Steiner's encyclopedic piece on Chicago[6] we learn that New Orleans musicians who came to Chicago early and found Chicago agreeable (except perhaps for the lack of familiar faces) sent letters to friends in New Orleans telling them how good it was to be in Chicago and encouraging them to make the move. Sidney Bechet corroborates the importance and force of these messages in his recollection of what Chicago was like shortly after he himself arrived there:

> About 1917 . . . a whole lot of musicianers started to leave New Orleans for up North, mostly for Chicago. . . . There was Laurence Duhé, Sugar Johnny, Roy Palmer, Tubby Garland, Wellman Braud, Minor Hall, Tubby Hall, Herbert Lindsay. . . . they was all writing back to New Orleans that work was plentiful, telling the New Orleans musicianers to come up. That's how Freddie Keppard, Bill Johnson, George Baquet, Kid Ory, Mutt Carey, Tig Chambers all come up from New Orleans. . . . it was a real excitement there.[7]

The excitement Bechet referred to grew out of the news that jobs were plentiful, that Chicago money flowed freely and was easier to come by than southern money, and that the sort of success being enjoyed by Bechet, Keppard, and others was available to all. For New Orleans musicians Chicago became Mecca, and once established there, they worked hard to entice others to join them.

According to Al Rose, "the first New Olreans jazz group to appear in the North" (and that later played in Chicago) was a band called the Original Creole Serenaders that included Freddie Keppard on trumpet, James Palao on violin, George Baquet on clarinet, and Bill Johnson on bass.[8] According to one commentator, Keppard's Original Creole Orchestra (not "Serenaders") came north for the first time in 1911 to play at the Grand Theatre in Chicago.[9] This may be the band that Jelly Roll Morton later called "The Freddie Keppard Creole Band"—a band that he said "was tremendous. They really played jazz."[10] The group originally led by Keppard clearly went through a number of changes in name as well as in personnel, and by the time Mezz Mezzrow heard them in Chicago Keppard was no longer the leader, the band was called the Original New Orleans Creole Jazz Band (although the men sometimes called it the Sugar Johnny Band or the Duhé Band), it included Bechet on clarinet and Lil Hardin on piano, and it was *this* band, Mezzrow said, that "really upset the town and paved the way for the rest of the New Orleans jazzmen in good old Chi."[11] (Mezzrow's unbounded enthusiasm often resulted in exaggeration.)

The roster of New Orleans musicians who went to Chicago includes, of course, many minor figures, friends of major figures, friends of friends, and so on, and the names were easily mingled, particularly before the historical or musical importance of the major figures became firmly established. Some came to Chicago and stayed; others came and went; still others moved easily back and forth. From reminiscences, memoirs, and various encyclopedias, we gather that between 1913 and 1917 the following musicians arrived in Chicago: cornetist Tig Chambers and trumpeter Sugar Johnny Smith, both born in New Orleans around 1880, and both performers in several Storyville nightspots; trombonist Zue Robertson, who had played in New Orleans with clarinetist A. J. Piron and John Robichaux; tuba and bass player Ed Garland, who played in New Orleans with King Oliver; trombonist Roy Palmer, who later worked in Chicago with Johnny Dodds and Oliver; bass player Wellman Braud, who worked in Chicago with Keppard and Lil Hardin; and Fred Hall, who worked in Chicago with Oliver and Armstrong. And the names run on.

The New Orleans musicians we have discussed so far were black musicians. Now we shall look at those white New Orleans musicians who came to Chicago, bringing with them *their* version of the New Orleans style. In May 1915, Tom Brown and his six-piece New Orleans band arrived in Chicago for an engagement at Lamb's Café. H. O. Brunn, in *The Story of the Original Dixieland Jazz Band*, tells us that Joe Frisco, a comedy dancer who had been doing a vaudeville turn at a club in New Orleans to the music of Tom Brown's band, had been sufficiently taken with their music to send for them six months later when he was hired to do a show at Lamb's Café.[12] Another account (the reports are inconsistent, but the truth is no doubt among them) tells us that Tom Brown's Band from Dixieland was imported to Chicago to replace Bill Johnson's Original Creole Orchestra.[13] Brown and his group, if not the first Dixieland group to go North (for "Dixieland" read "white"), were certainly among the first, advertising themselves as "Brown's Dixieland Jass Band, Direct from New Orleans, Best Dance Music in Chicago."[14] The band included Tom Brown on trombone, Ray Lopez on trumpet, Gus Mueller on clarinet, Arnold Loyacano on guitar, Steve Brown on bass, and Billy Lambert on drums. Except for Mueller and Loyacano, both of whom had worked in New Orleans with Laine's Reliance Brass Band, the rest of the band were relatively undistinguished performers. Several weeks after the band's arrival, Brown, learning of a clarinet vacancy in another band, sent for his friend, New Orleans clarinetist Larry Shields; Shields came, and when he did not fit into the other band, Brown persuaded his own clarinetist, Mueller, to trade places with

Shields (later, Shields would become prominent as a member of the Original Dixieland Jazz Band). With or without Shields, Chicagoans did not find the music of Brown's band especially engaging, and in August, about three months after their arrival, the band, under a new name—the Kings of Ragtime—left Chicago to do a vaudeville tour. After several unfortunate engagements, including one billed as "The Ragtime Rubes," it was clear that the band would be happier in New Orleans, and they returned home.[15]

Almost immediately, another band calling themselves "Stein's Band from Dixie" set out from New Orleans for Chicago to try *their* luck. Led by drummer Johnny Stein, with Nick LaRocca on cornet, Eddie Edwards on trombone, Alcide Nuñez on clarinet, and Henry Rojas on piano, the band had been "discovered" in New Orleans by Harry James, a Chicago nightclub manager, who booked them into Schiller's Café and advertised the group as "Stein's Dixie Jass Band." According to Stein, the band was "an overnight sensation," but then, "without warning, the four men left me holding the bag. They then reorganized, calling themselves 'The Original Dixieland Jazz Band.' "[16] Stein completed his engagement by hiring four New Orleans musicians who were already in Chicago, while his former colleagues replaced him by sending for New Orleans drummer Tony Sbarbaro. It was this band, the Original Dixieland Jazz Band, with Larry Shields replacing Nuñez, that would make the first jazz records.

Thus we see that the making of the historically important early white bands, playing what was called "jass," was as often fortuitous as it was calculated. New Orleans musicians in Chicago, black and white alike, used friends when they could; talent and ability were important, or course, but apparently not as important as friendship. John Steiner, reporting on the migration of New Orleans musicians who were eventually to form one of the most influential groups in Chicago—the New Orleans Rhythm Kings— wrote: "Several New Orleans men tried to convert Chicago musicians to their New Orleans style. In dismay at the inadequate results, New Orleans drummer Ragbaby Stevens . . . sent an invitation home to George Brunies to join him. George was reluctant to leave until Paul Mares, acting on Stevens' telegram, went North and soon wrote back to the effect: Come on in, the water's fine."[17]

The influx of musicians, black and white, together with a host of other circumstances, was to make Chicago in the twenties the jazz center of the world. Before we examine this phenomenon, and the manner in which Chicago jazz developed after the First World War, it will be worthwhile to stop here for a closer look at some aspects of Chicago's history from early times to the Great Black Migration of 1916–1920, the city's general economic and social significance, its early spirit, its rowdiness, crime, and political corruption, the growth and development of its Black Belt, and other influences that helped create an environment in which jazz could flourish. When we have explored these various Chicago elements, we should be able to look at the Chicago jazz scene, from the twenties on, with a deeper understanding of both jazz and the city. John Sirjamaki's *The Sociology of Cities* reminds us that in their early, formative stage "cities comprised urban communities which exercised a major part in the social and cultural events of that time."[18] In attempting to understand the relation of jazz to Chicago, it is therefore necessary to survey, even briefly, Chicago in its early years.

In its primitive days, what is now Chicago was a neck of land that lay between the Great Lakes and an unbroken succession of waterways to the Gulf of Mexico, and thus became the most convenient portage between the two. It was used by the Pottawottamies long before the first white men—Father Marquette and Louis Joliet—came in 1673. France owned it and used it until the British seized it in 1759 and held it for thirty-five years. Around 1790, the portage attracted its first permanent settler, Jean Baptiste Point de Saible, a well-educated French-speaking black with French leanings and connections.[19] In 1795 the United States, finally recognizing "the significance and importance of Chicago in the security of the western frontier," worked out a treaty with the

Indians which gave them a piece of land six miles square at the mouth of the Chicago River.[20]

In 1830, Chicago was platted, three years later it was incorporated as a village, and in 1837 it became an incorporated city divided into six wards. The city census taken that year showed 4,170 persons (including 104 sailors on Chicago-owned vessels and 77 blacks)[21] living and working in about 450 buildings, mostly "cheap frame structures referred to by visitors as 'mere shanties.' "[22] But the land boom and rampant speculation were just around the bend. The Illinois-Michigan canal connecting the lake with the Mississippi was completed in 1848; the railroads discovered Chicago, and by the beginning of the Civil War, the city was well on its way to becoming the nation's central shipping center. Although the city continued to grow steadily, in the years 1849 and 1850 the population growth was diminished by cholera epidemics. About 1,000 people were stricken, of whom 678 died. The disease attacked and spread quickly. "One theory of the spread of the disease," Edith Abbott wrote, "was that immigrants arriving from various parts of Europe where the cholera was epidemic were bringing in new cases, and this terrible disease was believed to have been brought up the river from New Orleans in an emigrant boat."[23]

After the Civil War, Chicago industry and shipping moved steadily forward, and, as Drake and Cayton summed up, "Chicago settled down to packing meat, shipping wheat, and making a fortune for Armour, Swift, Pullman, McCormick, Ogden, and Marshall Field."[24] State Street became the city's most important retail center through the efforts of such businessmen as Potter Palmer, Marshall Field, the Mandel Brothers, Abram Rothschild, Levi Leiter, and John G. Shedd, to name only a few. Its diverse manufacturing, shipping, and export sales constituted a formidable economic base, and between 1860 and 1890 Chicago business flourished. Cyrus McCormick continued to make reapers, George Pullman made sleeping cars, Marshall Field sold dry goods, and Swift and Armour became butchers to the world. Chicago's trans-

portation advantages appeared to be boundless. "In 1871 Chicago
was the hub of railroad systems embracing 10,750 miles of line,"
architectural historian Carl W. Condit wrote, "with aggregate annual revenues of $82,777,000. The carriers operated 75 passenger
trains per day to and from the city's terminals."[25]

Because of its fascination with moneymaking, the city had
little time for such amenities as paved streets, proper sanitation
facilities, decent housing for the poor, and adequate police and fire
protection. The woeful lack of firefighting equipment was clearly
demonstrated the night of October 8, 1871, when a fire started in
the O'Leary barn on Chicago's West Side, raged through the city's
narrow lanes and alleys, and burned its way to the lake. The fire
swept in all directions, and the majority of the city's buildings
burned like kindling. Condit tells us what the structures were like:

> About two-thirds of them were built wholly of wood, particularly the
> houses, stockyard structures, warehouses, railway facilities, and the
> many barns that were uniformly scattered over the urban area.[26]

Forty-eight hours after the fire started, property valued at $196
million was destroyed, about 300 people were dead, and about
100,000 were left homeless.[27] The city was rebuilt with iron, and
brick, and white, gray, and brown sandstone. Industry once more
boomed, but beneath the apparent prosperity, another fire smol-
dered: the bitterness and antagonism between labor and capital
that sporadically flared into violence, killing, and wounding, and
that provided provocative names for historians—the Railroad Riots
of 1877, the Haymarket Square Riot of 1886, the Great Pullman
Strike of 1894—all contributing to Chicago's early reputation as a
city burdened with violence.

From earliest times through the repeal of the Illinois Black
Code in 1865, many Chicago blacks (especially later, among the
middle class) believed that Chicago should be receptive to blacks
because Jean Baptiste Point de Saible, the first known settler, was
black. "The de Saible tradition," Harold F. Gosnell writes, "has

been used by a number of societies of colored persons in the city interested in building up race consciousness and civic pride."[28] For black and white alike, the spirit of Chicago may have been summed up by Lincoln Steffens in 1904, when he reported that "no matter who you are or where you come from, Chicago will give you a cheer and a first boost."[29] Several historians of Chicago believe that the character of early Chicago—its frontier spirit with its crime and violence—survived until the 1890s. Others, particularly Virgil Peterson, former executive director of the Chicago Crime Commission, "deplores this characterization as an excuse for the conduct of the public officials of that time."[30] Still, the idea of a special Chicago spirit is not without foundation. Here, for example, is another, less-well-known view of early Chicago, summarized by Archibald Byrne in "Walter L. Newberry's Chicago":

> Only a little probing beneath the surface reveals that early Chicago was very far from typical of frontier society. On the contrary, the city was cosmopolitan almost from its beginning; in weighted counterpart to the bass notes of the materialistic theme there sound always the higher tones of a cultural motif, a culture Chicago shared with the rest of mid-nineteenth century urban America and, to some degree, with the cities of Europe.[31]

If by "cosmopolitan" Byrne meant that the people of Chicago belonged to all parts of the world, then Chicago was certainly cosmopolitan. We need only look briefly at its ethnic makeup, its nineteenth-century enclaves, to see this point clearly. Before Chicago was established as a city in the 1830s, its inhabitants were most likely to be Anglo-Saxon, French, French-Canadian, and part Indian. The Irish arrived in great numbers in the 1840s, fleeing the great potato famine; Germans came, fleeing the revolutions of 1848; in the late 1840s and '50s the Scandinavians came, and German Jews came. They all came, even if they were not wanted. As John M. Allswang observed in *A House for All Peoples*, "In Chicago, as elsewhere, the immigrants were not always welcomed by Native-Americans."[32] By 1870 there were about 60,000 Germans (including Austrians and Bohemians), or 20 percent of the total population; and about 40,000 Irish, or about 13 percent of the total. In short, Chicago's Germans and Irish combined made up one-third of the total population.[33]

Transport cities, by their very nature, attract both the hopeless and the ambitious, and in the midst of Chicago's immense wealth and burgeoning industry (characterized by the World's Columbian Exposition of 1893, celebrating the four hundredth anniversary of the discovery of America, with its White City of 150 Roman, Greek, and Renaissance buildings along the lake shore), existed the most abject poverty, accompanied by the most violent crime. Squeezed into an area of about a third of a square mile, bounded by Halstead Street on the west, State on the east, Polk on the north, and Twelfth Street on the south, were the city's immigrant unfortunates. Agnes Sinclair Holbrook, commenting on the section in 1893, said, "This third of a square mile includes east of the river a criminal district which ranks as one of the most openly and flagrantly vicious in the civilized world, and west of the same stream the poorest, and probably the most crowded section of Chicago."[34] Of some comfort, perhaps, to its inhabitants, but to the horror of Chicago's temperance advocates, this area west of the river contained eighty-one saloons.

Little English was spoken in the immigrant district, and handmade signs announcing rooms for rent, say, or places that sold bread or mended dresses or shoes, were written in Italian, German, Russian, and Yiddish, to name only a few of the languages in use. Inhabitants of the section included persons from eighteen countries, including "seven Turks engaged in various occupations at the World's Fair."[35] The majority of immigrants worked in factories when work was available; others were self-employed, that is, engaged in working—usually at piece rates—at home. Among the poorest, we learn, "are chiefly pedlers, occasionally musicians and street-players [who] almost invariably live from hand to mouth, keeping up a precarious existence by irregular and varied occupations. Most of this class are very poor indeed . . . that is, they generally receive less than $10.00 a week, many less than $5.00."[36]

All through the nineteenth century, wherever slum areas developed in Chicago they were soon joined to vice areas. Vice, as we have seen, breeds crime, and from its earliest days the city of Chicago attracted those criminals who were bound to be, in Bessie Louise Pierce's gentle words, "accused of wrongdoing." Police reports showed that "thievery ranged from horse stealing and purloining hen roosts to robbery of the mails, the express, and the banks; pickpockets plied their trade with daring and success; counterfeiters deceived the unwary; and organized gangs created terror on all sides."[37] By 1849 there were over a hundred gambling houses on North and South Water Streets alone, and by the mid-1850s perhaps 150 sporting houses were paying graft to corrupt police, judges, and politicians. Later there were the usual attempts at reform followed by the usual raids.

Saloons and dram shops (which sold only liquor) also flourished—they were supposed to be licensed by the city, but it was charged that in 1854, of the 600 places that sold liquor, only 160 were licensed. One newspaper editor concerned with the strength of the forces of good and evil pointed out that for every church in the city there were seventeen drinking establishments. Saturday night was the busiest night of the week. "Then," Pierce noted, "the streets were filled with customers, and the haunts of vice were wide open, offering girls, music, liquor, and dancing."[38] From the 1890s until the findings of Chicago's Vice Commission in 1911 resulted in the closing of the city's red-light district, the district known as the Levee was Chicago's challenge to New Orleans's Storyville. It was called the Levee supposedly because early steamboat gamblers used it as their landing in the city, their place of relaxation, their snug harbor.

The old Levee, just south of the present Loop district, appears to have been located amid Chicago's railroad yards, bounded by Polk Street on the north, Twelfth Street on the south, Clark Street on the west, and State Street on the east. Railroad men, freight handlers, and those arriving or departing from the Dearborn Street Station found that a Levee joint was never farther than just across the street. On a remarkable color-coded street map compiled by Hull House workers around 1893 for the purpose of showing the weekly earnings of each family living in Holbrook's "third of a square mile" are not only the number of brothels in the district but their specific street addresses as well. Stepping out of the Dearborn Street Station, prospective clients had, for example, a choice of eight consecutive brothels between numbers 179 and 193 Plymouth Court.

Open prostitution, that persistent element in the evolution of jazz, was as necessary to Chicago's spirit and atmosphere as the Great Fire was to its architectural development. Of the several officially tolerated vice areas, the most important (if that is the word) was the Levee, which was afterward joined in the 1890s by a "new" Levee farther to the south. The old Levee was in the city's First Ward, and was controlled by two politicians, Michael ("Hinky Dink") Kenna and "Bathhouse John" Coughlin; when the "new" Levee established itself to the south, in the Second Ward, they moved in on the new prize. Hinky Dink had his own saloon, but he and Bathhouse John also used a place known as Freiberg's Dance Hall, which was:

> a hangout for thieves, whores, pimps, gunmen and small-time politicians who mingled nightly with visiting business and professional men from out of town or respectable neighborhoods in the city itself. Girls met their customers at Freiberg's, took them to the crib houses or cheap hotels surrounding it. Curiously, during the day the hall was often the scene for official political meetings to which came honorable or semi-honorable officials and candidates.[39]

Politics notwithstanding, the principal business of the Levee was prostitution. In 1900 the Everleigh sisters opened the Everleigh Club in the new Levee, and it at once became the most lavish and expensive brothel in Chicago, if not in the world. Wendt and Kogan describe this Never-Never Land:

Prices began at fifty dollars, and champagne was twenty dollars a bottle. . . . Customers were welcomed by the Everleigh sisters themselves. Negro servants accepted their wraps and escorted the guests to the card rooms or the ballroom, where women in evening gowns awaited them and a band played lively tunes. . . . Even the grand piano was leafed with gold, and the cuspidors, discreetly hidden by long velvet draperies that framed exotic murals, were gold-plated. Upstairs were gold, silver and copper rooms. . . . There were also a Persian room, a college room, a Pullman room fitted as a private railway car, a mirrored room covered from floor to ceiling and wall to wall with silvered glass.[40]

In 1911, the city fathers, in still another fit of reform, asked the Everleigh sisters to cease and desist, and they did. They retired to New York, presumably to live a more quiet life.

The Levee offered more than open prostitution; its patrons looked upon it as a complete social center. Scattered among the new Levee's sporting houses, gambling joints, barrel houses, cribs, and cheap hotels, and going by such engaging names as the "Bucket of Blood, Black May's, the Silver Dollar, the House of All Nations, and a place simply called Why Not?"[41] were the dance halls and concert saloons. Just before the axe fell in 1911 the Vice Commission could report that they had visited 250 saloons in which they identified 928 prostitutes. The majority of these saloons, the investigators reported, provided their customers with piano playing and singing and, in some instances, vaudeville acts. In addition, places to dance were frequently close by. There were about 275 public dance halls; later, when the attractions of the dance halls and those of saloons and eating places were combined, such Chicago establishments were called cabarets (in New York they were called nightclubs). By 1916, a good many of the social activities that formerly accompanied Chicago's high- and low-class prostitution—the vaudeville review, professional and semiprofessional solo and ensemble singing and dancing, public dancing, and eating and drinking—were rolled up into a native version of the cabaret, what Walter C. Reckless called "the first new manifestation of the jazz age."[42] Chicago newspaper headlines gave the cabarets more publicity than they deserved, and shrewd entrepreneurs, on the scent of easy money, opened cabarets in the expanding Black Belt on the South Side of the city, south of the Loop. Here whites could meet with blacks, in what were soon called black-and-tan cabarets, on a somewhat equal footing for dining, dancing, boozing, and whatever else pleased their fancy. "Once in the Black Belt," Reckless noted, "the cabarets exploited the musical tradition of the Negro who brought with him the 'blues' and a new type of jazz."[43]

In the years ahead there was to be continuous conflict between reformers and those who wished Chicago to be a wide-open city. In 1912, the year the vice districts were officially closed, a grand jury revealed connections between local politicians and vice syndicates on the South Side Levee, including the syndicate run by known gangsters "Big Jim" Colosimo and Johnny Torrio.[44] And two years after the district was supposed to have been shut down, an investigation by the *Chicago Tribune* showed three organized South Side vice rings, one of which was still led by Colosimo.[45]

The reformers were persistent. The Levee was officially closed and laws had been passed to forestall its reopening, yet only a year later Mayor Carter Harrison saw obvious indications that the district was, if not booming, then at least stirring again. In 1915 he appointed Major M. C. L. Funkhouser head of a Morals Division of the Chicago Police Department to enforce antivice laws, and, perhaps hoping to show that the law was not to be intimidated by the likes of Colosimo and Ike Bloom (owner of Freiberg's Dance Hall), the mayor revoked their licenses. The Levee's reaction was forthright: during the next eighteen months, the chief of the Morals Squad was stabbed in a Levee saloon (earlier, Levee leaders had offered him $2,200 a month to mind his own business), and a Morals Squad sergeant was shot and killed.[46] These criminal acts were a clear warning to the city that the Levee would not tolerate the interference of policemen.

After the revocation of Colosimo's and Bloom's licenses, it

took Big Jim five months to get his license restored; it took Bloom sixteen months to retrieve his; but by that time Chicago had a new mayor—William Hale ("Big Bill") Thompson—and the Levee crowd had great hopes for the future. Big Bill, they reasoned, would look after them. And he did. About a year after he took office, Big Bill Thompson abolished the Police Department Morals Division and made it crystal-clear that he looked favorably upon the idea of Chicago as a wide-open city. He defied his detractors "by approving the reopening of a number of Levee dives, including the notorious Cadillac Café, 'Polack Ben's' resort on Twenty-second Street, and Freddie Buxbaum's saloon, one of the city's vilest places, on the ground floor of the Marlboro Hotel, a brothel at State and Twenty-second streets."[47]

The rise and development of Chicago's vice areas, while they were essentially white-controlled, nonetheless brought forward a number of blacks who enjoyed the same power, influence, and wealth ordinarily reserved for white crime kings. Among the earliest of the black crime leaders was John ("Mushmouth") Johnson, who died in 1907. Starting as a porter in a white gambling house in 1880, he studied the gambler's trade, saved his money, and eventually was able to open a saloon and gambling house on State Street (right behind the eight consecutive Plymouth Court sporting houses we mentioned earlier), where he catered to railroad men and professional gamblers. Johnson ran his business as efficiently as any white czar, and staying in business was his priority. He knew how to do this as well as anyone in the Levee. During mayoralty campaigns he felt no compunction in giving Democrats and Republicans alike $10,000 each. He made his peace with "Hinky Dink" Kenna and "Bathhouse John" Coughlin, the First Ward's political leaders, and they saw to it that his establishments were not raided by the police. Johnson understood the connections between crime and politics. Harold F. Gosnell, in his *Negro Politicians*, the best survey of Chicago's early black crime leaders, points out one of Johnson's techniques. "While not directly concerned with other aspects of the political game, he urged Negroes to register and vote in the First Ward, he attended party conventions, and he was known as a political leader."[48]

When Johnson died, five years before the Levee was officially closed, his estate was estimated at $250,000. One of his successors waited just offstage. A black man, Bob Motts, had worked in Mushmouth Johnson's establishment as a porter, and some time after Johnson died Motts opened a combination saloon, cabaret, and gambling place in the Second Ward; in addition, he ran the Pekin Theater and, as the black population grew, made it a center of black social life. He bribed policemen and politicians alike, and, like his former boss, was active in getting out the district's black vote. Motts was followed by Henry ("Teenan") Jones, who had successfully operated a saloon and gambling place outside the Levee district until he was driven out by the "Hyde Park Protective Association," after which he opened *two* saloons in the Second Ward, the Elite No. 1 and Elite No. 2, a couple of blocks apart on State Street.

Daniel M. Jackson was not only the best known of the black gambling czars, but also the most interesting. Born in Pittsburgh in 1870, he graduated from Lincoln University in Pennsylvania and later came to Chicago, where his family opened an undertaking parlor at Twenty-sixth and State Streets. In 1900 he ran for county commissioner as a Republican and lost. His undertaking establishment, although operated as a legitimate business, was mainly a front for his several illegal enterprises. Gosnell reports that Jackson "was chiefly known as the head of a great syndicate that controlled vice, bootlegging, cabarets, and such gambling games as craps, poker, and policy."[49]

The areas in which Johnson, Motts, Jones, and Jackson could operate were clearly prescribed. Blacks in Chicago could not always choose where they wanted to live, and nearly all found themselves in the least desirable neighborhoods—the large vice districts. The reasons are clearly stated by the 1920s' Chicago Commission on Race Relations:

Ninety percent of the Negro population has always lived near the city's former segregated vice districts, partly because white sentiment excluded them from other neighborhoods, partly because rents in the neighborhood of vice were low enough to meet their meager economic resources, and partly because their weakness made their protests against the proximity of vice less effective than the protests of whites. . . . In fact, according to the report of the Chicago Vice Commission in 1911, at one time prostitutes were promised immunity by the police if they confined themselves to a certain area in which Negroes predominated.[50]

In 1910 the Chicago Vice Commission reported on 1,020 Chicago resorts for prostitution, and estimated there were "about 5,000 women who devoted their full time to the business of prostitution (including maids, madams, as well as prostitutes)."[51] The percentage of black women in Chicago engaged in prostitution at the time was so small as to be of no consequence; but during the next twenty years, the rise was phenomenal. Black neighborhood conditions helped provide a "proper" environment for prostitution and at the same time provided a benign environment for the development of jazz. The source of Chicago's relation to jazz, therefore, must be sought in the Great Black Migration of 1916 to 1920, which in turn resulted in Chicago's Black Belt. The political, economic, and social life of the Black Belt was strongly influenced by external factors, particularly the Thompson regime, and the effects of Prohibition. We now turn our attention to these subjects.

CHICAGO: THE WIDE-OPEN BLACK BELT

5

J ean Baptiste Point de Saible, the black man who was Chicago's
first settler, may have come from either Santo Domingo or the
Northwest Territory—his birthplace is unknown. He arrived
about 1790 and resided, until about 1806, with his Indian wife, two
daughters, and a son, near where the Michigan Boulevard Bridge
was later built. Although occasional blacks came to the city in its
earliest days, it was not until the decade between 1840 and 1850
that they began to arrive in any significant numbers. By then
"Chicago" had become a synonym for "freedom" among the supporters of abolition who assisted runaway slaves, and the city was
soon an important station on the covert escape route called the
Underground Railroad.

The federal Fugitive Slave Law, intended to punish those
giving aid and comfort to fugitive slaves, seemed to have little
deterrent effect in Chicago. Even though the law made it a crime
punishable by a five-hundred-dollar fine to shelter a fugitive slave
or to prevent his arrest, the city's sympathetic whites and free
blacks welcomed the arrival of hundreds of escaped slaves as they
were brought into the city. Some passed through, using Chicago as
a way station to Canada, while others sought hiding places and
tried to remain in the city. A few succeeded.

The number of blacks who stayed on was small, but it was
significant because the black population has grown continuously
since that modest beginning. The first Chicago census, in 1840,
showed that 53 out of a total population of 4,470 were black.[1] Still,
by the late 1840s there were at least ten blacks who owned property in Chicago's First and Second Wards. The black population
continued to expand; during the 1850s most of them lived on Clark
and Dearborn Streets north of Harrison Street, although a handful
of the more prosperous blacks bought property to the south,
around what was to be Thirty-third Street. After the Great Fire of
1871 and a lesser one several years later, the ensuing building
booms in the city's business district forced blacks to move still
farther south.[2]

Between the fires of the 1870s and the First World War, the

principal concentration of Chicago's blacks was on a thin strip of land between an upper-class white neighborhood and a lower-class white slum. Edith Abbott, whose special concern was Chicago's slum housing, describes more specifically the Black Belt's expansion:

> In the old days the South Side was divided into Negro and white areas stretching in parallel lines almost from the business district to Garfield Boulevard. Gradually the old "Black Belt" expanded in all available directions—to the south, to the west, to the east— everywhere except where it was checked by the pressure of business to the north. This movement went on simultaneously with the flight of the fashionable world to apartment-house life on the North Side.[3]

In the northern half of the South Side, along the carefully kept lake shore—the Gold Coast—were the fashionable mansions of the wealthy, later to become rundown rooming houses. Directly west was the north-south strip, or belt, in which most of the black population settled. (By 1920, the Black Belt was home for 90 percent of Chicago's black population.[4])

The continued concentration of blacks in this narrow belt brought continued isolation. Allan H. Spear sums up this aspect of the situation:

> As the pre-war era drew to a close, the Chicago Negro community was becoming an increasingly self-contained enclave within the city. Isolated from the mainstream of Chicago life, it had begun to pursue an independent course of development. Its leaders talked less of an integrated city, more of a self-sufficient Negro metropolis on the South Side. It remained to be seen whether such a goal was economically, politically, and socially possible.[5]

Between 1910 and 1920, Chicago's black population increased from 44,103 to 109,594, or 148.5 percent. In this same ten-year period, the migration to the North brought in about 61,000 blacks (an additional 4,000 were added through natural increase, that is, through the excess of births over deaths).[6]

When America entered the war in 1917, northern and southern social and economic forces combined to create the largest internal black migration in our history. While the migration had begun as early as 1916 when eastern industries began importing a southern black labor force, the migration to Chicago started in earnest a year later. The report of the Chicago Commission on Race Relations suggests a number of the reasons why blacks now began to arrive in Chicago in great numbers. There were direct railway lines to Chicago from many southern states, jobs appeared to be waiting in the mail-order houses, and labor was needed in the stockyards with their large packing plants and storage houses. And, as a special attraction, certain entrepreneurial organizations and their agents provided free transportation, or reduced fares for workers and their families. As the report relates, it "had the effect, on the one hand, of adding the stimulus of intimate persuasion to the movement, and, on the other hand, of concentrating solid groups in congested spots in Chicago."[7]

Some rumors, such as the one about jobs in the stockyards, had their basis in fact. The combination of the war in Europe and the lockout of European immigrants who had constituted the cheap labor force of the North created a theretofore unprecedented job market. The major Chicago industries, fearful of a labor shortage, sent agents south to encourage black workers to head for the Promised Land. And they came. During the Great Migration they came in the tens of thousands, especially from along the Mississippi Valley, to seek their fortunes. (It is worth noting that Louisiana-born blacks in Chicago in 1910 numbered 1,609, while by 1920 the number had increased to 8,078.)[8]

Weary of the old farm life, sharecropping, unemployment, Jim Crow laws, vestiges of Black Codes, lack of educational facilities, and widespread lynching, the migrants arrived ready to work in the stockyards, steel mills, and other defense industries. The majority were for the most part unskilled and uneducated, but full of dreams of a new way of life. Chicago seemed to promise a better life, or at least nothing worse than what they left behind. They came, liked—at first—what they saw (the freedom, the relatively high wages), and wrote letters to the folks down home, and *they* were encouraged to migrate. To reach what must have seemed like Beulah Land to the poor southern black, one had only to arrive at the terminus of the Illinois Central Railroad. From there, it was but a figurative step to the Black Belt, in the heart of Chicago's South Side, now well on its way to becoming deeply and thoroughly black.

Once they had found their way from the railroad station, or had been delivered by agents, to the addresses sent to them by friends and relations, the immigrant families had to find shelter. The Chicago Commission discusses the immigrant's housing problem upon his arrival:

> Prior to the influx of southern Negroes, many houses stood vacant in the section west of State Street, from which Negroes had moved when better houses became available east of State Street. Into these old and frequently almost uninhabitable houses the first newcomers moved. Because of its proximity to the old vice area this district had an added undesirability for old Chicagoans.[9]

The immigrants continued to come in the tens of thousands, and the intolerance of whites for black neighbors increased. The white ethnics, even the poorest of them, considered themselves superior to the blacks and moved out of their old neighborhoods when they could do so. Fear, no doubt, was an additional pressure that contributed to the flight of the better-off ethnics and native-born. The Black Belt encompassed Chicago's "official" vice district, and the important black newspaper *Chicago Defender* characterized the streets east of State as having "shooting and cutting scrapes" and "ragtime piano playing . . . far into the night."[10] The sound of guns and nighttime ragtime piano playing was, for the neighborhood whites, disturbing and frightening; what had previously been blocks of mixed black and white now became all-black blocks, and many neighborhoods became exclusively black.

The new black migrants had little understanding of the housing conditions they would face. They arrived expecting to find, rather easily, places to live in. They certainly recognized that they would have to earn money in order to pay rent, and they expected to do that. But that there would be *no* housing in the district where they had hoped to live—close to friends or hometown folk—was incomprehensible to them. In short, there were fewer dwellings available as new migrants continued to arrive in great numbers, and what was available was likely to place a nearly intolerable strain on their limited funds. Before the Great Migration, rent for a four-room tenement flat was eight to ten dollars a month, and a furnished room was two dollars to two-fifty a week, or about nine dollars a month. After the migration (and throughout the 1920s) the same sort of flat or furnished room rented for twenty-five to thirty dollars a month, and the migrants had no choice but to pay.

And the amount of rent asked had little relation to the condition of available dwelling places. The deplorable housing conditions new arrivals were expected to tolerate were mostly of long standing. Although Chicago had a sanitary code, the regulations were violated more than they were honored.[11] Under the heading "housing conditions," investigators made notations, of which the following are characteristic and fair examples: Plastering off in front room. Toilet off dining room. Toilet won't flush. Toilet used by four families. Sewer gas escapes from basement pipes; water stands in basement. No heat and no hot water. Window panes out. Large ratholes all over.[12]

Moreover, the high cost of housing and the scarcity of space led to a greater increase in rents for furnished rooms. Along Michigan Avenue, South Parkway, and other streets, the vacant, decaying mansions once owned by the rich could now be profitably rented to poor blacks, so were turned into furnished rooming houses. Moreover, as Abbott reported, "hundreds of tenements designed for one family, scattered all through the Negro residential areas, have been adapted for two or three families by the method of subletting furnished rooms in what used to be a one-family flat."[13]

Still the migrants came. As they continued to arrive, whites continued to leave for adjacent areas to the south (Hyde Park and Kenwood, for example), and were often followed by blacks soon unable to find space in the very neighborhoods the whites had so recently left. The situation was aggravated by a temporary halt in building construction caused by the war. And now white propertyowners sought ways to keep certain neighborhoods almost exclusively white, even when they had permitted some blacks to come into the neighborhoods earlier. These black residents were to be made unwelcome and held up as examples for other blacks intending to move into the area. Propertyowners' associations organized citizens' meetings, exhorting white residents to resist what they called the "mass invasion." The results of their efforts were described by Drake and Cayton:

> A wave of violence flared up and between July, 1917, and March, 1921, fifty-eight homes were bombed—an average of one every twenty days. Two Negroes were killed, a number of white and colored persons were injured, and property damage amounted to over a hundred thousand dollars.[14]

The mounting conflict and tension brought about by the housing problem, and later by labor problems, was finally brought to a peak in the summer of 1919 during Chicago's most tragic race riot. Starting with the drowning of a black boy on the shore of Lake Michigan at Twenty-ninth Street and a policeman's refusal to arrest the white man accused of stoning the black boy, the riot swept through the city for four days, ending with 15 whites and 23 blacks dead (accidentally and by murder), 587 injured, and about 1,000 left homeless.

Unskilled white workers believed the blacks, who were willing to work for less, would finally take their jobs from them, and that these black workers were therefore a genuine threat. There was, of course, some basis for the whites' concern. From the start of the Great Migration, one of the most powerful forces drawing blacks northward was reports of Chicago wages. In southern fields and factories, laborers' pay was as low as seventy-five cents a day; friends up North, southern blacks learned, were earning five to eight dollars a day.

It should be pointed out that in the period before America entered the First World War and the Great Migration got under way, the position of black workers in Chicago had been strictly prescribed, and they could not compete for jobs held by white workers. In earliest days, most were employed as domestic and personal servants. Black women took in washing and sewing, while nearly half the black men worked as porters, waiters, and janitors;[15] a relative handful worked as unskilled laborers in industry. It is revealing to note that at this time only 207 of 13,065 working men were musicians. White Chicago at this time boasted 2,692 musicians; by 1910 their number had grown to 3,442, while blacks in the same ten-year period increased from 207 to only 216.[16] The city was attractive to black musicians during the Great Migration. For them, as well as other southern blacks, the pay was better; moreover, Chicago had places where blacks could find jobs playing their instruments. In the decade between 1920 and 1930, 525 black men and 205 black women described their occupation as musician.[17]

One circumstance is unequivocal: before the war, the daily arrival of large numbers of white immigrants from Europe, willing to work for next to nothing, guaranteed there would be no shortage of unskilled and semiskilled laborers. As for the blacks, except for being called to work in stockyard and teamsters' strikes as scabs and strikebreakers, particularly in the first decade of the century, there was to be little place for them in industry and commerce until the war. During the war, of course, blacks were able to fill those posts previously held by immigrants from enemy countries, in addition to the new, war-inspired jobs where there was a critical labor shortage. (Of the total number working in the stockyards during this time, 70 to 80 percent were black.[18]) Once the United States had entered the war, numbers engaged in domestic and personal-service jobs declined dramatically, and by 1920 most Black Belt workers were employed in factories and mail-order houses; others worked in bottom-rung jobs in mills, foundries, and the stockyards; some black women, too, worked in factories, but most continued to find their most secure employment in domestic service. Compared to the wages they had received back home, black workers believed they were well paid. And they were—for blacks. The poorest jobs paid an average of fifty cents an hour, and even the least-schooled, least-skilled worker could count on an average of twenty-five dollars a week (we may recall that wages back home had averaged seventy-five cents a *day*). There was, of course, little hope for advancement, but the money was good while it lasted. While the revelation of the benefits of unionism came to the Black Belt relatively late, the musicians were aware of its advantages as early as 1902, when they formed a self-governing musicians' organization and charged the same prices as members of the white union.

For the new migrants, adjusting to daily life in the Black Belt was troublesome. Where to live and how to get a job were, of course, immediate and major concerns. Later, there would be a host of minor problems; chief among these (and the one most calculated to antagonize old Black Belt hands) was, as Spear put it, "the crude, rustic ways of many of the migrants, their inability to maintain accepted standards of cleanliness, and their traditionally sycophantic demeanor in the presence of whites."[19] It would take many years to modify and eradicate these social habits. Before migration, they had devised ways to keep themselves alive, to survive; thus, a simple change of scenery was not enough, at first, to alter lifelong modes of behavior. For some of the migrants, their southern habits and reflexes would never change; others, of course, learned rather quickly that while they could never move unimpeded in a world dominated by whites, there was nonetheless considerable opportunity for upward social mobility within the Black Belt itself.

Drake and Cayton's *Black Metropolis* (published in 1945 and

covering the 1920s and '30s), one of the most valuable studies of life
in Chicago's Black Belt, described each of its social classes—upper,
middle, and lower—as including a church-centered group, a non–
church-centered group, and a group of "shadies." Only a small
minority of the tiny upper class (about 5 percent of the black population) were church-centered; the majority emphasized culture,
refinement, and racial advancement; in addition, the upper class
included a small but powerful group that "earns its living in 'shady'
pursuits."[20] The middle class, less than a third of the population,
was divided roughly equally into church- and non–church-centered
groups, most of whom saw themselves as white-collar workers;
there was also a small middle-class group of shadies. The lower
class (about 65 percent of the total) may be divided into a church-
centered group, a small non–church-centered group, and a large
group of shadies. And pervading the entire lower class was the
Black Belt underworld—blacks preying on blacks and whites alike.
To understand why the Black Belt supported and, on occasion,
revered its underworld, we need to know the Black Belt's dominat-
ing interests, the lines of attention, the concerns of its individual
and community life. Drake and Cayton listed five of the most
important of these: Staying Alive; Having a Good Time; Praising
God; Getting Ahead; and Advancing the Race. We will touch
lightly on each of these important interests, leaving the second
most important—Having a Good Time—for the last, because in the
context of our discussion it is the most significant.

Staying Alive requires little explication; it is the black man's
struggle for existence against those whites who stand in the way of
his getting and keeping a good job. Praising God means having as
many churches and preachers and congregations as anyone wishes,
without interference. Getting Ahead is a clear and dominant drive,
the next logical step after Staying Alive.

> In its simplest terms this means progressively moving from low-paid
> to higher-paid jobs. . . . Individuals symbolize their progress by the
> way they spend their money—for clothes, real estate, automobiles,
> donations, entertaining. . . . Maintaining a "front" and "showing

off" become very important substitutes for getting ahead in the economic sense.[21]

Advancing the Race is equally clear. It means the purposeful cultivation of race pride and race consciousness as personified by such race heroes as Joe Louis, Jesse Owens, George Washington Carver, or other personalities in show business, athletics, politics, and the business world.

Having a Good Time is one of the most important features of life in the Black Belt. During the 1920s, the upper class found joy in church socials, bridge parties, dinner parties, dance clubs, and such other organized activities that appeared to emphasize their upper-class exclusiveness. The middle class, too, enjoyed church activities, lodge activities, social clubs, movies, dances, and working up their own fashion shows. For the lower class, Having a Good Time may have been more significant than anything except Staying Alive. The range of their good-time activities was great. Early on, some lower-class migrants discovered the YMCA, with its emphasis on sports and glee clubs; others found havens in one of the twenty Holiness churches west of State Street; for many others, however, Having a Good Time meant having a party, which required little equipment, was easy to arrange, and was cheap. Drake and Cayton describe a typical Black Belt party:

> The basic elements of a "party" are the same in most strata of American society: a deck of cards, a supply of diluted and disguised alcohol, and some "hot" music. . . . Acquaintances are always ready to "have a ball" on a moment's notice—sometimes a game of cards, occasionally a real "boogie-woogie."[22]

Like their New Orleans counterparts, Chicago's lower-class blacks were apparently obsessed with dancing, drinking, gambling, and more dancing, and these activities took place

> in the rear of poolrooms, in the backrooms of taverns, in "buffet-flats," and sometimes on street corners and in alleys. They will

"dance on the dime" and "grind" around the juke-box in taverns and joints, or "cut a rug" at the larger public dance halls.[23]

Many of the public dance halls operated in the shadow of the underworld, and with the help of those shadies on the underworld fringe. While the overwhelming majority of lower-class blacks learned to live with menial jobs for menial pay, others, particularly those characterized as shadies, learned to reap great benefits. Working closely with the underworld, these black men and women—gamblers, pimps, madams, racketeers, nightlife personages—found numerous ways to feed on the Black Belt's obsession with Having a Good Time. They also provided appropriate activities to accommodate those whites who saw the Black Belt as an exotic place in which to do a bit of slumming—a subject to which we will return in the next chapter.

Chicago's powerful underworld, with its czars and syndicates at the top and its seemingly endless number of subordinates, including shadies scattered throughout the Black Belt, could not have functioned without the help of even more powerful political and commercial forces. Gosnell summarizes the relation of the crooked politician to his underworld constituency:

> When asked to make campaign contributions or to produce results upon election day, the leaders of the underworld cannot very well refuse. When word is passed down from the gangster chiefs, all the beer runners, the proprietors of speakeasies, the book-makers, the burglars, the pickpockets, the pimps, the prostitutes, the fences, and their like are whipped into line. In themselves they constitute a large block of voters and they can augment their power at times by corrupt election practices. Personators, repeaters, chain voters, and crooked election boards are recruited from the ranks of organized crime.[24]

Members of the Black Belt underworld learned their lessons well from their white confreres in other parts of the city. They learned quickly which public officials could be trusted to support the best interests of the underworld, and in short order they learned how to control the black vote. Choosing the proper candidate and delivering the black vote became a vernacular art at which the black underworld excelled, and the result of their efforts may be observed in the person of William Hale Thompson—known to all Chicagoans as Big Bill. It is no surprise that Gosnell, in his invaluable study *Negro Politicians*, entitled his chapter on Big Bill "Mayor Thompson, the 'Second Lincoln.'" It may be worthwhile here to summarize the life of Big Bill Thompson, whose steadfast support of the underworld and its activities was so essential to the development and maturation of jazz in Chicago. To this end we turn to Chicago reporters Wendt and Kogan's *Big Bill of Chicago*, an important and penetrating study to which we owe much of what follows.

Thompson was born in Boston in 1867 and brought to Chicago the following year. His father, whose real estate deals would eventually make him rich, was elected to the Illinois Legislature, where he soon became the governor's aide. Young Billy seemed to have little interest in either of his father's occupations, and when he was about fifteen he left prep school to work for the Union Pacific Railroad, which later led to his taking a job as second cook on a ranch in Wyoming. Moving back and forth between semesters of business college in Chicago and life on the western range, he learned a little about accounting and considerably more about guns.

When Bill Thompson reached twenty-one, his father bought him a ranch in Ewing, Nebraska, perhaps to teach him the value of owning property. Bill justified his father's confidence in him by running the ranch with a profit of $30,000 over a period of three years. His father died soon after, leaving $2 million in real estate; Bill decided to remain in Chicago where he could look after his mother and take over his father's business. He was now twenty-four and full of high spirits, and while he enjoyed occasional visits to Frank Wing's high-class brothel on the Levee, he balanced this activity by joining the Chicago Athletic Club, where he became their star athlete. Big, easygoing, likable, rich, son of a politician, his entrance into politics seemed inevitable, and when rich bachelor friends persuaded him to run for his first political office in 1900, as a Republican candidate for alderman in Chicago's Second Ward, it seemed just the right thing to do.

He discovered that he enjoyed the rigors of political campaigning, and with the help of rich friends in the Second Ward he won his first election. The Levee was in the Second Ward, and included a number of lowlife establishments that made Storyville seem as safe as a Nebraska ranch. That the Levee was in the Second Ward seemed, to Thompson, only incidental; but the Levee, as he would learn, was a great and valuable prize. The improbable politicians Hinky Dink and Bathhouse John, who coveted this prize, gave Thompson his first hard lesson in politics by gerrymandering him out of the Second Ward and into the First, so that the Levee remained under their control. Thompson had much to learn, but he was a quick student. The following year he met Billy Lorimer, the Republican boss of Illinois, who later persuaded him to run for Cook County commissioner. Thompson ran, and again he won.

He was now happily married, but not altogether satisfied with his life. As time went on, he and Lorimer backed the wrong candidate for governor; Thompson lost his position in the First Ward, and his political career seemed bogged down. He turned once more to athletics, developed a taste for poker and for bourbon with a wine chaser, and when he was not out yacht racing—a sport he believed suitable to his social status—he helped Lorimer with his political machinations. In 1912, when Senator Lorimer's colleagues in the Senate ousted him for bribery, Thompson showed his loyalty by draping a flag over Lorimer's shoulders.

In 1914 he was put up for mayor. He campaigned vigorously and knowledgeably, especially in the Black Belt. Wendt and Kogan tell us: "He traveled everywhere in the Second Ward, where he was well known not only to his wealthy friends but to the Negroes, to whom he cried, 'I'll give your people the best opportunities you've ever had if you elect me!' " Later, he told them, "I'll give your people jobs. And if any of you want to shoot craps go ahead and do it. When I'm mayor the police will have something better to do than break up a little friendly crap game."[25] The Black Belt responded with unprecedented enthusiasm, and with the help of Fred Lundin, who had tried to pick up the Lorimer pieces, Big Bill won with the largest plurality ever given a Republican in Chicago; his reign was under way. "Let's have every crook out of here in sixty days!"[26] he said almost immediately, in a burst of reform. And he sounded as if he meant it. During his first two years as mayor, he settled a streetcar strike and forbade the sale of liquor on Sunday (except at Big Jim Colosimo's joint on the Levee, and other favorites), although he also made a shambles of the civil service system by putting about ten thousand loyal workers on the city payroll (for that privilege they each paid three dollars a month into a Big Bill presidential campaign fund).

During the third year of his reign, reform elements managed to have two of his most ardent supporters—his chief of police and the Second Ward's black alderman—indicted by a grand jury for graft, protection of brothels, protection of gambling joints, and several lesser infractions. At first the indictments held some promise, but the excellent defense provided by Clarence Darrow resulted in acquittal for both. Big Bill and his advisors could now think about using the growing Big Bill presidential campaign fund. Early in the European war, his advisors obstinately believed that Big Bill could gain favorable national attention, the sort of attention needed to run him for president, by vigorously and noisily opposing America's entry into the war. Big Bill liked the idea, and he set about learning his lines. When, however, the United States declared war in 1917, he continued to read the same lines, to make the same fatuous, isolationist speeches. No one apparently had told him not to, and his words of opposition to the war were not always enthusiastically received by those who pointed out that we were already *in* the war.

Nevertheless, the Black Belt continued to look upon Big Bill with great favor. They saw in him qualities they could appreciate, and they believed he understood them as well as any white man could. In plain words, drawling, sometimes with less than formal grammar, he told them what they wanted to hear. He promised jobs, special favors, free food for the poor, undisturbed crap games, an open Black Belt, and whatever else he thought would elect him. Black voters were enthralled, and they responded overwhelmingly. When Big Bill ran for mayor in four primary elections, the Second Ward, with a heavy black vote, enabled him to gather in over eighty percent of the Republican votes, and in almost every instance, as Gosnell noted, "the plurality which he piled up in the wards inhabited largely by Negroes was decisive in winning the nomination."[27] (In 1927, his best year, he received 93 percent of the black vote.[28]) Among Big Bill's early campaign assistants was the Reverend Archibald J. Carey, a black clergyman who later became Bishop Carey, and who in a speech before fifteen thousand blacks said, "There are three names which will stand high in American history—Abraham Lincoln, William McKinley and William Hale Thompson. . . . I helped elect him alderman; I helped elect him county commissioner; I helped elect him mayor; and my work will not be completed until I have helped elect him president."[29]

Big Bill was thankful for such public recognition of his worth. One way he showed his gratitude was by appointing blacks to jobs in city government, and, Gosnell notes, "as the size of his majorities in the Black Belt increased at each successive election, so the amount of recognition he gave this section in the form of patronage also increased."[30] More than any other politician, Big Bill, along with his political faction, made Black Belt inhabitants feel they were important. When new jobs came up he gave them a share, he protected them from over-zealous policemen, he treated them as if his interests coincided with those of the black community groups, and he did these things in such a way that "colored preachers could refer to Thompson as the 'Second Lincoln' and win applause."[31]

Outside the Black Belt, Big Bill's continued exhortations on staying out of a war we had already joined gave him the national press coverage his advisors had expected. They had, however, misjudged its direction. The general reaction to his statements on the war was summed up by Bishop George Herbert Kinsolving, of the Texas Diocese, who was reported to have said, "I think that Mayor Thompson is guilty of treason and ought to be shot."[32] This statement may have shaken his advisors a little, for they now thought perhaps Big Bill ought to run for the United States Senate instead, but Teddy Roosevelt spoke out against him and Big Bill lost the nomination. Politically, there was little he could do now except run for reelection as mayor. Although his enemies were gaining strength (stories of vice and corruption in the Chicago daily press seemed without end), he won the primary easily; on election day, however, he barely squeaked by his Democratic opponent. Soon after he resumed office, he widened streets, built a bridge, summoned the state militia to quell the 1919 race riot after it was over, and won for Chicago the national Republican presidential convention that would nominate Warren G. Harding. The worst was yet to come.

On January 16, 1920, Prohibition came to Chicago. Beer and liquor territories were being divided up by rival gangs, and the dam was about to burst. The Eighteenth Amendment to the Constitution forbade the manufacture, import, export, and sale of liquor to the public. The gangs of Chicago looked upon the new law as a joke, and enforcing the amendment was impossible. It seemed as if the Eighteenth Amendment, instead of preventing or curtailing the consumption of strong spirits (as the Anti-Saloon League and Prohibition party and Andrew Volstead had hoped it would), had in fact increased its consumption. People were now intent upon drinking anything resembling liquor, and the Chicago underworld, with the help of their friends in government, were ready to manufacture the liquor, to smuggle it in from outside, or both, and, either way, to guarantee that anyone who wished to break the law by buying a drink could do so.

Big Bill, recalling an old line, told his newly appointed police chief to "clear out the crooks!"[33] The chief acted promptly. The same evening 110 detectives raided everything in Chicago that even *seemed* illegal and locked up 800 allegedly dangerous men and women. They spent the night in custody; the next morning a few were fined $25 each, and nearly everyone else was let go scot-free. The people of Chicago no longer trusted Big Bill. Republican candidates backed by Big Bill were now losing elections; other political cronies were not only being indicted, but convicted. Even Governor Small submitted to pressure and was forced to return $600,000 to the state treasury.[34]

In 1921, it was difficult to know who could be trusted. A bevy of Big Bill's supporters, headed by his chief advisor Lundin, were indicted for tapping the public school treasury for over a million dollars. Again, defense attorney Clarence Darrow came to the rescue and the accused were acquitted. Now, however, the principal question was: Can Big Bill Thompson be reelected? The inner circle apparently thought not, and Big Bill was required to read a farewell message to the press. He would no longer be Chicago's mayor, but the underworld knew he was destined to return. Democrat William Dever served as mayor for four years, while the underworld consolidated its position in and around Chicago. Johnny Torrio, who had succeeded Big Jim Colosimo, passed the mantle to Al Capone. Earlier, Torrio and Colosimo had clashed over their beer business. Colosimo believed federal enforcement of the National Prohibition Act of 1919 would close their breweries. Torrio discovered that Prohibition agents, who were supposed to enforce the law, were to be political appointees—a circumstance he believed would be favorable to the criminal organization. Colosimo opposed Torrio's view, and, shortly after, Big Jim was murdered at his café on the Levee.[35] Now that his opponent was dead, Torrio, with the help of his new assistant, Al Capone, could go forward with his plans, and soon Capone could go forward with *his* plans.

Capone made it clear that he preferred Big Bill to Dever, and he showed his preference by hanging three portraits in his business office: George Washington, Abraham Lincoln, and William Hale Thompson. Big Bill was never more flattered. He took on Dever at the 1927 election, and on a platform of "America First!" emerged the winner. One of his first appointments as the new mayor went to Daniel A. Serritella, Al Capone's agent.[36] Capone, happy that he had backed the winner, opened a new office just a block from City Hall (presumably transferring his three portraits), and crime became Chicago's principal enterprise. The St. Valentine's Day Massacre two years later, in which seven supporters of George ("Bugs") Moran, Capone's archrival, were murdered, seemed anticlimactic. In 1931 Big Bill was defeated by Anthony Cermak, a political blow from which he would never recover. But during his colorful life, he had helped set the tone for Chicago and its night people; and jazzmen, had they thought about it, would have agreed that they owed Big Bill a considerable debt. He died in 1944.

CHICAGO JAZZ: NEW ORLEANS BLACKS AND CHICAGO WHITES

6

After the war and during the '20s, entertainment boomed in Chicago, and the nightspots where musicians could work seemed innumerable. Whether a musician read music or not, played sweet or hot, low-down or high-society, Chicago's nightlife accommodated him. For those musicians with much endurance and little ambition, there were the taxi-dance halls, where unattached men danced with unattached hostesses for 10 cents a dance, of which the hostess retained half. Between 1927 and 1930, thirty-six taxi-dance halls, scattered throughout the city, provided employment for musicians.[1]

As we have seen, the city had more than its share of cabarets, and these, again, were places where musicians of various tastes and abilities could find work. Cabarets, of course, required licenses, and those that were properly recorded at City Hall provide us with evidence of numbers. It is interesting to compare the number of Chicago's licensed cabarets before Big Bill Thompson's terms as mayor and after. In 1921, for example, just before he left office, there were 83 licensed cabarets; after Thompson left office, the number dropped to 16. During Mayor Dever's term the number of licensed cabarets crept up from 16 to 32; however, after Big Bill took on Dever and won the election, the number shot up to 65.[2] (It is important to remember that although cabarets were licensed by the city, not all cabarets applied for a license; many cabarets with violations of one sort or another, or those not willing to pay for a license, operated without benefit of license; therefore, the numbers shown above are actually minimums.)

In addition to the city's cabarets, musicians could also work in the new, underworld-controlled nightlife establishments called roadhouses that in the twenties began to proliferate outside the city limits. Automobiles were now becoming commonplace, and distance was no longer a deterrent to those looking for nightlife. The roadhouses were large, often palatial (the Garden of Allah, for one), and functioned as outsized cabarets. In 1929, in Cook County alone there were at least 171 establishments that fancied themselves roadhouses.[3] The principal jobs for Chicago musicians, however, were in the nightspots within the city. Reminiscences of Chicago musicians of the time show that their most vivid recollections were of jobs they held in gangster-controlled nightspots. Pianist Jess Stacy, who came to Chicago in 1925 from Missouri looking for work, remembers what it was like when work became scarce. "There was no choice but to work for the gangsters," he said. "They didn't pay much, but they didn't bother us either. . . . If you played the North Side you worked for Bugs Moran, and if you worked on the South Side, it was for Al Capone."[4]

Jazzmen were constantly aware, as they performed for customers, that violence in the mob-dominated clubs could break out at any moment. Guitarist Eddie Condon remembers working at a place called the Alcazar, where, "Occasionally Capone, the owner, dropped in. Then the doors were shut, Al changed a few hundred dollar bills and distributed the paper among his pals, and the party was on. There was no shooting while I was there but I decided not to push my luck; I quit."[5] Clarinetist Marty Marsala had similar memories. At one place he worked, Capone would come in with a number of his henchmen, change a few hundred dollar bills, hand them to his pals for distribution to all the help, including the band. "We got five or ten bucks," Marsala recalled, "just for playing his favorite numbers, sentimental things."[6]

Curiously, one of Capone's best-known places, the Four Deuces, had no music at all; still, it suggested the name for a place at 222 North State Street—the Three Deuces. Here is Benny Goodman's recollection of the spot:

> The best-known hangout for musicians at the time was a little hole-in-the-wall called the Three Deuces, on State Street. . . .
>
> The room downstairs, where they jammed, was a dismal, un-painted place, with wooden walls, and no covering on the floor. Over on one side was an old beat-up piano. Sometimes when you'd go in there sober it almost knocked you off your feet. If the boys were going good, you'd be just as apt as not to see the other fellows beating the rhythm on the wall with their hands when somebody took a chorus.[7]

Chicago musicians (including Goodman) found frequent employment at the then well-known Southmoor Hotel on Stoney Island Avenue; at Guyon's Paradise, at 128 North Crawford; and at the Rendezvous Cafe, which Goodman remembers as a gangsters' hangout owned by one Vince Drusy, who was shot to death.[8] "Rendezvous" was apparently a much-favored name. Bix Beiderbecke worked at one Rendezvous on North Clark Street, while Condon remembers working with Mezz Mezzrow at another, Ike Bloom's Rendezvous on Randolph Street. Similarly, the North Side Paradise, where Goodman worked, had its namesake in the Black Belt, at Thirty-fifth and Calumet, where white jazzmen went to hear clarinetist Jimmy Noone playing behind Bessie Smith's singing. The club was something less than a Paradise. "Rats as big as your arm," Condon said, "prowled around casing the customers. . . . The place was small, unventilated, gin-soaked, and had been slept in by everyone but George Washington."[9] The names of the various nightspots were more fanciful than descriptive, and seem to have been drawn out of a hat. The Vanity Fair, for example, was an unprepossessing cabaret at Broadway and Grace Street where Art Cope, a local violinist, on occasion led a band; the Friar's Inn, at Wabash and Van Buren, was a gaudy basement cabaret with outrageous prices where the New Orleans Rhythm Kings were first billed as the Friars' Society Orchestra. The penchant for French names brought on the Deauville, on Randolph Street, distinguished principally by its doorman; and King Oliver once played at a spot called the Chez Paree.

"Garden" and "Gardens" were favorites. New Orleans jazzmen Paul Mares and George Brunies could be heard occasionally at the Blatz Beer Garden at North and Halstead. Condon, who had once played at the Palace Gardens, a cabaret on North Clark Street, recalls the surrounding neighborhood. "There were five blocks almost solid with cabarets—The Derby, The Erie, Liberty Inn, 606, etc., *ad infinitum*. Most of them were like the Palace Gardens, which had a small band with hag singers going from table to table moaning gold-toothed ballads full of moons and Junes."[10]

"Gardens" were not only cabarets, but also dance halls. Midway Gardens, across from Washington Park, was the South Side's biggest dance hall, where at times Benny Goodman played with Art Kassel's band.

Independent ballrooms as well as those in hotels provided further employment. Jobs were in good supply at the Cascades Ballroom at Sheridan and Wilson; at the Columbia Ballroom on North Clark, where trumpeter Muggsy Spanier once played in a band called Sig Myer's Druids; at the Randolph Hotel (later the Bismarck), where the ubiquitous Goodman once played; at the College Inn, in the Sherman House, where the band of Isham Jones was often featured; and at the Stevens Hotel, which opened in 1927 with a ballroom to accommodate four thousand dancers.

Although the best-paying jobs went to Chicago's white musicians willing to play "sweet," some black musicians with similar proclivities were able to find work outside the Black Belt. The steadiest employment for blacks, however, was to be found in the Black Belt, and by the end of the twenties the focus of Black Belt nightlife was on Thirty-fifth Street and a half-dozen blocks between State Street and South Parkway—Wabash, Michigan, Indiana, Prairie, and Calumet Avenues. The Pekin, on State Street, was where Tony Jackson's ragtime piano was heard; and Bill Bottom's Dreamland Cafe often resounded to the music of Joe ("King") Oliver and Sidney Bechet. The Elite No. 2, stomping grounds for pianists Tony Jackson, Jelly Roll Morton, and Earl Hines, was on Thirty-fifth and State, as was the DeLuxe Cafe, up a flight of stairs over the DeLuxe Saloon and Poolroom, and Bechet and Keppard played at the DeLuxe at the same time King Oliver held forth at the Pekin. A few blocks over, on Thirty-fifth and Calumet, the Sunset Cafe had Carroll Dickerson's band with Earl Hines on piano when Armstrong joined them in 1926. Joe Glaser, who later managed Louis Armstrong, said, "They all worked for me. I owned and managed the Sunset and a couple of other places on the South Side. The Sunset was the biggest black-and-tan club west of New York."[11] Diagonally across the street was the Plantation, where

Oliver had blown his horn, and right next door, one flight up, was the Nest, where young, aspiring white jazzmen went regularly to hear clarinetist Jimmy Noone and others (the Nest later became the Apex Club).

Jimmy Noone got around. At various times he could be heard at Paddy Harmon's Dreamland Ballroom, where he and Freddie Keppard had worked in Doc Cook's orchestra; together they had also worked at the Lorraine Gardens; and, moving a bit farther south, Noone had played the Eldorado Club at 55th and Garfield. Musicians who worked the smaller clubs and cabarets moved frequently, and for good reason. For example, the Entertainer's Cafe, a South Side black-and-tan spot which on occasion featured Earl Hines, was closed up by the authorities in 1922, reopened a year later, and was once again padlocked for still another year.[12] For musicians looking for steady employment, it was clearly better to be employed in a police-protected nightclub than in one that was not. The *Chicago Tribune* reported how the system worked.

> The difference between a protected place and one not so favored is best illustrated by these facts: The "Black Four Deuces" at 2222 Dearborn Street is often raided and is about to close up in disgust. Bud Gentry's place, 2222 Indiana Avenue, and the one at 2222 Wabash Avenue never are molested by the police and never will be closed up until some one acts.[13]

Certain nightspots demand attention for their historical significance, that is, for their connection with early jazzmen. Fritzel's Arsonia Cafe, for example, at Madison and Paulina Streets, outside the Black Belt, featured the Perez band, imported as a group from New Orleans in 1915. The Café de Paris has importance only because it was later called the Lincoln Gardens (and associated with King Oliver and Louis Armstrong), and still later called the Royal Gardens. Kelly's Stable, a converted barn on the North Side, is associated with Johnny and Baby Dodds; Johnny remembered that "everything inside it was painted black, and the stalls were still there from maybe twenty or thirty years before. It even smelled horsey."[14]

And the names roll on, coming from the memories of Chicago musicians like a jazz improvisation: LaRue's Dreamland, the Granada, the Club Ambassador, the Club Havana, the Vendome Theater where Armstrong appeared with Erskine Tate, Frolic's Cafe on Twenty-second Street off Wabash, the Savoy Dance Hall, the Arcadia Ballroom, the Fiume, the Rose Garden, the Open Air Gardens, the Dusty Bottom Cafe, the Grand Theater on Thirty-first and State which Ramsey and Smith believed "witnessed the debut of New Orleans music in the North,"[15] and the wonderfully evocative Dago Frank's. "The very first place I worked," blues singer Alberta Hunter recalled, "was Dago Frank's on Archer and State Streets. That was a place where the sportin' girls hung out." From there Alberta moved to Hugh Hoskins's club on Thirty-second and State, and afterward to the Panama on Thirty-sixth and State where, she recalled, they employed two piano players, dancers, and a variety of singers including Bricktop. (The big time, for Alberta, came when she moved on to the Dreamland, where King Oliver's band was playing.[16])

"The greatest single event in Chicago's early jazz history," Albert McCarthy wrote in his *Big Band Jazz*, "was the arrival of King Oliver in Chicago."[17] There is no question that Oliver and the musicians he gathered about him have to be reckoned among the historically most significant figures in early jazz. Oliver was born in New Orleans in 1885 (or earlier). Probably self-taught, with occasional words of advice from old marching bandsmen, he eventually was able to join the Onward Brass Band, the Eagle Band, and others, meanwhile supplementing his income by working as a butler. At age twenty-five, after working with a number of Storyville bands, legend has it that he stood on a Storyville streetcorner, pointed his trumpet at the café where Freddie Keppard was holding forth, and played a blues so full of surprise, adventure, and power that he was, from that moment on, established as "King."

In 1918 he arrived in Chicago, where he alternated playing

with Laurence Duhé's New Orleans Jazz Band and Bill Johnson's Original Creole Band, replacing Johnson as leader in 1920. After a year of scuffling in Chicago, he toured California, then returned to Chicago in 1922 where he opened at the Lincoln Gardens. The following year he asked Armstrong to leave New Orleans to join him, and in July 1923 Armstrong arrived in Chicago to join the band in which the best qualities of the New Orleans style were to find their culmination. In addition to Oliver and Armstrong, the band now included Honore Dutrey on trombone, Johnny Dodds on clarinet, Baby Dodds on drums, Lil Hardin on piano, and Bill Johnson on banjo. It is worth noting that except for Lil Hardin, who was born in Memphis, all the members of Oliver's Creole Jazz Band were born in New Orleans.

While the Creole Jazz Band was in Chicago, its principal association was with the Lincoln Gardens, a huge, barnlike structure at Thirty-first and Gordon that provided space for six- to seven hundred dancers. Frederick Ramsey, Jr., one of the best of the early jazz historians, provides us with an important eyewitness account of the band during an evening he spent at the Lincoln Gardens:

> There were no waltzes played at the Lincoln Gardens, the customers liked the Bunny-hug, the Charleston, the Black Bottom. . . . Joe tooted a few notes down low to the orchestra, stomped his feet to give the beat, turned around, and they were off on a new piece. . . . Lil Hardin bit hard on her four beats to a measure, while the deep beat of Bill Johnson's string bass and the clearly defined foundation of Baby Dodds' drum and high-toned, biting cymbal filled out the "bounce" and kept the others sweeping forward. This motion led to a climax, a point beyond which the breathless pace of the music seemed doomed to fall, unless something would intervene. Then Joe and Louis stepped out, and one of their "breaks" came rolling out of the two short horns, fiercely and flawlessly.[18]

Edmond Souchon, a New-Orleans-born jazz historian, had seen and listened to Oliver at the "Big 25" club in Storyville and at

Tulane University fraternity dances. Later, he heard Oliver in Chicago, and when Oliver's Chicago recordings were made, he compared the early New Orleans Oliver with the later Chicago Oliver. In Chicago, Souchon recalled, "his sound was not the same. It was a different band, a different and more polished Oliver, an Oliver who had completely lost his New Orleans sound." It was Souchon's view that Oliver "was trying to sound like a big white band." In summing up Oliver's early New Orleans style, Souchon said:

> It was rough, rugged, and contained many bad chords. There were many fluffed notes, too. But the drive, the rhythm, the wonderfully joyous New Orleans sound was there in all its beauty. This is what the recordings made in Chicago missed. Those records even miss conveying the way that Oliver was playing in Chicago when I heard him.[19]

It is likely that Souchon was correct in his view—not that Oliver's early style was better or worse than his later style—but that there were distinct differences in Oliver's manner of performance, depending entirely on the makeup of his audience. In New Orleans his audiences had been essentially all black or all white, and he sensibly provided his audiences with the musical style he believed they preferred. Sidney Finkelstein discusses an aspect of this complication:

> The Negro community for whom Oliver played in Chicago was different from the Negro community in New Orleans. The music that Oliver played was still New Orleans in its march tempo, its rag, blues and stomp content, its collective music making and self-absorption in the music on the part of the players; but it also reflected the new Chicago audience. The opportunity to make records, as well, induced a greater attention to technical detail and formal organization, making the music a found out unity with beginning, middle and end.[20]

The key figure in the development of jazz during this period was Louis Armstrong. He was born in New Orleans in 1900, grew up in the slums "back o' town," and at age thirteen was remanded to the Waifs' Home for firing a gun outdoors—a gun he had found at home. In the Waifs' Home he received sufficient instruction on the cornet so he could play in the Waifs' Band. About a year later he was released, and soon was competent enough to play for local picnics and parades and, somewhat later, to play in a Mississippi riverboat band. Between the ages of eighteen and twenty-two he continued to improve his technique and enlarge his tone. He worked frequently with Kid Ory, and by 1921 he was generally acknowledged to be the best trumpeter in New Orleans; he had in fact already turned down an offer from Fletcher Henderson to join his band in New York.[21] But when Oliver, his boyhood idol, asked him to come to Chicago the following year, Armstrong was filled with excitement and anticipation.

It is important to remember that Oliver himself had left New Orleans in 1918, and thus had already been subject to four years of refining influences when Armstrong joined him. When Oliver heard him play, Armstrong later recalled, he "stopped me playin' all those variations."[22] Armstrong was so thankful to be in Chicago with Oliver that he would have played any way Oliver wished. Armstrong believed he owed a considerable debt to Joe Oliver— not just to Oliver the musician, but to the Oliver who sometimes suggested, jokingly, that he was Armstrong's stepfather and who treated him as a son. Armstrong invariably addressed Oliver as Papa Joe, and the younger man's loyalty to Papa Joe required him to remain Oliver's subordinate in the Creole Jazz Band for the next two years. By this time he and Lil Hardin had discovered each other, and in February 1924 they were married. With his wife's encouragement, he left Oliver and took a job as first trumpet in Ollie Powers's Dreamland band, and several months later, Lil Hardin's confidence in him more than justified, he accepted Fletcher Henderson's offer to come to New York.

After nearly a year with Henderson, Armstrong returned to

Chicago. He would never again allow himself to be subordinate to any individual or any group, for he was now clearly a master of solo improvisation. He joined up with Lil Hardin, who now had her own band at the Dreamland, worked for a while with Erskine Tate's band at the Vendome Theater, then moved on to work with Carroll Dickerson's band (with Earl Hines on piano) at the Sunset Cafe. "In the course of his stint at the Dreamland," Hadlock noted, "Louis put the finishing touches on his musicianship, his creative outlook, and his reputation as the best jazz trumpet player in the land."[23]

Although he had appeared on records earlier—with Oliver's band in 1923, then with Henderson's band, and had also provided background for several blues singers in New York—he was now ready to make records as a leader. First with his Hot Five (Kid Ory on trombone, Johnny Dodds on clarinet, Johnny St. Cyr on banjo, and Lil Hardin Armstrong on piano), then with his Hot Seven, and later with a group including Earl Hines, Armstrong turned out a batch of recordings between 1925 and 1928 that were to establish for good his artistic and historical significance. By 1929 the Chicago jazz world was at Armstrong's feet, and he was ready to take on New York.

Before the First World War, few Chicago musicians were familiar with the sound of the New Orleans style. After the war, the situation changed. Two factors were responsible: the sound of New Orleans music coming out of so many South Side nightspots, and the release of records by *white* New Orleans musicians, specifically the New Orleans Rhythm Kings—the most powerful, most pervasive influence on Chicago's young, white, aspiring jazzmen. The group included at the outset Paul Mares on trumpet, George Brunies on trombone, Leon Rappollo on clarinet, Elmer Schoebel on piano, Jack Pettis on saxophone, Arnold Loyacano on bass, and Frankie Snyder on drums (later, Loyacano was replaced by Chink Martin, Snyder by Benny Pollack, and Lew Black was added on banjo). The original group was led by Paul Mares, who brought them in 1921 from New Orleans to Chicago, where in their initial appearance they were known as the Friars' Society Orchestra. It is worth noting that of the original seven members, according to bass player Loyacano, only he and Schoebel, the pianist, could read music,[24] but, as we mentioned earlier, not being able to read music in the 1920s (or *saying* one couldn't read) seems to have had a certain cachet.

Imitating the New Orleans Rhythm Kings became a popular pastime. After listening to some of their records in 1922, a group of students from Chicago's Austin High School were moved to form a band in imitation of the New Orleans Rhythm Kings' style. Jimmy McPartland, a leader of the group, recalls how they were initiated into the style while visiting their favorite ice cream parlor: On hand was a record of *Farewell Blues* by the New Orleans Rhythm Kings. Taken with the fresh sound of the band, the boys got together a number of instruments, organized their own group, and by listening to a few bars of the record and repeating it over and over, trying to reproduce what they had just heard, they managed in a few months' time to learn by rote a good many of the NORK recordings. "The New Orleans Rhythm Kings," McPartland later said, "that was our model."[25] The Austin High Gang, as they were called, included Jimmy McPartland on cornet, Frank Teschemacher on clarinet, Bud Freeman on saxophone, Jim Lanigan on tuba, and Dick McPartland on banjo; these early members were later joined by Davie Tough on drums and Dave North on piano, and the group called themselves the Blue Friars.

For an exhaustive listing of Chicago's major and minor white musicians of the period, the studies by John Steiner, Richard Hadlock, and Albert McCarthy are indispensable. It will be worthwhile, for our purposes, to survey briefly the most significant of these jazz figures. Let us begin, then, with the general group of musicians known as the Chicagoans, of whom Hadlock said:

> There were many Chicagoans in jazz, but they are usually discussed as a group, for most of Chicago's young jazzmen of the twenties who became important were part of a loosely knit single gang, the core of

which was an almost fanatic, exclusive inner clique. These men listened, practiced, worked, recorded, drank, and finally found fame together. They regarded themselves as a kind of musical family.[26]

Not all of these Chicagoans were natives—more important was holding the right beliefs and living what might be called the jazz life. In this regard, Wingy Manone, New Orleans trumpeter, was acceptable as a Chicagoan; and so were Volly De Faut, Arkansas clarinetist; Rod Cless, Iowa clarinetist; and Jess Stacy, Missouri pianist. Chicagoans fell into two broad categories: those who were part of the earliest group—first-string Chicagoans, in Hadlock's phrase, and not generally known outside the Chicago area; and those from outside Chicago who joined or were adopted by the group. In addition, both groups include those whose historical position was dictated by the early period and those who became famous later. In either case, no list would be complete without mentioning drummers Ben Pollack, Dave Tough, George Wettling, and Gene Krupa; trumpeters Bix Beiderbecke and Muggsy Spanier; pianist Joe Sullivan; clarinetists Mezz Mezzrow, Benny Goodman, and Pee Wee Russell; the Austin High School group mentioned above; singer-leader-promoter Red McKenzie; and the ubiquitous banjoist Eddie Condon, whom Dave Dexter described as "a combination pitchman and plectrum-plucker, confidence man and atomic blast."[27]

The best-known out-of-towner adopted by Condon and his friends was Bix Beiderbecke. "For them," Neil Leonard wrote in his *Jazz and the White Americans*, "Beiderbecke was the incarnation of the esthetic morality."[28] Beiderbecke lived the arch-Bohemian life—without ties, and without responsibility except in his great passion for music—and he loved liquor. He died in 1931, when he was twenty-eight, and since that time his life and his work have received the sort of mythic treatment and veneration usually reserved for saints—the whole culminating in Sudhalter and Evans's *Bix: Man and Legend*, which closes with a fifty-six-page month-by-month chronology of Beiderbecke's life.[29] Beiderbecke's very existence was of the highest importance to the young Chicagoans, and we will return to him again shortly to discuss his musical influence on the Chicago scene. First, however, it is necessary to discuss briefly the elements of the musical style New Orleans jazzmen brought to Chicago.

The basic musical style brought up from New Orleans was a collective improvisation performed on three wind instruments—cornet or trumpet, clarinet, and trombone—and a variety of rhythm instruments drawn from piano, bass, drums, banjo, guitar, and tuba. The cornet or trumpet played the lead, staying close to the melody, the trombone punched out and defined the harmony below, while the clarinet embroidered and embellished a line above—the three voices creating the impression of three independent parts—all against the steady, unaccented beat of the rhythm section. Although there were frequent solo improvisations, the essential element of the style was *collective* improvisation based on variations of the original tune or on the simple, original chords that underlay the tune. The bases for these improvisations were the relatively fixed standard forms of the blues, rags, marches, stomps, and original compositions by the jazzmen themselves, usually cast in these forms. In King Oliver's Creole Jazz Band with its rich ensemble, Oliver's and Armstrong's frenetic solos, Johnny Dodds's pushing arpeggios, and Baby Dodds's steady beat, we find the culmination of New Orleans style.

The formation of the style occurred essentially in New Orleans. A group of its practitioners would then move the New Orleans style to Chicago, where it was refined and polished to a state of considerable elegance. In his definitive study *Hungarian Folk Music*, Béla Bartók discusses a system by which peasants develop a homogeneous musical style. We may note, in what follows, that the system can be related to the development of the New Orleans style and, later, to the style as it matured in Chicago:

> Performance by peasants, exactly as performance by a great artist, includes a good deal that is almost extemporization. . . . It is obvi-

ous, indeed, that no essential alteration of a musical element can come from one individual peasant. And there can be no doubt that with peasants who people *one geographical unit*, living close to one another and *speaking the same language*, this tendency to alter, in consequence of the affinities between the mental disposition of individuals, works in one way, in the same general direction. It is thus that the birth of a homogeneous musical style becomes possible.[30] (My italics.)

While Bartók's "geographical unit" is, in our context, the city of Chicago, we need to remember that there were people from other places who tried "speaking the same language." For example, clarinetist Pee Wee Russell, who is generally counted among the foremost second-string Chicagoans, and who was born in St. Louis, disliked the term *Chicagoans*. Many of those who called themselves (or thought of themselves) as Chicagoans, he pointed out correctly, were not in Chicago when the Chicagoans' ideas were being formulated. Furthermore, many had their musical training elsewhere. Russell believed that it did not matter so much where one came from; what mattered was the ability to "play good jazz."[31]

Russell's view is widely held. The best-known Chicago jazzmen were not always among the best, that is, if knowledge of music, technical ability, and a creative imagination are qualities we expect from the best. For every Armstrong, Goodman, and Russell, there were dozens of what we may call jazz personalities whose chief concern was to live the jazz life and whose ability and imagination were more closely tuned to public relations and providing good news copy than to creating significant jazz improvisations. Personalities like Eddie Condon and Mezz Mezzrow and Red McKenzie were more interesting to the public and to the press than their music was. Condon was the nonpareil white jazz talker (about pianist Joe Sullivan's hands: "He could play a tenth and reach for a drink at the same time; he has studied piano for twelve years including a stretch at the Chicago Conservatory of Music."[32]). Mezzrow was the forerunner of Norman Mailer's "white Negro," extolling the virtues of marijuana and a sort of jazz primitivism. McKenzie was best known as co-leader of the McKenzie/Condon Chicagoans and for his kazoo playing. The prevailing anti-intellectual idea—the jazzman as noble savage—was that jazz played by an untrained, unschooled musician (who, say, had taught himself the fingering of his instrument), whose work seemed untouched by any rational process of thought, was, in some unexplainable way, of greater worth than jazz produced by a trained musician. That the press and general public find untrained artists more *interesting* than those who are trained is certainly true, and frequently leads the reader to the notion that the jazz arena is dominated by untrained types and unusual personalities. The facts, however, show the contrary. Benny Goodman is a case in point.

Goodman's autobiography shows that he would have liked to be one of the young Chicagoans, but in their sense he was not first-string. His clarinet playing was rooted in traditional techniques; he could read music; and his tone was at once classical and lovely—words that would have made the young Chicagoans ill at ease, to say the least. Goodman's position as viewed by Chicago's black jazzmen, however, was quite different. Although black jazzmen, on the whole, were not especially interested in the views and performances of aspiring white Chicagoans, they made exceptions, and Goodman was one of them. Such New Orleans clarinetists as Barney Bigard, Albert Nicholas, and Jimmy Noone, all of whom were trained by members of the Tio family, recognized in Goodman's playing a tone, technique, and spirit not unlike their own. Hadlock reminds us, "It was a judgment not so readily bestowed upon Teschemacher and others in the young Chicago gang."[33] We may note that Goodman and Noone (as well as Buster Bailey) had studied privately with Franz Schoepp, who had taught at the Chicago Musical College and had played clarinet in the Chicago Symphony.

There were several band leaders who toured regularly and in whose bands Chicagoans frequently found employment and an opportunity to renew acquaintances while working in other cities. One of the best known was Jean Goldkette, who was born in

France and led a band in Detroit during the 1920s. At various times he organized bands that included Beiderbecke, Jimmy McPartland, and other Chicago jazzmen. In 1927 Beiderbecke was with a Goldkette band in Detroit, and, as Goodman recalled, Bix "ran up to Chicago one Sunday night with two fellows from Jan Garber's orchestra, which was also playing Detroit at the time." They all went to hear Armstrong and Hines at the Sunset Cafe, and Jimmy Noone at the Nest, and roamed around until morning when they could catch an eight-thirty train back to Detroit, Goodman tagging along. In Detroit they continued drinking and listening to records in Bix's room until it was time for him to go to work. They accompanied him to the Greystone Ballroom where, still high, they entered through the back door. "We finally heard the band," Goodman recalled, "and it was plenty good, with fellows in it like Venuti, Don Murray, Irv Riskin, Frank Trumbauer, Steve Brown and Chauncey Morehouse. We got back to Chicago the next day."[34]

Beiderbecke is significant not only because he was a cult hero, but because in his role as a devil-may-care wandering minstrel he played and heard a great deal of music of diverse styles in many cities and, afterward, by anecdote or through his own playing, brought to those of his constituents with lesser talent and mobility the latest sounds, the latest ideas—the latest musical news, as it were. Between the ages of sixteen and twenty-one he heard Armstrong and riverboat jazz bands, played with a society dance band in Chicago and a theater band in St. Louis, and joined what was later called the Wolverine Orchestra in a tour of Ohio and Indiana. In 1924, at twenty-one, he arrived in New York to spend a few days with Red Nichols, who introduced him to the playing of Tommy and Jimmy Dorsey; a week later he was back in Chicago playing at the Rendezvous Cafe on North Clark Street; several months later he joined the musicians' union in St. Louis and played with Frank Trumbauer's orchestra. By 1926 he was back in New York playing in Jean Goldkette's orchestra in a "Battle of Music" opposite Fletcher Henderson's band. Another tour in 1927 took Beiderbecke to Detroit, and back to New York, where he made records with Trumbauer, Joe Venuti, Eddie Lang, Adrian Rollini, and others; he afterward joined Paul Whiteman's band on a tour that included a three-week stay in Chicago, where he renewed his friendship with the Chicagoans. He stayed with the Whiteman band, on and off, until his death in August 1931.

The playing style of those who considered themselves first-string Chicagoans was, in one sense, indigenous. Rhythm was more important to them than melody or harmony. The pianist provided heavy, on-the-beat chords, four beats to a bar; the banjo reinforced steadily the pianist's chords; the bass player leaned heavily on the first and third beats of the bar; and the drummer set up the steady pulse and filled in the spaces between phrases. The saxophone became an important addition to the ensemble, and solo improvisation became more important than collective improvisation. Although they purposely kept their stylistic interests parochial, they were no doubt aware that a good many "foreign" influences moved regularly in and out of Chicago in the persons of jazzmen based outside Chicago and touring bands. Later, the more adventurous among them felt strong enough to test their ability in other cities—away from home base. In 1926, for example, a band including most of the now-grown-up Austin High School Gang were booked into a ballroom in Detroit, where they found themselves in competition with Fletcher Henderson's band.

The dissemination of jazz came about in a number of ways: individual instruction of a student by an experienced teacher; mutual instruction and exchange of musical information; the unconscious absorption of influences as a result of listening to music and musicians in new environments; the conscious absorption—imitation and "stealing"; the music-publishing business (for example, the sale of Louis Armstrong's *125 Jazz Breaks for Cornet* published by Melrose Brothers in 1928); and radio broadcasts that included jazz. However, the most effective means was through phonograph records. Records were inexpensive and were sold everywhere. Clarinetist Buster Bailey provided an important example of the influence of records when he recalled his early days as a musician in Memphis. "In 1917," he said, "we began to improvise after hearing recordings of *Livery Stable Blues* and stuff like that. Also some of the boys had drifted up from New Orleans. . . . So the first I heard of the New Orleans style was on records."[35]

Finally, we need only mention how the *ur*-Chicagoans, the Austin High Gang—before they discovered the records of the New Orleans Rhythm Kings—listened to records by Paul Whiteman, Art Hickman, and Ted Lewis. Mezzrow, who saw himself as guru to the young Chicagoans, tells us about the effect of an Armstrong record on his disciples:

> I brought the record home to play for the gang, and man, they all fell through the ceiling. Bud, Dave and Tesch almost wore it out by playing it over and over until we knew the whole thing by heart. Suddenly, about two in the A.M., Tesch jumped to his feet, his sad pan all lit up for once, and yelled, "Hey, listen you guys, I got an idea! This is something Bix should hear right away! Let's go out to Hudson Lake and give him the thrill of his life!"[36]

The importance and influence of records in the history of jazz cannot be overestimated. For the seminal jazz figures in all cities, records were the stuff that shaped and molded their tastes, technique, and ultimately their very lives. Here, in Barry Ulanov's account, we learn something of the popularity of records in the mid-1920s, with particular emphasis on Black Belt favorites:

> In 1926 sales of records in America reached a dizzying new high of 151,000,000 disks. In Chicago, on June twelfth of that year, the Consolidated Talking Machine Company (Okeh Records) celebrated the phenomenal success of records with a "Cabaret and Style Show" at the Coliseum. For about ten thousand people, Okeh's Chicago recording manager, the pianist Richard M. Jones, gathered together the stars of his label. There were the big bands—Carroll Dickerson's Sunset Cafe Orchestra, Charlie Elgar's Arcadia Ballroom Band, Dave Peyton's Peerless Theatre Orchestra, Doc Cook's Dreamland

Ballroom Orchestra, Erskine Tate's Vendome Syncopaters. Al Wind brought down his Dreamland Cafe band, King Oliver the Plantation Cafe Orchestra, and Louis Armstrong led his Hot Five through an actual recording as the climax of the evening.[37]

Since the gathering was clearly a Black Belt promotion, it is no surprise to see listed among the musicians the names of those blacks most prominent in Chicago in the mid-1920s; yet, of these, only Armstrong and Oliver were at all well known outside the city. Nevertheless, several of the others named attained high local prominence, worked regularly, and provided jobs for their better-known sidemen. Doc Cook came from Louisville, Charlie Elgar from New Orleans, and Erskine Tate from Memphis, all arriving in Chicago before the Great Migration; by the '20s they were among Chicago's established band leaders. Cook played at the Dreamland Ballroom for nearly six years; during that time he employed Freddie Keppard, Jimmy Noone, and Hot Five banjoist Johnny St. Cyr. Erskine Tate had a hand in shaping young Armstrong; his specialty was theater jobs, which he preferred to dance hall jobs, and when he persuaded Armstrong to join his theater band it was the best move (as time would prove) for Armstrong to make. As Hadlock noted, "Working [on trumpet] with Tate brought a new audience to Armstrong—an audience of young people, conservative middle-class fans, and musicians who couldn't afford the Prohibition prices of after-hours nightclubs."[38] Carroll Dickerson employed clarinetist Buster Bailey as early as 1922, but is best known for having employed Armstrong in his band at the Sunset Cafe after Armstrong returned from his stay with Fletcher Henderson (it was Dickerson's 1929 band that went to New York and played there under Armstrong's name).

By the late '20s, it was plainly evident to ambitious jazzmen, black and white alike, that the focus of jazz had shifted from Chicago to New York. Many, of course, had already made the journey earlier, some to remain and to flourish in New York's jazz atmosphere, some to stay on in relative obscurity, others to return to Chicago for revitalization or to nurse their wounded pride. At the same time, there was another jazz scene developing, somewhat independently, in Kansas City, Missouri, whose principal jazz figures would eventually leave Kansas City to meet up with their Chicago counterparts in New York. To understand how this process came about, we must now turn our attention to life in Kansas City.

KANSAS CITY: THE DEVELOPMENT OF ITS SPIRIT

7

On April 30, 1803, Napoleon Bonaparte, anxious to dispose of the French holdings known as the Territory of Louisiana, arranged to "cede and grant" the territory to the United States for $15 million. Six months later Congress authorized Thomas Jefferson to complete the Louisiana Purchase and take possession of the land. In 1804, the new land was divided at the 33rd parallel, the southern part becoming the Territory of Orleans and the northern part the District of Louisiana. The following year the District of Louisiana became the Territory of Louisiana—a designation which held for seven years. In 1812 the Territory of Orleans was admitted to the Union as the State of Louisiana, and to preclude confusing the name of the new state with the still-existing territory, the Territory of Louisiana was renamed the Territory of Missouri.

As the Missouri Territory attracted settlers, the advantages of statehood became apparent, and between 1817 and 1819 citizens of the territory petitioned Congress to allow them to form a state government. Most of the new residents were southerners and had assumed that Missouri would be a slave state; free-state proponents in Congress, however, opposed the increase in number, and hence political power, of the slave states. A bitter struggle between partisans on all levels of government resulted in the Missouri Compromise of 1820, which provided that, while Missouri could enter the Union as a slave state and Maine as a free state, slavery would be banned elsewhere west of the Mississippi and north of Missouri's southern boundary. Missouri was thus admitted into the Union in 1821.[1] About twenty years later an area near the mouth of the Kansas River, known locally as "the Kaw," was platted as the "Town of Kansas." (*Kansas*, *Kansa*, and *Kaw* were renderings of the Indian name; Kansas also meant "smoky wind," or prairie fire.) In 1853 the Town of Kansas became the City of Kansas, but it was not until 1889 that it officially became Kansas City.[2]

With the platting and early development of the Town of Kansas, three villages could now supply necessities to those traveling the Santa Fe Trail—Independence, Westport, and Kansas. Independence stood at the head of the trail and specialized in wagon outfitting and, along with Westport, provided lodging for travelers. The Town of Kansas, on the Missouri River's edge and confined by towering bluffs, included a few stores and a few warehouses. The rock levee on which it stood made a first-rate steamboat landing; otherwise, it seemed a pointless place to build a town, and there was apparently little reason for anyone to do so. Senator Thomas Hart Benton, traveling up the Missouri on a steamboat in 1845, thought otherwise. As the boat approached the Kansas Landing and the site which would later become Kansas City (the three towns linked together), he is reported to have said to a group of men on deck, "Gentlemen, there is the gateway to India."[3] Although Benton spoke with a politician's exuberance, his words were not entirely an exaggeration. It was at the confluence of the Kansas and Missouri rivers, at the Kansas Landing, that the Missouri reached closest to the Southwest; and it was here that steamboats traveling the river channel from St. Louis delivered their cargoes, saving westward-bound travelers the long overland journey.

A year after Senator Benton's "gateway" remark, the outbreak of the war between the United States and Mexico brought the Kansas Landing to the attention of the military. The need for speedy shipment of men and guns to the Mexican war made the Kansas levee, with its natural rock ledge, the logical point of departure. The time advantage in using the Kansas levee was evident to everyone after the end of the war in 1848, with the California Gold Rush of 1848–49, when tens of thousands of men and wagons came through the territory. Independence, whose position at the head of the Santa Fe Trail had given the town a monopoly in wagon outfitting, lost its dominance first to Westport and eventually to the Town of Kansas. By the 1850s, wagon freighters (like the military before them) discovered the advantages of starting from steamboats on the Kansas levee. Kansas citizens were delighted to accommodate them, and the Town of Kansas now became the center of the wagon-outfitting business.

The town was now well on its way to becoming something more than a steamboat landing on the Missouri. Here is a moderate booster's view of the city's position as a municipality in the late 1850s:

> The rugged bluffs were still there—but the legal right to issue bonds for public improvements had been established. It was far from being a beautiful city—but a city hall had been built, some streets graded or macadamized, the first telegraph service introduced, and, highly important, property values were booming.[4]

Other "streets" were added from time to time by digging through the bluffs; the highest was the West Bluff, which towered two hundred feet above the steamboat landing and the levee district. The streets were cut through every which way, zigzagging and crisscrossing each other with no apparent logic except to provide some sort of access up from the rock levee. "By the time of the Civil War," Darrell Garwood tells us, "the uptown section, above the bluff, had acquired one good three-story brick hotel, the Pacific House, and several lesser hotels; two daily newspapers, a theater called an Opera House, and a residential section stretching toward Westport."[5] Down on the levee, land speculators accompanied by brass bands greeted steamboats arriving with brass bands of their own playing for dances on the steamboat decks. It was a time of building and merrymaking, and the city would continue to grow until the Civil War interrupted its expansion.

The Town of Kansas grew rapidly. Although population figures for the area before 1860 vary widely (estimates made by public officials, travelers, and others), the first official census in 1860 showed Westport with 1,195 people, Independence with 3,164, and Kansas City with 4,418.[6] Rapid growth increased the city's social problems. For example, in 1857, when the city had a population of about 1,500, its only official law enforcement was provided by a chief of police, a regular force of two policemen, and a supplementary force of ten on call for night patrol. The city's nightlife, even then, appears to have required special monitoring. During this same year, citizens of the town enjoyed watching 1,500 steamboat landings with their attendant loading and unloading of passengers and merchandise. Such activity filled the townsfolk with pride and the hope of honest boom and prosperity. Kansas was their city, and they wished to see it develop not only as a transport city but also as a good place to live.

Not everyone in Kansas City watched the steamboat landings with pride; there were those who watched the docking and unloading with an eye to the main chance. The constant coming and going of itinerant workers, well-heeled travelers, and gullible visitors gave the levee's riverboat gamblers, con men, pickpockets, and prostitutes a remarkably dependable clientele, and the saloons were the principal marketplace. "Drinking saloons abounded," a visitor to the city in 1857 reported, "and everything wore the accidental, transitory look of new settlements."[7]

The city's frontier spirit, its violence, its shrill laissez-faire may easily be attributed to its peculiar location. For those hardy characters—the traders, mountain men, pioneers, and adventurers—who prepared to leave the civilizing influences of the East for the unknown dangers of the Great American Desert, Kansas City was in a sense their Last Chance Saloon. As Garwood put it, "Kansas City . . . was nurtured by the East, but it was literally the place where the West began."[8]

Kansas City was also in many ways where the conflict between North and South began. Although the Missouri Compromise of 1820 permitted unrestricted slavery in the new state, the Compromise was effectively repealed in 1854 by Stephen A. Douglas's Kansas-Nebraska Bill intended to enable Kansas to enter the Union as a slave state on the principle of "squatter sovereignty," that is, if the settlers themselves wished to have it that way. The border between Kansas and Missouri now became more than just a geographical boundary. Proslavery men from Missouri and other slaveholding states headed for Kansas to file squatters' claims, and abolitionists from the North (among them John Brown and his five sons) also made for Kansas to file claims. Each side hoped for victory over the other, or at least a standoff. After the first elections in 1854 and 1855, the slavers appeared to have won. (With 2,905 Kansans eligible to vote, the slavers had somehow managed to muster 6,307 votes.[9])

The beginning of the Civil War in April 1861 gave both sides a license to use violent means, as it were; looting and killing could now be viewed as patriotic acts necessary to the survival of one's own nation. While Missouri's leaders favored secession, the people did not, and at first some thought Missouri would be allowed to remain neutral. The hope of neutrality proved to be wishful thinking. Each side set up its own government, and the prosecessionists declared their secession from the Union and joined the Confederacy. By now, however, the state was under control of the Union army, and the secessionists were a government in exile. Missourians were torn between the two causes; of those who fought in the Civil War, 100,000 joined the Union Army and 30,000 the Confederate.[10]

Throughout the Civil War, guerrilla parties—self-styled defenders of the faith—who were fed, sheltered, and protected by sympathizers in rural communities, roved through Kansas City and the surrounding countryside pillaging, burning, terrorizing, and murdering. Guerrillas from Kansas, across the border, were known as Jayhawkers, while those who operated out of the brush immediately surrounding Kansas City were the Bushwhackers. The best known of the Confederate Bushwhackers was William C. ("Charlie") Quantrill, who led his own force of about a hundred men. In August 1863, several bands of Bushwhackers numbering about 450, under the command of Quantrill, grouped forces for a raid on Lawrence, Kansas. En route they murdered ten men they identified as Union men and a farmer who just got in the way. Once in Lawrence, they simply shot anything that moved, made their way from the streets into the houses, commandeered the town's saloons, and, full of drink, took potshots at unarmed men and children. They attacked the town's business district and burned

185 buildings, some of which still held townspeople. Quantrill's order to his men had been, "Kill every man big enough to carry a gun." When the massacre finally came to an end, the dead included 150 men and children.[11] Four days after the massacre, the Union commander at Kansas City retaliated with his General Order No. 11:

> The famous—some say infamous—order directed the evacuation within 15 days of all persons living in Jackson, Cass, and Bates Counties and in part of Vernon County. Excepted were the inhabitants of certain towns. Grain and hay were to be removed "within reach of military stations," after which the fields were to be burned.[12]

Throughout the war, Quantrill remained unscathed and a hero to his guerrilla band, including one of its youngest members and his most apt pupil, fifteen-year-old Jesse James. In May 1865, a month after the war was officially over, federal troops finally caught up with Quantrill and he was mortally wounded. Soon after, Jesse, now nineteen, and his brother Frank, twenty-three, formed their own band of robbers and murderers, including the three Younger brothers, of whom Cole, twenty-one, another Quantrill alumnus, continued to carry on in the spirit of Quantrill, first specializing in bank robberies and later in train robberies, with incidental murders along the way. The James gang operated for fifteen years after the war was over, and before the gang broke up they became the best-known criminals in America.

The spirit in which Missourians looked upon Jesse James is worth noting because it helped create and sustain the atmosphere in which Kansas City later developed. While the James boys and their band were not acclaimed as heroes, neither were they looked upon as cold-blooded murderers. Missouri, we must remember, had a fair share of southerners, and, after all, the reasoning went, the James boys had fought for the *southern* cause. Were they, unreconstructed Missourians reasoned, to be despised just because the South had failed? Garwood discusses this interesting point:

Missourians looked on the James boys with mixed feelings; . . . since they repeatedly escaped, they came to symbolize the resentment which Missourians felt for the "law" which had been imposed during and after the war. . . . Whatever its basis, the fact remained that the James boys and their fellow bandits always had more friends than the men who hunted them.[13]

"The plague of banditry," in Arthur M. Schlesinger's phrase, came to an end when, in 1881,

the governor of the state joined with various railway and express companies in setting a price on the heads of Jesse and Frank James. Tempted by the heavy reward, a member of the gang treacherously killed Jesse several months later. Frank voluntarily gave himself up and, after several futile attempts to convict him, quietly lived out the rest of his life as a decent member of society.[14]

The war years brought the early prosperity and growth of Kansas City to a virtual halt. In the postwar years, however, the atmosphere of crime and violence notwithstanding, the city was once more on the move. Although there were a number of factors that figured in the boom of Kansas City's postwar decade, one of the most significant came about because of the difficulties Texas cattlemen were having bringing their cattle to market. Shortly after the war, Texans were desperate to find ways to bring their herds to railroad shipping points without having to stop for fences. Abilene, Kansas, suitably and safely (Wild Bill Hickok was marshal) located 150 miles west of Kansas City, became the first railhead. In order to win out over competing cattle towns (particularly, heavy opposition from Leavenworth, Kansas), Kansas City put up the Hannibal Bridge across the Missouri, completing it in 1869 after three years of construction, and thus connecting the city with seven railroad lines.

With the construction of the Hannibal Bridge, Kansas City was now the western rail center closest to where the cattle-town railway spurs could connect with other rail systems. And it was to here, along the Kansas River bottomlands (called the West Bottoms), that the cattle were shipped, unloaded, fed, rested, reloaded, and sent on their way to Chicago. For five years Kansas City functioned as middleman between the western cattle industry and the Chicago stockyards. In 1871, Kansas City took the bull by the horns, so to speak, and opened the Kansas City Stock Yards. Large packing firms (Armour, for one) found the location attractive, and according to contemporary accounts, "by 1874 it was possible in Kansas City in a single day to slaughter and dress 2,000 cattle and 6,000 hogs."[15]

Kansas City became the arch-cowtown, taking the play away from such places as Abilene and Dodge City, and attracting the West's best-known gunmen, lawmen and outlaws alike. Wild Bill Hickok spent three years in Kansas City, and such fast draws as Wyatt Earp, Doc Holliday, and Bat Masterson (as well as the spirit of the James boys) gave Kansas City considerably much of its cowtown tone and saloon atmosphere. The building of the Hannibal Bridge brought large numbers of men looking for jobs; it also brought those who victimized them. Citizens trying to contain the inevitable disorderliness created a vigilante organization, but crime and violence continued unabated. Reports on the quality of life in Kansas City in the postwar decade sound curiously like reports from New Orleans and Chicago. Reference is made to the "large number of abandoned characters," the thieves, the gamblers, and the general uselessness of the Kansas City police force. In 1870, a year after the bridge was completed, the police force included twenty-three policemen without uniforms and a marshal; moreover, in a city with a population of somewhere between twenty and forty thousand, there was no official police station and only two small "lockups."[16]

Gambling in Kansas City became a major industry, pushing other business aside' as it spread throughout the city. The artist George Caleb Bingham, known for his painting "Order No. 11," rented out some property he owned in order to supplement his income. Here he describes why his venture failed: "The numerous gambling holes and kindred establishments, by driving proper business to other quarters, have so reduced my rents that I have been compelled to paint portraits this winter for the support of my family."[17] In 1874 Bingham became the Kansas City police commissioner, and during his tenure is reported to have led raids against at least two hundred gamblers—surely a case of poetic justice.

Unlike Bingham, most solid citizens could do little to affect the city's burgeoning lowlife; instead, they turned their efforts to works which would benefit the city's permanent, homeloving residents. Shortly after the war was over, a school board began the organization of a Kansas City public school system, and by 1870 over three thousand students were attending schools. Graded and paved streets were also considered essential, and in 1870 horse railroad companies built street railways covering the main parts of the city. Two years later, the city formed its first fire department, with two firemen. In 1883 the Cawsmouth Electric Light Company, with a grand total of five employees, built a powerhouse in the West Bottoms (one of the company officers had seen electric arc lights at the Centennial Exposition in Philadelphia in 1876), and electric light service was made available.[18] It was now plain to all that a way had to be found to connect the railroads in the West Bottoms with Quality Hill and the rest of the city. For a dozen years, a cable car had been successfully used in San Francisco—a vehicle that was a match for Kansas City's hills and steep inclines—and in 1885 the cable car was introduced to Kansas City.

The growth and transformation of Kansas City from the late nineteenth century through the 1930s were firmly tied to the fortunes of Jim and Tom Pendergast, who between them forged the Pendergast machine—the most infamously successful political machine in its time—and, who, as we shall later see, brought about exactly the right circumstances for jazz to flourish. In 1876 twenty-year-old Jim left St. Joseph, Missouri, where he had grown up and attended school, and arrived in Kansas City looking for work. He moved into a furnished room in the West Bottoms, found his first job in a packing house, then moved on to an iron foundry where the work was more in keeping with his massive, muscular build. Jim soon discovered that he could drink in two hundred Kansas City saloons—if he wished—and could gamble almost anywhere. The city's principal industry may have been cattle, but gambling—on anything, apparently—was but a step behind. William M. Reddig discusses this interesting phenomenon:

> The gambling industry attained a high state of development in Kansas City in the 1870s. The faro banks at Marble Hall and No. 3 Missouri Avenue were famous throughout the West. . . . the citizens exercised their financial genius at chuck-a-luck, faro, three-card monte, roulette, high five, keno, poker and, occasionally, craps. They bet on horse races, dog fights, free-for-alls with rats, cock fights and, in an extremity, they played fly-loo. This last game called for rare judgment, the players placing their money on common houseflies and guessing which one would move first, in what direction and how far.[19]

After five years of lying in wait for the main chance, Jim Pendergast's ship (or, rather, his race horse) came in when Climax, whom he had bet on heavily, won; this windfall enabled him to buy a combination hotel and saloon in the West Bottoms, which he gratefully named the Climax.[20] He later sold the Climax Saloon, kept the hotel, bought two more saloons—one in the West Bottoms and another in the North End—and was now considered by all to be a successful West Bottoms entrepreneur. He was now ready to turn his attention to West Bottoms politics.

The West Bottoms, along with the adjacent North End, were to become Jim Pendergast's kingdom. The West Bottoms, bounded on the west by the Kansas state line, on the north by the Missouri River, and on the east by Quality Hill, was the center of Kansas City's industrial district. Its poor streets and mean neighborhoods took in not only the city's packing houses, railroad yards, and factories, but a population of low-income blacks and whites living in dingy slum tenements and wooden shacks. In his authoritative book *The Pendergast Machine*, Lyle W. Dorsett describes conditions there:

> The ubiquitous junk shops and second-hand stores on Ninth Street were patronized by these low-income laborers, most of whom lived in overcrowded tenements and shanties. The perennial problem of open sewers and gutters coupled with overcrowded living conditions, constantly threatened the inhabitants with disease and added to the unpleasantness of their surroundings.[21]

(The North End, aside from the district called Little Italy, also included the neighborhoods where the majority of the city's prostitution and crime were contained.)

William Allen White, arriving in Kansas City in 1891 to work as a reporter on the *Kansas City Journal* just as Jim Pendergast was about to come into his own, described the city as

> an overgrown country town of a hundred thousand people. It was consciously citified, like a country jake in his first store clothes. It had one ten-story building, and a score of buildings from five to seven stories. Its business area comprised a dozen blocks in something like the center of the town. To the west of the business area were the packing houses. . . . Around them were the small industries of the city and the stockyards, which smelled to high heaven. And of course fringing these were the shabby, unpainted homes of the workers. North of the business district was the red-light area, segregated and properly policed. South of the business area lived the ruling class in lovely homes surrounded by green lawns, with spreading elms, massive oaks, a few walnut trees, and young evergreens.[22]

White lived first in the Centropolis Hotel, "a third-rate hostelry down near the edge of the red-light district, but still the haunt of old Missouri cattlemen who remembered it in the days of its royal prime," and later he moved into the Midland Hotel, a first-class hotel with a dining room he could not resist, for, as he put it,

I certainly was a sincere and competent eater in those days. On the breakfast menu were baked oysters, and broiled oysters with strange sauces. I learned to like them even for breakfast, along with pancakes, fried potatoes, and fruit. At lunch and at dinner I wandered through the bill of fare as a Sultan might stroll through his harem.[23]

The Democrats had originally divided the city into six wards, and later a rearrangement of ward boundaries put nearly all of the West Bottoms into a new First Ward. Voters in the wards elected a chairman who appointed a committee that chose the delegates to a convention where candidates for the city's political offices came for support. Whoever controlled the chair controlled the delegates, and, to a large extent, the candidates. By 1892 no one questioned the fact that "Big Jim," as he was now called, was the political leader of the First Ward. For his debut he was elected as an alderman to the city council, then reelected in 1894 against massive opposition from the Republican and Independent tickets and the Kansas City press. Apparently no one wanted Jim to win except his laboring friends and his customers in the West Bottoms. They came to his saloon to cash checks, to ask and receive small political favors, to leave full of good cheer, and eager to support Big Jim when he asked them to; and when thirty-eight men were arrested for gambling in a room over his North End saloon, the North End's sympathy went to Alderman Jim.

Jim ran for alderman again in 1896, was again elected, and continued his good works. He put up a bail bond for a black inhabitant of the First Ward and the blacks cheered; he cast the deciding vote against the gas company, whose franchise enabled them to sell gas for $1.60 per thousand cubic feet, in favor of another company that offered to sell gas for a dollar per thousand, and his fellow hotel owners cheered; in the wintertime he visited his constituents, making sure none were cold or hungry, instructing grocers, butchers, bakers, and coal sellers to provide their wares to the needy and send the bills to Jim Pendergast.[24]

Jim's North End saloon was a block away from the courthouse

and City Hall, and was the favorite gathering place for city officials and lawyers and (when it seemed politic) their clients, generally those involved in gambling and liquor. The saloon was also the headquarters of a syndicate led by the gambler Ed Findley, who had twenty-two employees working in Jim's saloon alone and who ran gambling games in saloons all over the North End. Jim's election to the City Council, the location of his North End saloon, his connection with the gambling syndicate, his influence in the Kansas City Police Department, and the strong support of his constituents made him, by 1898, not only boss of the First Ward's West Bottoms, but of the Second Ward's North End as well. His greatest power, however, was still to come.

In the 1900 mayoralty race, Jim favored James A. Reed over his Republican opponent; Reed won overwhelmingly and believed he owed it all to Jim. To show his appreciation, he turned over to Jim the sort of patronage that was tantamount to handing him Kansas City. Jim had his younger brother Tom appointed superintendent of streets; he arranged to have Democratic firemen replace Republicans in the fire department; and Jim's man became deputy license inspector. The control over the police department that Reed gave him was, for Jim, best of all. "Between 1900 and 1902," Dorsett noted, "Jim Pendergast named 123 out of the 173 patrolmen on the force."[25]

In 1898 the State of Missouri controlled the police through the governor's power to appoint the police board. This arrangement suited Jim just fine—the governor of Missouri was a Democrat, and Jim had strong state government connections. Republicans believed the city would do better with local control (particularly if they could elect a Republican mayor and city council), and so they stumped for home rule of the police. Reports, perhaps exaggerations, claimed the city tolerated 600 saloons (and their associated activities: gambling, prostitution) as well as 147 houses of prostitution whose 554 inmates earned an average of $50 a week each and whose fines to the city totaled over $3,000 a month.[26] The revenue to the city notwithstanding, Republicans wished to break Democratic control. A three-fifths majority vote would bring about home rule and give Kansas City citizens control over their own police department. At election time Jim rallied the wards he controlled, and the home rule cause was crushed.

In 1904, with the election of a Republican mayor, Jim lost his patronage; at the same time, however, the inhabitants of the First Ward, demonstrating their unswerving fealty, elected Jim their alderman for the seventh time. Jim carried their banner for another six years, retiring in poor health in 1910, when he is reported to have counseled his people to "take Brother Tom; he'll make a fine alderman, and he'll be good to the boys just as I've been."[27] And so it was. Tom was elected, and shortly after, in November 1911, Jim died.

Tom Pendergast took over the machine his brother had built in the West Bottoms, and before he was through expanding its power the whole of the city and parts of the county were under his control, and in the highest reaches of state and federal government Kansas City came to be known as Tom's Town. Tom Pendergast was born in 1872, and when he arrived in Kansas City at the age of eighteen, brother Jim, already a successful saloonkeeper, put him to work as a bookkeeper in his West Bottoms saloon. Under Jim's tutelage Tom learned the ins and outs of First Ward politics, and at age twenty-four he was appointed a deputy county marshal; at twenty-eight he became Kansas City's superintendent of streets, and two years later, with the support of the Goats, as Jim's faction was called (the rival Democratic faction was called the Rabbits), he was elected county marshal. Tom now began building on his brother's foundation. Dorsett observes Tom in a characteristic gesture:

At Christmas time in 1903, Tom used his own money to purchase fourteen turkeys and all the trimmings to brighten the holiday for 120 inmates in the Jackson County jail. This sort of conduct had a dual effect. It added not only to the immediate stature of the Pendergast machine in places like the rough and tumble river wards, but also to the number of men who would not forget Tom when he ultimately took over the Goat faction.[28]

When Tom became alderman, Kansas City had a population of about twenty-five thousand. New neighborhoods were growing rapidly, and citizen concern with reform grew alarmingly. A Society for the Suppression of Commercialized Vice took aim at Tom's Jefferson Hotel and Cabaret, whose principal attractions appeared to be gambling, prostitution, indoor shootouts, and unrestrained boozing. Tom was unperturbed by the reformers, and treated them good-naturedly until 1916, when the county, led by the nationally based Women's Christian Temperance Union, mounted an election for statewide prohibition. (The drys lost the election by losing St. Louis, but that they could force an election at all was significant.) What the local drys had initiated, the 1918 wartime Prohibition Act completed. But Tom had outwitted them all; just before the end he sold out his liquor interests. Furthermore, the city took a piece of property on which Tom's hotel stood—in order to widen the street, it was said—and a condemnation jury awarded him $79,550 for a hotel and cabaret that had outlived their usefulness.

By the mid-1920s Kansas City was governed from an office in the Jackson Democratic Club at 1908 Main Street, which was two blocks from the railroad yards, only a few minutes from Tom's Ready-Mixed Concrete Company (which supplied the concrete and asphalt used on city streets and in public buildings, without competitive bids), and a few blocks from what had been the T. J. Pendergast Wholesale Liquor Company—a liquor interest he revived after the war. In short, 1908 Main Street was Tom's command post. Tom welcomed callers, and visitors with problems always left with a satisfactory solution. He was an executive who, at least in the early days, did not believe in delegating authority; he took his position as boss literally, and apparently so did everyone else.

Everyone, that is, except the reformers. In 1925, a nonpartisan city charter was accepted by the voters that would take the business of running Kansas City out of the hands of the politicos and put it in the hands of a nonpartisan city manager, a businessman with no axes to grind, beholden to no special interests, no faction, and working only in the best interests of the people of Kansas City. To the reformers it looked like an enlightened, progressive solution to the problem of corruption. In November, the results of an election for city councilmen gave the Democrats a five-to-four majority. Since the new city manager was to be chosen by the majority of the council, Tom Pendergast was called in, and he helped them select, and then elect Henry F. McElroy, a Jackson County judge who was also an established businessman and a friend of Kansas City's commercial interests. Tom also helped elect Harry S. Truman. Reddig observes McElroy's position in the business community and his relation to Tom:

> Henry McElroy seemed to be the ideal man for the task from both the commercial and political points of view. Bankers, real estate men and merchants knew him as a shrewd and hard-headed operator, a man who had started from scratch, understood the value of a dollar and made a pile. Boss Pendergast knew him as a thoroughly dependable disciple of Tom Pendergast.[29]

For the next four years, McElroy proved that Tom's confidence in him was justified. Every Sunday, McElroy—whom some saw as an honest country bookkeeper—came to Tom's house to report and to receive instructions. The Ready-Mixed Concrete Company expected to continue supplying the city with concrete, without competition and at its own prices. Tom told McElroy who was to go on the city payroll, for what purpose, and at how much salary. Eventually the city carried a payroll that averaged over half a million dollars a month.[30] By the time the city finished a municipal airport, acquired two bridges over the Missouri River, and expanded its consumer services (not the least of which were street repairs and maintenance), McElroy had managed to run up a substantial deficit. As a fair country bookkeeper, however, he was able to hide the deficit, and the city continued to receive credit regularly from local bankers. McElroy, however, was appalled at the amount of money being spent by the police department. Chief Miles, no favorite of the Goats, bore the brunt of McElroy's new-found parsimony. Reddig shows us McElroy in action on this occasion:

> He began by objecting to the size of the police budget, arbitrarily refusing to pay certain expense bills of Chief Miles and other items. He held up the wages of policemen for months at a time, upset the police benefit fund and otherwise demoralized the department. He made an issue over a bill for fifteen dollars for flowers for a slain officer and staged a hammy comedy act over a clothes cleaning bill for the police. To one touching plea for money needed to pay the police wages, he replied with a letter advising that the officers be fed castor oil.[31]

Tom Pendergast became the boss of Kansas City because he made a constituency wherever he could find it and because he showed no ethnic prejudice in rewarding his supporters. He was, of course, delighted when Michael Ross, an Irishman, helped him run the First Ward in the 1920s. When Ross, however, lost his power in 1928 to Johnny Lazia, an Italian, Tom adjusted easily. The North Side's Little Italy had always been one of Tom's strongholds and now, with Johnny Lazia as his liaison, the district's inhabitants (85 percent of whom were of Sicilian descent in 1929) could be safely tucked away until their votes were needed.[32] With Tom's blessing, Lazia became the most powerful criminal in Kansas City. Maurice M. Milligan, the district attorney who was later to smash the Pendergast machine (he prepared the federal government's case against Tom in 1938) wrote: "I was not altogether ignorant of the positions occupied in the Pendergast empire by City Manager McElroy and the shadowy racketeer, Johnny Lazia. I did not need to be told that Kansas City's police setup was rotten, that crime was rampant, and that vice was flourishing. Justice, on anything less than a Federal scale seemed blind or inept, or both."[33] In 1928 Lazia was thirty-one years old. Despite his immigrant parents, his Little Italy street training, and his eighth-grade education, his manner was that of a persuasive and high-powered salesman. An ambitious youth, he had worked as a clerk in a law office, perhaps hoping to become a lawyer. No doubt impatient with his financial rewards as a clerk, at eighteen he engaged in a holdup which brought him $250 in cash, a gun battle which ended in his capture, and a prison sentence of fifteen years that was later reduced to twelve. Young Johnny was an exemplary prisoner, and with recommendations from the Jackson County attorney and two Democratic party leaders, his parole was granted by the Democratic lieutenant governor. Of his twelve-year sentence, Lazia served a total of eight months and seven days.[34] Once outside the prison walls, he spent the next ten years in small political organizing tasks, gambling, a bit of loan sharking, and helping others to help themselves. Now he was about to have the chance of a lifetime—the chance he had been waiting for.

To the casual observer, Lazia's relation to Tom appeared to be straightforwardly political. When Lazia overthrew Mike Ross, he reorganized the North Side Democratic Club. The club was a legitimate party organization, Lazia was its boss, and the organization acted in the best interests of Tom Pendergast and his friends. But Lazia was, in fact, a crooked gambler and ex-convict who needed only a slight push in the right direction to turn Kansas City into one of the nation's principal crime centers. The push came in 1932 when home rule was finally established in Kansas City and control of the police department went to City Manager McElroy, who yielded in favor of Boss Tom, who decided that Lazia deserved to have this incredible plum, and in short order both the police department and the underworld knew that on matters criminal, Lazia (with Tom's protection) held the key and the sword.

When Lazia made his debut as Little Italy's boss, ordinary citizens of Kansas City had already endured a decade of relatively unrestrained crime. In 1928, a citizens' group concerned with protection from criminals (eighty-nine people had been murdered in Kansas City that year) arranged for a study of the police department by the Kansas City Public Service Institute, directed by August Vollmer, later professor of police administration at the University of Chicago. Vollmer's study and report corroborated everyone's worst fears. Between 1920 and 1928, murders in the city increased over 100 percent; armed robberies increased 60 percent; while business burglaries decreased slightly, and residence burglaries decreased 65 percent. Clearly, during this decade, Kansas City criminals no longer found business and residence burglaries as profitable as murder and armed robbery.

In 1928 the city endured 4,275 auto thefts, with an overwhelming number taking place between Fourteenth Street and Thirty-first Street, between Troost and the state line (encompassing the red-light district). The Public Service Institute's survey was "welcomed" by the Kansas City Board of Police Commissioners, as were the institute's recommendations for "an effective system of employment and promotion" and the training of patrolmen. At first, the commissioners announced "the policy of eliminating political considerations in all work of the Department." Later, the announcement turned out to be no more than a stalling tactic. A year after the report was made, the institute announced: "So far, . . . the chief failure has been that the Commissioners have not yet adopted the reorganization plan, standards for entrance to the department, or a scientific method of selection and training of men. These are being considered, but little has actually been done." With the establishment of home rule, a great deal would happen in the police department, but exactly contrary to anything recommended by the institute. Under home rule, Lazia "advised the Chief of Police on matters pertaining to the underworld, . . . took his regular cut in the manifold gambling rackets, and was master of the 'fix.' "[35] Kansas City racketeers paid for his protection, prostitution was rampant, and Kansas City was "safe" for gangsters and murderers from all over mid-America. As D. A. Milligan put it, "With the possible exception of such renowned centers as Singapore and Port Said, Kansas City probably has the greatest sin industry in the world."[36]

As an ex-convict himself, Lazia showed his concern for the welfare of his peers, although the small-minded might consider his generosity as at least uncharacteristic. However that may be, he arranged for sixty ex-convicts to become policemen, and in 1934, 10 percent of the Kansas City police force possessed known criminal records.[37] With the chief of police and the department in his hip pocket, Lazia was able to furnish all the ingredients that made Kansas Ctiy as attractive as any of America's other jazz cities. Observed Milligan:

> When the underworld flocks to Chicago, New Orleans, Miami and Kansas City, it has to be entertained on a wild and lavish scale. It demands music, women and gambling tables, and while engaged in the pursuit of "high life" it wants protection from snoopers, reformers, and policemen who may be a bit overzealous in upholding the law. Under John Lazia and other Pendergast henchmen Kansas City provided this freedom from molestation.[38]

Lazia, incidentally, by his success, created the atmosphere for his own demise. In 1934, he died in commonplace gangland fashion—machine-gunned to death by rival gangsters. Seven thousand people attended his wake, including Tom Pendergast, McElroy, and police director Higgins.

District Attorney Milligan recognized an important corollary to the "high life" of Kansas City, and although the contemporary jazz scene will be taken up at length in the next chapter, it is worthwhile to give special notice here to Milligan's keen observation on Kansas City jazz:

> In Kansas City a whole new school of jazz music was born. Bennie Moten, Count Basie, Walter "Hot Lips" Page, Andy Kirk and others kept the Reno Club and other hot spots jumping with rhythm. I am no authority on jazz, and must take the word of others about this phase of Kansas City's cultural renaissance. The only point I would

like to make is that all this flourished during the Pendergast era and because of it.[39]

Ross Russell, jazz historian, puts it another way:

> A rising gangster element, attracted to Kansas City by a permissive political climate, operated the nightclubs, just as they had in Chicago and New Orleans. The gangsters were familiar with jazz and respected its value as a means of bringing in customers and selling booze, which is where the profits lay. . . . Unusual circumstances brought about near ideal working conditions for jazz musicians in Kansas City that lasted for almost a decade and a half. Granted the isolating factors that separated Kansas City from the popular culture of America, the creation of a new jazz style was a possibility.[40]

It is certain that Tom Pendergast received a prodigious share of the cash that passed through the hands of Lazia and his underworld organization. In addition, he received special money from what we may call his associates in white-collar crimes. The precise amount Pendergast received will never be known, but it is a shock to learn what big money it must have been. Where, then, one might ask, did the money go? How did Tom use it? Why was so much money necessary? Here, in Garwood's summary, are Tom's major ongoing expenses:

> He lived expensively in a $115,000 French Regency house on Ward Parkway in the best part of town. He traveled some, two or three times to Europe with his family, and to political conventions and horse races, keeping a suite at the Waldorf-Astoria in New York when he was in the East. At home, he acquired a stable of race horses in adjacent Platte County, to which, before going to his dumpy political office, he sometimes drove to watch his horses exercise at daybreak. He had a weakness for wagering excessively on his own and other people's horses.[41]

Betting on horses surely contributed to Tom's downfall. The enormous sums he wagered and almost always lost required a constant flow of cash from all sources. (In 1938, Charlie Carollo, Lazia's successor, gave evidence in federal court that he collected protection money from gambling joints that he turned over directly to Tom or to Tom's secretary. Collections from only nineteen of these came to $103,275 in 1938, of which Tom got about 40 percent; the rest was divided among others in the syndicate.[42])

In 1935, for a brief moment, Tom Pendergast may have thought he had found a solution to his immediate cash problems and a way to replace the huge amounts he had gambled away. One day in January, Tom met with Charles R. Street, a representative of the Great American Insurance Company, to negotiate a rather ticklish financial arrangement, as fraudulent as one would wish. The money was indeed big. Back in 1929, insurance companies operating in Missouri had increased their premiums by 16⅔ percent—an increase the policyholders and the state superintendent of insurance believed was unwarranted. A court order permitted the companies to initiate their increase, but tied up the money until the state and federal courts could make a final decision. During the next six years the impounded increase totaled almost $11 million, and the insurance companies grew tired of seeing what they believed was their money continuing to pile up. Tom Pendergast, they thought, held the key to the strongbox, and Street offered Tom $200,000 to arrange for the state to give up the battle and, of course, the cash. Tom seemed reluctant to act for that kind of money, and Street upped the ante to half a million. This time Tom seemed more agreeable. When several months passed and nothing happened, Street raised the offer to $750,000, and Tom went into action. By the time he had recruited his necessary partners in crime—including the latest superintendent of insurance—and had given his partners their shares of the payoffs, he was left with $305,000. Tom kept his promise and did what he was asked to do, the insurance companies received about $5 million as their share—but now Street saw no reason to pay Tom the last $300,000 of the $750,000 agreed upon.[43]

While $300,000 was a substantial amount of money to be "cheated" out of, there was little Tom could do. Obviously, he could not sue. Besides, he was too busy worrying about the collapse of his own financial empire. Desperately trying to recoup his losses, he was betting as much as $5,000 on a single horse race, and most racetracks offered as many as six or seven races a day to bet on. At that rate, and for a loser, Tom's $305,000 cut of the insurance bribe did not last long. Later, the government showed that in 1935 Tom's bets on the horses totaled $2 million and his net loss was $600,000. Between 1925 and 1935, it was estimated that he had gambled away $6 million.[44]

In 1939 District Attorney Milligan presented a federal court with a full exposé of Tom's participation in the insurance fraud and showed evidence that Tom had been guilty of income-tax evasion between 1927 and 1937. The evidence was incontrovertible, and Tom, sick at heart and in poor health, was found guilty of the charges. He was fined $10,000 and sentenced to fifteen months in prison. When City Manager McElroy heard the bad news he resigned. (McElroy died a few months later, after which it was discovered that he had left Kansas City a deficit of nearly $20 million.) Tom served fifteen months in the federal penitentiary at Leavenworth. Before his death in January 1945, he spent his remaining years sadly watching the decline of his once-powerful machine.

Reformers were on the march. The city's nightlife had been forced underground; nightclubs, cabarets, gambling joints, and bawdy houses suffered wholesale closure, and the nightspots no longer offered jazz musicians the economic sanctuary they had so long enjoyed. Kansas City jazzmen were now forced to move on, to seek new, more cordial environments (New York, for one), and to compete with their counterparts from New Orleans, Chicago, and New York itself. They had had, nonetheless, an exciting time of it while it lasted. They had watched and participated in the simultaneous growth and development of Kansas City as Tom's Town and as a jazz center, producing a music that would later be called Kansas City style, or Kansas City jazz—to the growth and development of which we now turn our attention.

KANSAS CITY: THE JAZZ DEVELOPMENT

8

In 1898 Jenkins' Music Store—the largest manufacturer and seller of musical instruments in Kansas City—offered to supply the *world* with their mandolins and guitars. The Jenkins factory made five thousand of these instruments that year. The *Kansas City Journal*, appealing to the pride and, perhaps, sense of duty of civic-minded citizens, reported that "in the Sandwich Islands . . . guitars and mandolins manufactured by J. W. Jenkins' Sons furnish music and amusement to thousands. . . . If it is your desire to see Kansas City forge ahead and at the same time secure for yourself the best mandolin or guitar in the world," why, then, buy a Kansas City mandolin or guitar.[1]

There is no record of the number of Jenkins-made mandolins and guitars purchased by Kansas City citizens for use at home. Playing parlor music is, of course, a private concern, and its purpose is frequently more social than musical. Considering the relative cultural isolation of Kansas City in the 1890s, it seems safe to say that whatever music was played in Kansas City homes was of no great moment. This premise is given additional weight by Henry J. Haskell, a Kansas City newspaper editor who, evaluating the city's cultural strengths and weaknesses, demolished its private musical life in a mordant reference to Atchison, a town about forty miles from Kansas City. "Ed Howe," Haskell wrote, "once said of Atchison that for fifty years every girl in town had practiced on the piano until she had driven the neighbors crazy, but Atchison had not produced a single musician. Broadly speaking his remark applies to Kansas City."[2]

Although there is little question that many of the city's residents enjoyed some sort of music at home, we are on safer ground discussing public performances, particularly the music of local brass bands and the great visiting concert bands of the day. The decade of the 1890s was the heyday of the touring concert band, with such figures as John Philip Sousa, Frederick Neil Innes, Thomas Preston Brooke, Patrick Gilmore, and others setting the pace (if not the standard) for small-town Sunday afternoon band concerts in all parts of the country. Contests among rival bands from cities and towns around Kansas City were frequent, and challenges were commonplace. In one significant instance, a black band from Sedalia challenged a black band from Kansas City—to no decision, since, as the *Sedalia Times* reported, "The band contest that was to be held in Lexington today between Sedalia and Kansas City colored bands has been called off on account of the latter backing out."[3] In an 1889 enumeration of brass bands of the West, we find a band listed simply as the Kansas City Band.[4] This was most likely the Kansas City Municipal Band that played regularly in Kansas City's Electric Park and was led by a Professor Tremaine.

In 1891, when William Allen White was a reporter for the *Kansas City Journal*, he heard Patrick Gilmore's band, for the first time, in Kansas City's Warder Grand Theater, and was overwhelmed. Gilmore's professional sixty-piece band was touring Missouri, and at its peak challenged John Philip Sousa. The band, White wrote, "was like something from another world, created by other creatures than the human beings I had known." White was an amateur musician, had studied organ, and was delighted when the *Journal's* music critic took him along on his concert rounds. "I heard good music wherever I could," White wrote; "life was certainly one round of joy in Kansas City."[5] Later, after showing he enjoyed a bit of singing and hilarity, White was offered the opportunity to participate in a Chamber of Commerce minstrel show to raise funds for a civic enterprise. "I was made an end man," White wrote exuberantly, "did a turn of buck-and-wing dancing, sang a song, and thought myself quite a figure in Kansas City affairs."[6]

In 1899 Kansas City opened its new convention hall, and at its grand opening on Washington's birthday thousands of visitors came, not only to explore the city's newest and proudest structure, but to enjoy the concerts by John Philip Sousa and his concert band. During this visit the people of Kansas City were likely to have heard Sousa's special arrangement of "Doc Brown's Cake Walk" by Kansas City composer Charles L. Johnson.[7] Sousa, the "March King," had the best-known band in America, and his name was synonymous with band music. Around the turn of the century he showed interest in "coon songs," cakewalks, and ragtime, and later he acknowledged his awareness of favorable public reaction to what he called "syncopated music." By 1924—the word *jazz* was in common use by this time—Sousa took special notice of the "new" music. H. W. Schwartz discusses Sousa's band during this period:

> Sousa's band in 1924 was comprised of seventy-five men, which was not remarkable; but what was remarkable was that he carried eight saxophones: four altos, two tenors, a baritone, and a bass. Another remarkable feature of his programs that year was the half hour devoted exclusively to syncopated music. The small dance bands called this type of music "jazz," but what Sousa and his men presented to the public was only a lame sort of jazz, and calling it syncopated music avoided a lot of controversy. This concert band, unquestionably an excellent one, could no more play authentic jazz than the Sousa band of 1904 could play true ragtime.[8]

Nonetheless, what Sousa was playing in 1924 was *called* jazz, just as what he had played in 1904 had been called ragtime. Another important concert band leader much taken by ragtime was Thomas Preston Brooke. In 1902 Brooke and his Chicago Marine Band left Chicago to play concerts in New Orleans, after which the band turned around and made their way back, completing their tour in Kansas City. Since the ragtime craze was sweeping the United States, Brooke regularly devoted entire concerts to band arrangements and transcriptions of ragtime, playing to packed Kansas City houses. Schwartz, in his excellent *Bands of America*, compares Brooke and Sousa on this point:

> Brooke demonstrated his pioneering in band music and his keen understanding of what the people wanted to hear. This was two whole years before Sousa risked playing ragtime at the St. Louis World's Fair, although Sousa is reputed to have played some ragtime in 1900 in Paris. Brooke started playing coon songs and the cakewalk almost from the day he started his Chicago Marine Band,

and he is probably the first bandmaster who had the temerity to devote a whole evening's concert to ragtime tunes.[9]

Military bands were a favorite in Kansas City, and no holiday, no special event, seemed complete without their brassy rhythms. According to jazz historian Dave Dexter, Jr., who grew up in Kansas City,

> the first bands to appear in [Kansas City] were . . . military bands. Arthur Pryor played the 1914 Fraternal Order of Eagles convention and composed a striking new tune, the *Heart of America March*, in honor of the event. John Philip Sousa immediately chose it as the official Camp Funston song, and played it with his world-renowned band for years afterward.[10]

(The "Heart of America March" was dedicated to Edwin J. Shannahan, an important member of Tom Pendergast's Goat faction; as leader of the local service club preparing to host the Eagles' national convention, Shannahan named Kansas City "the Heart of America."[11])

To those seeking entertainment in Kansas City before the First World War, the city's legitimate theaters were important— the best known of these were the Orpheum, Empress, Gaiety, Willis Wood, Hippodrome, and, later, the RKO Missouri and the Pantages (later the Tower Theater) on Twelfth Street. Kansas City musicians, however, had a special interest in those theaters where they could find employment. They favored, for example, Valentine Love's Theater Comique, where melodramas were alternated with singing and dancing; Martin Regan's Fountain Theater, where shapely waitresses served drinks during the stage performances; the Standard Theater at Twelfth and Central, where the fancies danced and preened, which opened in 1900 and later became the Folly Theater, a burlesque house; and Joe Donegan's Century Theater, whose specialty was also burlesque.

As some saloons were changed into cabarets, jobs for musicians became more plentiful. One of the best known of these saloon-cabarets before the First World War was Tom Pendergast's Jefferson Hotel cabaret where, as one reporter put it, "Cabaret entertainers wandered from table to table singing sensuous songs."[12] Newer hotels also furnished dining and dancing to Kansas City's more sedate, white merrymakers, which in turn created jobs for local dance bands as well as for touring bands from out of town. Dancing went on at the Baltimore Hotel where, on occasion, young Jack Teagarden played his trombone, and at the Bellerive Hotel Terrace Room, where during the 1920s and '30s one danced to Ben Pollack's orchestra or Glen Gray and his Casa Loma Orchestra. The Muehlebach Hotel also provided dance music. The Coon-Sanders band (Carleton Coon and Joe Sanders), a popular band formed just after World War I, played together for fourteen years and finally reached the pinnacle of their fame through their performances from the Muehlebach Plantation Grill, broadcast over radio station WDAF. And for those Kansas City dancers who wished to dine in one place and dance in another, there were two dance halls to accommodate them—the Pla-Mor on Main Street and the Century at Thirty-sixth and Broadway.

The larger hotels and dance halls flourished mainly in the '20s and '30s, providing jobs for bands large and small. In the early 1900s, most of Kansas City nightlife was conducted in saloons like Jim Pendergast's on St. Louis Avenue below the West Bluff at Twelfth Street, or at his place at 508 Main Street, uptown. West Ninth Street, in the West Bottoms near the Missouri-Kansas state line, boasted twenty-four buildings, twenty-three of which were saloons.[13] By 1914, though, the construction of the Union Station southeast of the Bottoms disrupted West Bottoms social life (particularly along Union Avenue), and the activity moved uptown. The overwhelming majority of saloons, basement joints, and other nightspots, because of their size, location, or for economic reasons, were likely to feature solo blues singers or ragtime piano players, if they thought they needed to offer entertainment at all.

Except for these pianists and blues singers, all our references to this point have been essentially to white entertainers, white musicians, and the white citizens of Kansas City. Black entertainers and musicians (like their counterparts in New Orleans and Chicago) were known to the city's black community long before they became popular with the white community. Black entertainment for black audiences in black districts reached a position in Kansas City in the 1920s where it became economically propitious to construct theater buildings exclusively for this purpose. Two illustrations show how such buildings were used both in their heyday and in their decline. The New State Theater, at Eighteenth and Highland, was built in 1924. Five years later it became the Boone Theater (named in honor of Blind Boone, a ragtime pianist), and still later it became the Old Armory Building. The Eblon Theater, at Eighteenth and Vine, was built in 1923. Later it became the Cherry Blossom (where blues singer Jimmy Rushing performed), and still later the Chez Paris.[14]

Kansas City blacks provided steady support in the '20s for black entertainers working the black theaters. Black show business folk visiting Kansas City were usually booked into the city by the Theater Owners Booking Association (TOBA), and generally played the Panama, Eblon, or Lincoln Theaters. The pool of talent included such blues singers as Ma Rainey, Bessie Smith, Alberta Hunter, Ida Cox, Lizzie Miles, and Bertha ("Chippie") Hill. Occasionally these singers traveled with their own small bands or ensembles, some of which—Ma Rainey's Georgia Minstrels, for one—had some jazz orientation. By the early '20s the increasing popularity of jazz (as well as easy transportation) brought to Kansas City the touring bands of such jazzmen as King Oliver, Fletcher Henderson, and Duke Ellington.

Under the Pendergast regime, from the 1920s to the '30s, Kansas City was a wide-open city. For musicians, these were to be the golden years. There were over fifty nightspots between Twelfth and Eighteenth Streets, and for anyone who could make music, economic opportunities seemed limitless. The district, roughly six blocks square, was bounded by Highland Avenue on the east,

Eighteenth Street on the south, Forest Avenue on the west, and Twelfth Street on the north. (The "Twelfth Street Rag," by Euday Bowman, certainly one of the most familiar of all ragtime piano pieces, was published in Kansas City and was named for this Kansas City street.) From west to east the streets included Forest, Tracy, Virginia, Lydia, The Paseo, Vine, and Highland. The principal intersections of the district were at Twelfth and Paseo and at Eighteenth and Paseo; half a dozen streets to the east, the intersection of Fourteenth and Cherry was the center of what may have been the least restrained red-light district in the country. (In 1940, in an atmosphere of Kansas City righteousness, the nightspots in and around Eighteenth and Vine were shut down. In 1976, citizen groups, by means of Urban Renewal, made plans to restore and rehabilitate the old area.)

Exploring the city's nightlife after the First World War, those looking for a good time could take their choice and hear blues singers, ragtime, and small ensembles in hundreds of Kansas City nightspots. Armstrong used to refer to the music of unrestrained and untrained uptown blacks (as well as those from the section he called "back o' town," where he grew up) as rough music, compared presumably to the smooth music by downtown Creoles. For rough music there was the Antlers, in the West Bottoms across from the Armour Packing Company; the Ozarks Club at Seventh and Wall; or the Hole in the Wall at Independence and Harrison, where Joe Turner, at age thirteen, sang the blues. The Lyric Hall, near Eighteenth and Forest, gave Kansas City–born saxophonist George E. Lee and his blues-singing sister Julia their start in the music business. And just up the street, at the Panama Club, Benny Moten and a six-piece band opened right after the war. Roy Searcy, a blues pianist still playing Kansas City clubs in 1976, recalled early jobs he played at the Rendezvous Club near Eighteenth and Troost, the El Capitan Club on Highland, and Bernie's Cocktail Lounge "near the old Pla-Mor Ballroom."[15]

The best single survey of Kansas City nightlife during the Pendergast regime is found in Ross Russell's chapter "Kansas City

Clubs and Night Life" in his *Jazz Style in Kansas City and the Southwest*, to which we owe much of what follows. Nightspots were scattered all around town, some along the edges of the district, some downtown, and included the Amos & Andy and the Greenleaf Gardens, both near Twelfth and Cherry; the Hey-Hay Club on Fourth and Cherry; the College Inn, later the Club Continental, at Twelfth and Wyandotte; the Bar Le Duc at Independence and Troost; the Hi Hat at Twenty-second and Vine; Elmer Bean's Club at Eighteenth and Harrison; and the Novelty Club at Sixteenth and McGee, where the house band consisted of Count Basie, Walter Page, Jo Jones, Hot Lips Page, and Lester Young— all playing for three dollars a night each.

The clubs, however, clustered near the intersections of Twelfth and Paseo (except the important Reno Club, on Twelfth, ten blocks west of Paseo), and Eighteenth and Paseo. Russell, tracing the complex of nightclubs near these intersections, noted, near Twelfth, the Boulevard Lounge, and Cherry Blossom; and, near Eighteenth, the Panama Club, Subway Club (which later became Lucille's Band Box), Elk's Rest, and Old Kentucky Bar-B-Que. In addition, there were three dance halls exclusively for blacks: the El Torreon Ballroom; the Roseland at Fourteenth and Troost; and, at Paseo and Fifteenth, Paseo Hall, which was the largest and could accommodate three thousand dancers. While the number of nightspots in the district is estimated to have been about fifty, the grand total of Kansas City nightclubs during this period (exclusive of saloons, bars, and other assorted drinking spots) has been estimated at between two and five hundred.[16]

Three nightclubs—the Sunset, the Subway Club, and the Reno Club—require special attention because of the significance of the jazzmen who either played in these clubs or were influenced by the jazz they heard when they came to listen. The Sunset Club at Eighteenth and Highland, the southeasternmost edge of the district, was run by Felix Payne, a crony of Tom Pendergast's. Earlier, Payne had operated a saloon in Tom's First Ward and later operated the Twin Cities Club in the West Bottoms, right on the

Missouri-Kansas state line, thus enabling him to break the laws of two states simultaneously. After Prohibition was enacted, Payne hired a black manager, a black bartender (singer Joe Turner, whose voice was carried over an outdoor loudspeaker and whose blues shouting could be heard for blocks around), and a two-piece house band and, with Tom Pendergast's blessing, declared the premises of the Sunset Club open for business. The two-piece house band had a drummer and boogie-woogie pianist Pete Johnson. "With Pete Johnson on the piano," Russell said, "and a good drummer, the two pieces were a whole rhythm section in themselves. They were so effective and popular with jazz musicians that the Sunset became one of the earliest and most popular places to jam."[17]

At its peak, the Sunset Club was "the boss club of Kansas City." The best jazzmen in Kansas City often played at Sunset jam sessions, and on occasion included Lester Young, Ben Webster, and, later, Charlie Parker. Just down the street from the Sunset was the Subway Club, on Eighteenth and Vine—in a basement, of course, and, like the Sunset, owned by Felix Payne. Attending the Subway jam sessions became the rule for visiting jazzmen, particularly during the swing era, when Benny Goodman, the Dorsey brothers, Coleman Hawkins, and others stopped off to listen to the Kansas City regulars, to be seen, and, when appropriate, to sit in.

The Reno Club, on Twelfth between Cherry and Locust, run by Papa Sol Epstein, was far and away the favorite spot of Kansas City jazzmen. Catering to both blacks and whites, but with separate facilities, including separate dance floors, the Reno provided a complete evening of dancing and entertainment at reasonable cost in an atmosphere of security and protection (Epstein's membership in the Pendergast syndicate guaranteed his customers protection from police raids). Cheap drinks, four floor shows every night, and a good dance band made the Reno one of the city's most attractive nightclubs. For Kansas City jazzmen, however, the Reno's principal attraction was its jam sessions.

The jam session was a great boon to the nightclub entrepreneur. The essential ingredients for a potentially successful jazz club required only a swinging rhythm section of two or more jazzmen, a raised platform large enough to accommodate visiting hotshots, some tables and chairs, and a bartender who was reasonably honest. And while jobs for musicians were always plentiful, their wages were kept to a minimum. When Count Basie played the Reno Club, band members worked from nine in the evening until six in the morning, seven nights a week, and received eighteen dollars a week each. They were grateful for the work and the opportunity to jam. (After World War II, the jam session became "illegal" in the nation's major jazz centers. In an effort to force nightclub operators to share their profits from customers coming to hear jazzmen who jammed free of charge, the Musicians Union prohibited the advertising of such sessions and the jazzmen from participating without pay.)

Garvin Bushnell, a jazz clarinetist who played in a touring band accompanying singer Mamie Smith in Kansas City in 1921, recalls listening to seventeen-year-old Coleman Hawkins, who had joined the pit band of the Twelfth Street Theater. Hawkins was already "running changes" and Bushnell was considerably impressed. With others, however, he was less impressed:

> We heard music at several cabarets in Kansas City. I wasn't impressed. We felt we had the top thing in the country, so the bands didn't impress me. It may be, now that I look back, that I underestimated them. The bands in the Midwest then had a more flexible style than the eastern ones. They were built on blues bands. They had also done more with saxophones in Kansas City. Most bands included a saxophone. They just played the blues, one after another, in different tempos. It was good, but after we'd heard Oliver and Dodds, they were our criterion. I also heard blues singers in Kansas City, just like Joe Turner sings, and they did impress me.[18]

The jazz played in Kansas City before the 1920s would in any case have been nothing unusual; that is, there would have been nothing to identify it specifically as Kansas City jazz. Still, whatever jazz was going on was not to the taste of Kansas City's more conservative citizens. As the *New York Times* reported in 1922: "In a speech before 1,000 teachers, the superintendent of schools in Kansas City, Missouri, warned, 'This nation has been fighting booze for a long time. I am just wondering whether jazz isn't going to have to be legislated against as well.' "[19] Whatever sort of jazz the school superintendent wondered about prohibiting, his remark shows that jazz, the word, at least, had currency in Kansas City.

The development of the jazz style known as Kansas City jazz came a bit later and must be sought in the jazz played in Kansas City from the mid-1920s to about the mid-'30s. That development will be found not just in the work of Kansas City–based jazzmen (although their contributions were basic) but in the work of those southwestern jazzmen who came to Kansas City, studied the scene, returned to their respective territories, and then either returned to Kansas City or, as carriers, moved on to other territories.

The jobs were in Kansas City, and for musicians bent upon pursuing the jazz life Kansas City was obviously the place to be. Other of the Southwest's residents, although not especially interested in jazz or in the jazz life, were nonetheless equally attracted to Kansas City. To cattlemen, farmers, and businessmen from ten states, Kansas City was the West's major city. Here they sent their products, or brought them, received their money, and stayed on just long enough to revitalize themselves with a bit of hotel living, risky gambling, easy women, and jazzy music, after which they would once again be fit to resume the monotonous, reputedly austere life of the Great Plains.

Musicians in the states immediately north, south, and west of Missouri, as well as those in Texas, found Kansas City equally attractive. Kansas City was Mecca. The vibrant life of the city attracted itinerant bluesmen, gospel shouters, street bands, riverboat musicians, ragtime piano "professors," and, finally, the full-fledged jazzmen of the Southwest's "territory bands." In his seminal jazz study "Kansas City and the Southwest," Franklin S. Driggs adds the states of Missouri, Nebraska, and Iowa to those of the traditional Southwest (Texas, Colorado, Arkansas, New Mexico, and Oklahoma).[20] While the major cities in these states, Driggs observed, had dance bands that usually performed on home ground, they traveled with some regularity out into the surrounding territory to play in communities too small to mount their own bands. These bands were known as territory bands. Driggs comments on their subsequent proliferation.

> From the middle 1920's until the Second World War, industrial developments throughout the Southwest, coupled with population shifts and increases, created a very heavy demand for dance work that led to the organization of band after band, until well over one hundred were operating with regularity in that part of the country. . . . As the 1930's wore on, even the territory outfits gave way to better bands from other areas, which then set themselves up in cities other than the ones in which they had originally been based.[21]

In any study of jazz in Kansas City to the mid-1930s, five figures dominate the scene: Benny Moten, Walter Page, Harlan Leonard, Andy Kirk, and Count Basie. There is little question that, of these, Moten was the most important, or at least first among equals. Moten will therefore be our point of departure, followed by brief sketches of the others and their contributions to Kansas City jazz.

Benny Moten was born in Kansas City in 1894, and as a youth took up the baritone horn, then switched to piano, studying with Charles Watts and Scrap Harris, both of whom had studied with Scott Joplin. At twenty-four, Moten played with small groups in several Kansas City clubs, and during the next five years worked his way around the city until a record company representative, Ralph Peer, taken by the sound of Moten's band, persuaded him to record a number of sides for Okeh Records. The earliest known photograph of this band was taken at Paseo Hall, at Fifteenth and Paseo, probably late in 1923 or early in 1924, and shows Willie MacWashington on drums, Le Forest Dent on banjo, Vernon Page on tuba, Thamon Hayes on trombone, Lamar Wright on trumpet and French horn, Harlan Leonard on alto and baritone saxophones, Woody Walder on clarinet and tenor saxophone, and Moten on piano.

In 1928 Moten took his band east for the first time, on a successful six-month tour of upstate New York, and returned to Kansas City the conquering hero. Two years earlier he had forsaken the idea of the small jazz ensemble and had worked constantly toward building a "big" band. In 1926 his band included two trumpets or cornets, a trombone, three saxophones, and a rhythm section (piano, banjo, tuba, and drums); by 1930 he was using three trumpets and two trombones. On an eastern tour the following year, Moten took along Walter Page on bass and Count Basie to spell him on piano (both Basie and Page had appeared with Moten's band on Victor recording dates in 1929 and 1930). For the tour he bought a large number of big-band arrangements that diminished the rough, driving force of the band; the tour turned out to be a depressing failure. Some members of Moten's band then took jobs with other leaders or tried to form their own bands. Moten tried to reorganize his forces, but he was never able to re-create his earlier success. In 1935, while undergoing a tonsillectomy, he died when his jugular vein was accidentally severed. His untimely death resulted in the band's eventual dissolution, but Moten's contribution to the history of jazz in Kansas City is matchless.

When Walter Page joined Benny Moten's band as a bass player around 1930, he was already a long-established Kansas City jazz figure. Born in Gallatin, Missouri, in 1900, he attended Lincoln High School in Kansas City where he had tuba and string bass instruction from Major N. Clark Smith, the Lincoln High music teacher responsible for training many of Kansas City's later jazz musicians. After his graduation Page gigged around for a year, and early in his career played a date with young Benny Moten. Apparently unsatisfied with his rather meager musical background, and perhaps inspired by Major Smith, Page left the Kansas City scene to work for a degree at Kansas State Teachers College, where he majored in music for the next three years. He then joined a road-show band, and for the next several years traveled with it throughout the Southwest; he finally took over as its leader in 1925. The Ritz Ballroom in Oklahoma City became the band's headquarters. Originally called the Oklahoma City Blue Devils, the band was now called Page's Blue Devils, and in due time he added Buster Smith on alto saxophone, Eddie Durham on trombone, Oran ("Hot Lips") Page on trumpet, Jimmy Rushing on vocals, and Bill Basie on piano (Basie would later be named "Count" by a Kansas City radio announcer).

In a 1928 battle of bands (in which the winners were determined by audience applause) Page's band defeated Jesse Stone's band, the Blues Serenaders. Stone was considered to have the best band in Missouri and Kansas—outside Kansas City. But Page was not satisfied; he wished to vanquish everyone *inside* Kansas City, and that meant Moten; and after Moten he hoped to challenge Alphonso Trent, who led the best band in Texas. In a regional battle of bands in Paseo Hall, Page finally won over the best Moten's band could muster. Moten did not take his loss gracefully. In what was perhaps his only defense against Page's band, Moten persuaded trombonist Ed Durham and Count Basie to leave the Blue Devils and join *his* band. He offered them salaries Page could not afford to pay, and the loss of these men to Moten's band caused the Blue Devils considerable frustration and lowered their morale. Within a short time, because of lack of bookings and financial problems, other sidemen were persuaded to leave Page, and although the band still included Buster Smith (who became leader) and Lester Young, the band never recovered. At its peak, Page's Blue Devils may easily have been the best band in the Southwest. "The rhythmic flow and riff settings in the Blue Devils," Driggs wrote, "became the basis of the best Moten band, and of Count Basie's own band of the late 1930's."[22] Page's individual contribution to jazz bass playing is summed up by jazz critic Stanley Dance when he compares two sides of a Benny Moten recording in which Basie is heard with and without Page's bass. "Basie is heard on both sides, but the characteristics of what might be called the 'Basie rhythmic effect' are not really evident until he is joined by Walter Page, a bassist, bandleader, and well-schooled musician with whom he had previously worked. . . . The tremendous drive he and Basie created together was the fundamental source of inspiration on the . . . session."[23]

Harlan Leonard, we may recall, appeared in ,the 1923–24 photograph of Benny Moten's band. At the time the photograph was taken, Leonard had just graduated from Lincoln High School, a year behind Walter Page's class. Leonard was born in Butler, Missouri, in 1905, moved to Kansas City, and at fourteen took up playing the clarinet in the high school band under Major N. Clark Smith's direction. Shortly after, he switched to alto saxophone, taking lessons with Paul Tremaine, a local teacher whose father led the Kansas City Municipal Band. Leonard worked hard at his musical studies, determined to be a professional musician, and by the time he was ready to graduate at seventeen he could hold his own in groups playing around the city, including participation in some recording sessions with George E. Lee and His Novelty Singing Orchestra.[24] Moten, ever on the lookout for musicians to improve and expand his band, noticed young Leonard's clean tone, facile technique, and ability to read, and hired Leonard to lead his saxophone section. Leonard was to remain with Moten for the next eight years. When Moten made wholesale changes in the band personnel for an eastern tour in 1931, Leonard, unhappy with the direction Moten had taken, decided it was time to leave. Others in the band, concerned with Moten's changeover to an "eastern style," felt as Leonard did. Half a dozen men left Moten, formed their own band led by Thamon Hayes, and after several years of trying to find themselves, finally became the Kansas City Rockets with Harlan Leonard as the leader. The band could now continue to champion what was for them the true Kansas City brand of jazz.

Andy Kirk did not arrive in Kansas City until he was thirty-one years old and a fully matured musician. He was born in Newport, Kentucky, in 1898, and grew up in Denver where he received his earliest musical training with, among other teachers, Paul Whiteman's father. Kirk left Denver playing tuba with George Morrison's society band to tour Cheyenne, Salt Lake City, and small towns in Colorado. He then quit Morrison's band to join Terence ("T") Holder's jazz-oriented territory band in Dallas. Eventually, the usual territory band difficulties arose—money, bookings, changes in personnel—and in 1929, while the band was playing the Winter Garden in Oklahoma City, Holder left the band and Kirk became the new leader.

George E. Lee, who later came down with his band from Kansas City to replace Kirk's in Oklahoma City, arranged for Kirk to work at the Pla-Mor Ballroom in Kansas City. During the following winter, the band's success at the Pla-Mor resulted in recording dates with Brunswick, tours in the Midwest, and Kirk's marriage to jazz pianist Mary Lou Williams. In 1930 Fletcher Henderson, while playing Kansas City, heard Kirk's band and arranged to have Kirk replace him at the Roseland Ballroom in New York. Kirk's New York appearances, including one at the Savoy Ballroom in Harlem, were unprecedented successes, resulting in additional recording dates and road tours. The East was now in the throes of the Great Depression, and Kirk returned to Kansas City. Kirk later recalled:

> The work was still good in and around Kansas City even though the depression was going full blast. After that summer we went on tour . . . around the Southwest but nobody had any money to go into the theaters with. . . . When we got back home there was no depression. The town was jumping! . . .
> We stayed right around Kansas City, working all the other good spots in town like the El Torreon Ballroom. We'd get the finest acts out of Chicago to play in the night clubs in Kansas City, because they weren't working regularly.[25]

The Depression had little debilitating effect on Kirk's career. By 1935, Kirk and his band were again touring upstate New York, and his career as a band leader was on the upswing. In the years ahead

Kirk would be fortunate enough to have the right manager, the right bookings, and the right band making the right records. For a series of recordings for Decca in 1936, Kirk's Clouds of Joy included Earl Thomson, Harry Lawson, and Paul King (who had replaced Irving "Mouse" Randolph) on trumpets; Ted Donnelly on trombone; John Williams, John Harrington, and Dick Wilson (who had replaced tenorman Ben Webster) on reeds; Claude Williams on violin; Mary Lou Williams on piano; Ted Robinson on guitar; Booker Collins on bass; Ben Thigpen on drums; Pha Terrell, vocals; with Kirk himself on baritone saxophone. The band's recording of "Christopher Columbus," followed by "Until the Real Thing Comes Along," brought Kirk the success and national recognition that were to be his for the next decade.

Like Kirk, Count Basie was not a native of Kansas City. William ("Count") Basie was born in Red Bank, New Jersey, in 1904. As a child he studied piano with his mother, and later, in New York, he came under the influence of Harlem jazzmen, particularly Fats Waller, whose place he took as piano accompanist for a vaudeville act. In the late 1920s he took a job with a road show traveling west, and after a while found himself stranded in Kansas City without friends, without money, and, in his words, "just a kinda honky-tonk piano player."[26] He found a job at the Eblon Theater playing background music for silent movies, and stayed there for almost a year. He then wrote a letter to Walter Page (he had met Page in Tulsa earlier, during his disappointing tour, and had sat in with the band at the time) asking Page if he knew of any jobs. Page offered him the piano job with his band, and Basie joined the Blue Devils.

About a year later, Basie left the Blue Devils and joined Benny Moten's band. When Moten died in 1935, his brother Bus, who played accordion, ran the band for about six months, but its old vigor was gone and the band broke up. After freelancing for a while, Basie then organized his own band for a job at the Reno Club. The band Basie put together seemed to synthesize the best qualities of Page's Blue Devils and Benny Moten's old band, and eventually included Ed Lewis on trumpet; Eddie Durham on trombone; Buster Smith, Lester Young, and Jack Washington on saxophones; Jo Jones on drums; Walter Page on bass; Jimmy Rushing, vocals; and Basie on piano. A local short-wave radio station, W9XBY, regularly broadcast the shows from the Reno Club. Both John Hammond, a jazz entrepreneur, and Benny Goodman (whose band was playing in Chicago at the time) heard Basie's band over this station and in 1936 persuaded Willard Alexander of the Music Corporation of America to handle Basie's bookings. The band left Kansas City in the hands of the agency that had made Benny Goodman King of Swing, with dates at the Grand Terrace Ballroom in Chicago and the Roseland Ballroom in New York, along with a contract to record twenty-four sides for Decca that would include "One o'Clock Jump" and "Jumpin' at the Woodside," and Basie was on his way to making Kansas City jazz one of the best-known jazz styles in America.

Excellent and extensive treatment of individual Kansas City pianists, reedmen, brassmen, and rhythm men will be found in the work of Driggs, Dexter, Russell, Schuller, and Horricks.[27] For the present, however, an enumeration of the best-known Kansas City bands (apart from those we have looked at more closely) may be sufficient for our purpose. All of these bands and their leaders flourished in the 1920s and '30s and contributed to the musical atmosphere of the city. Dave Lewis led a band about 1920; Jesse Stone, who was born in Atchison but raised in Kansas City, led the Blues Serenaders; the bands of George E. Lee provided a training ground for many Kansas City musicians, including Charlie Parker, and Lee's sister Julia was one of the city's best blues singers. The Thamon Hayes orchestra also included many of Kansas City's well-known sidemen: Woody Walder on saxophone, Ed Lewis on trumpet, Baby Lovett on drums, and Harlan Leonard on saxophone; Tommy Douglas, an arranger and reedman who was born in Kansas, spent four years at the Boston Conservatory of Music and worked all over the East, Southwest, and Midwest but considered Kansas City his home base; pianist Paul Banks led his

Syncopating Orchestra with the ubiquitous Ed Lewis on trumpet and Jap Allen on tuba; and Allen, graduate of Lincoln High School, had his own band between 1927 and 1930, which included Kansas City–born Ben Webster on tenor saxophone, who was to achieve his lasting fame through his later association with Count Basie.

The ten years of important jazz activity in Kansas City fall within what is called pre-swing (principal figures besides Basie, Moten, and others from Kansas City were Armstrong, Fletcher Henderson, and Duke Ellington) and the early years (1934 to 1936) of the swing era. As an entity, therefore, the Kansas City style must of necessity include musical elements and characteristics also found in the styles of New Orleans, Chicago, New York, and lesser centers. We need touch only lightly upon those aspects common to all; our discussion here will deal for the most part with those aspects of style peculiar to Kansas City.

Let us consider first the size of Kansas City bands. Starting in the early 1920s with the New Orleans idea of three individual voices (cornet, clarinet, and trombone) and a rhythm section, the Kansas City bands grew slowly and steadily toward the big band that included groups of like instruments—in short, the idea of a brass section (trumpets and trombones), a reed section (saxophones and a clarinet or two), and a rhythm section. In New York the big-band arrangement (requiring five or six brass, four or five reeds, and three or four rhythm) was developed essentially by Don Redman for Fletcher Henderson's orchestra; Ellington, too, from 1926 on, had been working on increasing the size of his sections;[28] in Kansas City, the archproponent of the big band was Benny Moten. In 1923 Moten's band had six players, in 1924 eight players, and in 1926–27 ten players—two trumpets or cornets, trombone, three saxes, piano, tuba, banjo, and drums. From this point on, it was but a step to the standard big-band instrumentation of the swing era: five to seven brass, four or five reeds, and three or four rhythm—just about the size of Count Basie's band once he was established in New York.

Of the individual jazz-band instruments to come into their

own in Kansas City in the '20s, the saxophone is by far the most important. Jazzmen from all parts of the country considered Kansas City the nonpareil saxophone center. Coleman Hawkins and Chu Berry frequently came to Kansas City to try their hands against the likes of Buster Smith, Budd Johnson, Tommy Douglas, Dick Wilson, Lester Young, and Ben Webster. During this same period the tuba was gradually replaced by the string bass. The stiff and heavy punctuation of the four-four rhythm by the tuba, characteristic of early Kansas City style, in which the emphasis was placed on the first and third beats or the second and fourth beats, became a flowing, steady, walking, one-two-three-four in the plucked-string bass playing of Walter Page. That changeover created a fluid rhythmic pulse (later taken up by the rest of the rhythm section) that the tuba had been incapable of producing, and provided the rest of the band with a bouncing, swinging foundation on which to build exciting structures.

An easily identifiable formal characteristic of the Kansas City style is the "riff"—an initial musical figure or phrase repeated by an instrumental section as a background for an improvised solo, or against the rest of the ensemble (see Figure 1). Where two or more

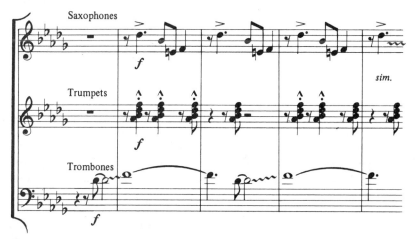

Figure 1 Characteristic riff figures.

riffs oppose one another, with each section alternating contrasting riffs, the effect is that of a call-and-response. "The riff," Ross Russell wrote, "became the signature of the Kansas City band. When Kansas City bands assumed a place of national leadership in the mid-thirties, the riff became the signature of the swing band, and of swing itself. Benny Goodman's *Sing, Sing, Sing* and Glenn Miller's *In the Mood* were riffs inspired by original Kansas City models."[29]

Next to the riff, the most important musical structure in the Kansas City style is the instrumental 12-bar blues, which together with the 32-bar popular song form (usually designated AABA) came to dominate the period. Although the musical forms of both the New Orleans style and early Kansas City style—blues (in 8-bar phrases), stomps, and rags—continued in use through the 1920s, by the 1930s the 32-bar form and the 12-bar blues form enjoyed their greatest currency. Both were originally vocal forms, based on the structure of the lyrics. The 32-bar form consists of 4 stanzas of 8 bars each, in which the first, second, and fourth stanzas are sung to the same tune, while the third stanza (sometimes called the bridge or release) is sung to a different tune and usually in a different key. The desire on the part of black bands to share the commercial success of white bands who specialized in arrangements of such AABA songs as "Yes Sir That's My Baby" or "Dinah" inevitably led to black-band arrangements of similar material.

Concerning the 12-bar blues, however, the situation worked in reverse. Gunther Schuller notes the changeover from the vocal blues to the instrumental blues:

> Before the 1920s the blues existed at a separate social-cultural-musical level from that occupied by orchestras playing in hotels or dance halls. Once the blues had broken through into the middle-class urban realm, however, the larger Southwestern orchestras quickly adopted the form and used it more consistently than bands anywhere else.[30]

The 12-bar vocal blues consists of 3 musical phrases of 4 bars each against which three lines of words are sung. The line of words for phrase 1 is repeated for phrase 2, and a new line is sung to phrase 3. (E.g., "Every mornin' I hear my baby cry/[repeat]/If she don't stop, she gonna lose me bye and bye.") What is significant for the instrumental version of the 12-bar blues is that each of the three phrases has a different set of chords (for example, in the key of C: C-C-C-C^7/F-F-C-C/G-F-C-C), enabling an improvising soloist to continually create fresh melodies against the "fixed" chord progression of the blues. The great vocal blues tradition of the South and Southwest became, in the instrumental solo version of Kansas City jazzmen, particularly in the night-long jam sessions, the final examination.

Hsio Wen Shih in "The Spread of Jazz and the Big Bands" points out that early jazzmen, black and white, came from all parts of the country, and that all these musicians could not have learned to play jazz simply by listening to records because few records existed before the early 1920s—the time during which these jazzmen were developing their craft. He notes that jazzmen listened to music, all right, but they listened to "live" music, particularly in those theaters catering to black audiences and specializing in black musical entertainment. The stages of these theaters provided a place where the sound of music from distant jazz centers could be heard on the spot by those unable to visit those centers. Hsio cites the Howard Theater in Washington, D.C., where Ellington heard Luckey Roberts; and a black vaudeville house in Pittsburgh, where Mary Lou Williams heard Lovie Austin and her band[31] (and we have earlier referred to the black theaters of Kansas City). These theaters and others like them scattered throughout the South and Southwest brought the sound of traveling musicians and bands to local jazzmen, and often provided jobs for the local bands as well. Frequently, traveling bands upon their arrival would count on adding local musicians temporarily, in order to save on travel expense. Finally, bands from several cities were often performing in a major center at the same time and were able to hear each other.

Kansas City, we will recall, had jobs for jazzmen. In the 1920s and '30s jazz was one field of endeavor (sports was another) where opportunities for a black man were constantly developing. There were few others. When Fletcher Henderson came to New York in 1920 with his degree in chemistry from Atlanta University, no one cared much and no employer was interested; but he had no difficulty finding work as a piano player—a position which apparently threatened no one. Men of Henderson's and (in Kansas City) Walter Page's caliber, along with Don Redman and others with advanced training or degrees in music, not only helped train the jazzmen in their bands by sharing their theoretical knowledge, but developed the harmonic and structural changes that resulted in the big-band jazz style.

Although we shall discuss Fletcher Henderson's work in the section on New York jazz, we wish to note here that one of Henderson's principal New York competitors was a band called the Missourians. The band came to New York from St. Louis in 1924 as Wilson Robinson's Syncopators. A year later they opened at the Cotton Club in Harlem, where they were replaced by Duke Ellington in 1927, and the band left New York known as the Missourians. At various times the band included Kansas City jazzmen Eli Logan on alto sax, DePriest Wheeler on trombone, Leroy Maxey on drums, and Lamar Wright on trumpet (of these, Logan was well known in Kansas City and Wright was best known, having played in Benny Moten's band from 1923 to 1928). The Missourians returned to the Cotton Club in 1931 with Cab Calloway as their new leader and went on to become one of New York's favorite bands. Concerning five of the Missourians' recordings, including "Ozark Mountain Blues" and "Market Street Stomp," Schuller wrote:

> In these numbers the band was at its best and displayed an elemental, fiery drive that probably no other band in New York could match. . . . as driven by Leroy Maxey's drums, with Lamar Wright's boisterous trumpet solos and George Scott's madcap clarinet embellishments and the band's overall intensity, the Missourians must have given Henderson and Ellington many an uneasy night.[32]

Before we close the chapter on Kansas City, it may be worthwhile to remind ourselves of the widespread jazz activity throughout the Southwest, of which Kansas City was the principal center. The principal carriers, of course, were the territory bands and their sidemen. Many of the bands played jazz only occasionally, while others were not jazz bands in any sense. A number of these groups considered themselves novelty groups or show bands, but nearly all played for dancing. Some bands thought of themselves as readers—society bands—playing smooth dance music for sedate dancers, while the nonreaders played a rough, vigorous jazz which was as much for listening as for dancing.

It is often difficult to classify a band or its sidemen from the personal reminiscences of the men involved, particularly when the band has left no recorded evidence. What *is* evident, however, is that many of the sidemen, especially those with high ability and ambition, moved at will from one band to another and from one territory to another. Here is a sampling of territory bands, brought together from a wide variety of sources.

The most nearly complete record we have is of the bands based in Texas. In Amarillo, Gene Coy's Happy Black Aces; in Austin, the Deluxe Melody Boys and the Royal Aces; in Dallas, the Alphonso Trent orchestra (including reedmen James Jeter and Hayes Pillars, whom we will meet again in St. Louis), the Blue Moon Chasers, the Moonlight Melody Six, and Jimmie's Joys; in El Paso, Ben Smith's Blues Syncopators and the Doc Ross orchestra with Jack Teagarden on trombone and Wingy Manone on trumpet; in Greenville, Eddie Battle's Dixie Stompers; in Houston, Milt Larkin's orchestra, Nat Towles's orchestra (well known in Omaha as well), Johnson's Joymakers, and Peck Kelley's Peck's Bad Boys, including Teagarden on trombone; in San Antonio, Troy Floyd's Shadowland Orchestra with Herschel Evans on tenor saxophone, Don Albert's Ten Happy Pals (drawn in part from the Shadowland Orchestra), and Clifford ("Boots") Douglas's Boots and His Buddies; in Wichita Falls, the Southern Trumpets, who moved on to Dallas where Jack Teagarden joined them; finally, and perhaps best known, in Tyler, Texas, Eddie and Sugar Lou's Band, with trumpeter Hot Lips Page.

In other territories we find, based in Oklahoma City, Doc Ross (the earlier, El Paso, Ross) and his Jazz Bandits (later, as he moved about the West, the band became his Texas Cowboys); in Tulsa, Salva Sanders and his alliterative Southern Serenaders; in Helena, Eugene Crookes's Synco Six, the forerunner of Alphonso Trent's Texas band; in Milwaukee, the Grant Moore orchestra; in Little Rock, the Brady-Bryant Peppers and Chester Lane and the Original Yellowjackets; in Omaha, Clarence Love's orchestra, Lloyd Hunter's Serenaders, and the Omaha Night Owls, who later became Red Perkins's Dixie Ramblers; at various places in the state of Kansas, Art Bronson's Bostonians, which included sixteen-year-old Lester Young; in St. Louis, the Jeter-Pillars orchestra, Charlie Creath's Jazz-O-Maniacs, the Mound City Blue Blowers, with banjo, comb, and Red McKenzie on kazoo, Oliver Cobb's Rhythm Kings, who later with Eddie Johnson became the Crackerjacks and still later, under Winfield Baker, the Original St. Louis Cracker-jacks (St. Louis was also the headquarters for the Streckfus river-boats carrying bands organized by and sometimes led by Fate Mar-able); finally, in Cincinnati: the delightfully provocative Zach Whyte's Chocolate Beau Brummels.

By the mid-'30s, aspiring jazzmen from all over the country were forced to acknowledge that the jazz life of America was cen-tered in New York, and all regional musical victories and successes had meaning only as a prelude to the departure for New York. We close this chapter with the words of Ross Russell, whose body of work is basic to any study of Kansas City jazz: "If the musicians came to New York from all parts of the country, the musical ideas that provided the material and inspiration for their experiments were those that had been gathered together in the American Southwest and concentrated in Kansas City during the Pendergast era."[33]

NEW YORK:
PROHIBITION,
POLITICS,
AND
HARLEM

The two major social factors in the development of big-band jazz were the Great Depression and the repeal of Prohibition, and both materially affected the employment of musicians. Big-band jazz, for example, could not have reached its peak during the early 1930s if employers had been required to pay musicians enough to live on. Crucial events in the development and proliferation of big-band jazz occurred during the Depression, when labor—anxious musicians included—was willing to work for almost any wages. New York jazzmen, like their Kansas City counterparts, were willing to work for two to four dollars a day; but unlike Kansas City (where the work was abundant, if not the pay), New York had few places for jazzmen. The repeal of Prohibition, as we shall see, solved the unemployment problem for jazzmen in New York, and big-band jazz subsequently flourished there. To grasp the full impact of this social phenomenon on the development of jazz in New York, we must look at the state of jazz during Prohibition, as well as after its repeal.

Between 1918 and the repeal of Prohibition in 1933, the "noble experiment" spawned swarms of gangsters, racketeers, bootleggers, saloonkeepers, nightspot operators, and customers only too willing to aid and abet them. The enforcers of Prohibition, the persistent tormentors of bootleggers and their customers, were agents of the Bureau of Internal Revenue. The agents raided places suspected of illegally making or selling liquor and arrested those involved. The efforts of the agents were not well met by the underworld, nor was the general urban public in sympathy with those efforts. Often, after successful raids and arrests, agents were made to realize they were losing ground as they watched lawbreakers fined a pittance and released, or saw their cases dismissed from court.

For New Yorkers who enjoyed going out to drink, the low point may have come when Major Maurice Campbell, national Prohibition administrator of New York State, with the help of 270 agents, set out to put a stop to drinking in the city. Choosing New Year's Eve 1929 to display their determination, Campbell's agents made nineteen raids and arrested fifty ordinary citizens celebrating the New Year. Campbell's timing was at least unfortunate, and New Yorkers saw him as a nosy spoilsport. Soon after, twenty-five of Campbell's agents raided the Hotel Manger (later called the Taft), the Cornish Arms, and the Central Park Casino, and attempted to have these places padlocked for selling their guests club soda, ginger ale, and ice—presumably because these ingredients could be mixed with liquor. Major Campbell's righteousness notwithstanding, New Yorkers saw his actions as desperate and petty.[1]

During the same period, a feud arose between Campbell and New York City Police Commissioner Grover Whalen. Campbell saw New York's drinking problem as a local issue and wanted Whalen's policemen to monitor the city's thirty thousand speakeasies. Whalen claimed that for each speakeasy it would take three policemen working eight-hour shifts to do this, a task that would add $45 million a year to the police budget. Furthermore, Whalen observed, Prohibition enforcement was a national problem, not a local one—at least, not a problem for New York. New York was, after all, the nation's nightlife capital and entertainment was a major industry there. The press agreed with Whalen's view, as did those who ran New York nightlife and those who helped support it.

Government raids notwithstanding, new nightclubs sprang up in New York at a phenomenal rate. Stanley Walker, in his good-natured anti-Prohibition work *The Night Club Era*, mentions "seventy or more profitable centers of night life" in New York, of which the following were raided at least once between 1924 and 1933: Peter's Blue Hour, Gallagher's, Peek Inn, Metamora Club, Club Borgo, Beaux Arts, Silver Slipper, Helen Morgan's club, Larry Fay's club, Texas Guinan's club, the Jungle Club, Club Richelieu, and the Biarritz. For a number of nightlife figures, government raids were indispensable to the advertising and promotion of their establishments. Places like Helen Morgan's and Texas Guinan's thrived on the publicity. Daily tabloid stories and pictures of clubs and their inhabitants during and after raids made club owners as well known as movie stars. When the famous Belle Livingston's five-floor "country club" on East Fifty-eighth Street was raided by Prohibition agents and Belle was found guilty of selling liquor illegally, she was given thirty days in prison; upon her release she traveled back to midtown Manhattan in an armored car sent by Texas Guinan. And the press covered the story, of course.

"Although competition was murderous between the clubs," Walker wrote, "and the constant raidings made the business extremely hazardous, the gay life continued through the years. . . . The profits were too large to give up." The profits came from such characteristic sales as ten dollars for a pint of whiskey, a dollar for a small bottle of club soda, and two dollars for a pitcher of water.[2] In keeping with the outrageous prices in the clubs were their frequently pretentious names: Café de Paris, Folies Bergère, Moulin Rouge, Bal Tabarin, Montmartre, and Monte Carlo. In these clubs, for a cover charge of from five to twenty dollars, customers could dine, buy liquor and setups, watch a floor show, and listen to a band that provided, in Stanley Walker's phrase, "swift dance music." While serious drinkers needed little more than the corner speakeasy to entertain themselves, others who were looking for a night on the town also wanted entertainment; their principal consideration in choosing a nightspot (after they had made sure that liquor was available) was the lavishness of the floor show, or that the club at least provided music.

As in most cities, jazz could be heard in some places while others provided little or none. Most jazz nightspots in New York were to be found uptown, in Harlem, and we will discuss the Harlem spots in the following chapter. Most of the other places were downtown, generally in mid-Manhattan. Jazz-oriented sidemen played wherever the work was—dance halls, clubs, recording studios. If the job called for jazz, well and good; if not, one played with the society bands, show bands, studio bands, and hoped for a change. The greatest number of jobs of course went to those who played for the most part popular, or "commercial," music. Benny Goodman, who was a successful freelance in New York in 1929, describes the relationship between those musicians who played "hot" and those who didn't:

Musicians who played hot were pretty much of a clique by themselves. They hung around in the same places, made the same spots
after work, drank together and worked together whenever they had
the chance. In New York they even had one place that was pretty
much their own—a dive called Plunkett's on West 53d Street, where
the liquor was cheap and the credit liberal. It was listed, in the
'phone book, for special reasons, as the Trombone Club.

None of us had much use for what was known then and probably
always will be, as "commercial" musicians. . . . The saddest thing,
always, was a recognized hot man who went in for that sort of work
because he made good dough and got steady work around the
studios.[3]

The commercial musicians Goodman referred to could play
with bands that accompanied floor shows or revues, after which the
bands would provide popular dance music for the customers. They
could be found working, for example, at the Trocadero, where
Fred Astaire and his sister Adele danced; at Ciro's, where Clifton
Webb danced before he became a legitimate theater actor; at the
Lido, which featured torch singer Libby Holman; at Texas
Guinan's club, where Ruby Keeler danced and sang; at the
Casanova, where Helen Kane became famous as the "boop-boop-
a-doop" girl; at the Hollywood, where Nils T. Granlund, known as
N.T.G., produced one of New York's most lavish floor shows; or at
the Silver Slipper, which featured the team of Clayton, Jackson,
and (Jimmy) Durante.

Well-trained musicians with proper connections could make
their way into those established bands with "big name" leaders
who worked regularly in the city's best-advertised clubs—with
Roger Wolfe Kahn, for example, who owned Le Perroquet, and
who also had his own band there which included Eddie Lang on
guitar, Miff Mole on trombone, and Joe Venuti on violin; or the
Heigh-ho, with Rudy Vallee's band, and Vallee's frequent rendi-
tions of the "Maine Stein Song"; or the Midnight Frolic and the
Palais Royal, both of which took turns hiring the famous Paul
Whiteman and his orchestra; or the Little Club, a basement room
under the Nora Bayes Theater on West Forty-fourth Street, where

the still aspiring Benny Goodman played his clarinet, and which earlier had been the Club Alabam where Fletcher Henderson's nine-piece band worked for three hundred dollars a week.

Black bands did not often play at the downtown nightspots. The most popular ones, of course, did, and Duke Ellington is perhaps the best-known example. He played at the Hollywood Cabaret, a basement club on West Forty-ninth Street and Broadway, later called the Club Kentucky, for almost five years (taking over from what had been Elmer Snowden's Washington Black Sox Orchestra, with Ellington on piano); Ellington also played at the Plantation, on Fiftieth and Broadway. The principal outlets for black jazzmen, however, were uptown, in such established jazz clubs as Small's Paradise, the Bamville Club, the Cotton Club, and the Nest Club, and in such dance halls as the Rose Danceland, and the Savoy Ballroom. On the other hand, if a black band became sufficiently popular and well known, they were welcome to play at the Roseland and Arcadia Ballrooms on Broadway, the city's foremost dance palaces, featuring the best bands in the city. Lesser black bands could play at, say, the Waltz Dream Dance Hall on Fifty-third Street, where trumpeter Bubber Miley played before he joined Ellington's band, or in the mid-Manhattan taxi-dance halls (in 1933 the city licensed seventeen taxi-dance halls in the Times Square neighborhood alone, from Forty-second Street to Fifty-seventh Street, where many of the taxi dancers charged— unbelievably—one penny a dance).[4] One downtown spot where black jazzmen could find work deserves special mention: the Hot Feet Club at 142 West Houston Street in Greenwich Village, where on occasion one could hear Fats Waller on piano and Chu Berry on tenor saxophone.

While the New York nightlife scene was not dominated by the underworld (there were simply too many nightspots for the underworld to operate them all), there is clear evidence that many of the most notorious underworld figures were considerably involved, if not directly then through partnerships or by taking a percentage of a nightspot's profits. The pickings were too good, and too easy. In Stanley Walker's view:

New York, in its worst spots, never did have a reputation of excessive purity, but after prohibition these bad spots assumed a vastly more complicated and serious aspect. Bank robbers, murderers, bomb-throwers, confidence men and all stripes of racketeers began taking an interest in booze. They had an interest in night clubs and speakeasies where nice people thought they had to go to have a good time. Time and again it has been shown that police officers either were in the pay of such places, or were friendly with the owners, or had some vague connection which would have made it embarrassing for them to proceed against the joints.[5]

Larry Fay must have had some "vague connection." He managed to run Larry Fay's club despite having been arrested forty-six times. Another criminal, Red Sheehan, ran the Rendezvous Club before he entered Sing Sing; and still another gangster, Richard Whittemore, who was eventually hanged for murder in Baltimore, operated the Club Chantee. But none was a patch on Owen Madden, sometimes known as Owney the Killer. With a record of forty-four arrests and after eight years in Sing Sing, Madden returned to New York where, with various partners, he took a hand in running the Cotton Club; the Silver Slipper; one of Texas Guinan's clubs; and a seemingly endless number of speakeasies whose owners were dependent on Madden for their liquor supply. When the Plantation Club opened in Harlem in 1930 in competition with Madden's Cotton Club, its new owners persuaded Cab Calloway and his orchestra to leave the Cotton Club and work for them. Two nights later, "friends" of the Cotton Club management smashed up everything inside the Plantation Club, and one of the new owners was found murdered.[6] Shortly after, one of Madden's Cotton Club partners was found murdered; the police, however, found no connection between the murders of the two club owners. In the end, the Plantation was closed down and the Cotton Club continued to flourish.

Although the Cotton Club and a number of other major Harlem nightspots were run by white downtown gangsters, many of the lesser clubs were run by Harlem's own, lesser gangsters. The best known of these was Barron D. Wilkins, whose cabaret, the

Exclusive Club on 134th Street and Seventh Avenue, was among the most popular black-and-tan spots in the city. The pattern of Wilkins's life was characteristic of those blacks who operated on the fringes of the underworld. Wilkins was born in 1861, came to New York from Washington, D.C., and Norfolk in the early 1900s, and opened a downtown resort on 37th Street near Eighth Avenue which later became the social headquarters for boxing champion Jack Johnson. Constant complaints about violence in Wilkins's place brought frequent police raids. Wilkins operated a number of places around the city and eventually opened the Exclusive Club where, although his entertainers were black, the majority of customers were white. He became involved in many sports enterprises and provided financial backing to black boxers (Jack Johnson among them) and to black baseball teams. He gambled heavily on horse races and in craps games; to the Harlem underworld he was known as "the man with the big bankroll." It was general knowledge among black criminals trying to escape the police that Wilkins could be counted on for getaway money. In May 1924, Wilkins was confronted in front of his cabaret by Yellow Charleston, a gambler and drug addict who, having just killed another gambler, came to Wilkins and asked him for a hundred dollars. When Wilkins said he didn't have that much money. Charleston shot him dead.[7]

As we have already seen in New Orleans, Chicago, and Kansas City, men like Barron Wilkins, with their questionable operations, could not have functioned without the cooperation of politicians, policemen, and the underworld. In the mid-1860s, the New York State Legislature established a state commission to control municipal police, an act New York City's Democratic majority saw as an infringement of home rule and a device to give Republicans patronage they presumably had not earned. In 1870, William Marcy ("Boss") Tweed—"one of the very rich men in the Metropolis, Boss of Tammany, master of the entire machinery of the State government, executive, legislative and judicial, the Court of Appeals the sole exception"[8]—drafted a charter that was to return control of New York City's police to a four-man board appointed by the mayor. Although bipartisan at the outset, after 1890 the board was dominated by Tammany Democrats, and business between the police, politicians, and the underworld flourished. In 1894, Captain Timothy Creeden testified before a State Senate committee that he had paid a police commissioner fifteen thousand dollars for his captaincy (a captain's salary at the time was three thousand dollars a year). Inspector of Police Alexander S. Williams owned an estate at Cos Cob, Connecticut, and a fifty-three-foot yacht, paid for mainly from his share of monthly gambling house collections. William Devery, who became chief of police in 1898, so outraged the State Legislature by his dictatorial conduct that they abolished his office as well as the four-man board and placed total control in the hands of a single commissioner. The new commissioner then appointed Devery as his first deputy commissioner, and the underworld breathed a sigh of relief.

The reasons why firm ties developed between politicians, police, and the underworld are summarized by James F. Richardson in a passage that applies not only to the city in the 1890s but to the 1920s and 1930s as well:

> Police corruption arose primarily from the desire to punish and control behavior many people considered harmless. When the law attempted to make the sale of alcohol, sex, or betting slips illegal, it ran counter to the moral codes of sellers, buyers, and many policemen—who taken together constituted a sizable portion of the city's population. Those whom the law would regulate or suppress made every effort to capture control of or at least influence the police. Since policemen often had more in common with the gamblers and the drinkers than they did with the moral reformers, it is not surprising that they took money from the former to ignore violations of laws passed by the latter. The political masters of the department shared this conception of proper police performance.[9]

Lowlife resorts abounded in nineteenth-century New York. A good survey of such resorts patronized by both blacks and whites may be found in Herbert Asbury's *The Gangs of New York*. Of special interest is the late-nineteenth-century resort called the Black and Tan, located in the basement of 153 Bleecker Street, in Greenwich Village, and operated by one Frank Stephenson. That some sort of music accompanied the Black and Tan's nightly activities is evident from Asbury's report on the curious behavior of owner Stephenson:

> It was his custom to sit bolt upright in a high chair in the center of his resort, and remain there for hours without displaying any other sign of life than the baleful glitter of his eyes. His establishment was largely frequented by Negroes, but the women were all white and appear to have been quite abandoned. Four bartenders served drinks over a long counter, and behind each was a long dirk and a bludgeon which were frequently used to silence fractious customers. The closing hours of the Black and Tan, as of the other principal resorts, were enlivened by the cancan and licentious displays.[10]

Perhaps no single instance shows more succinctly the relationship between politicians, police, judiciary, and the underworld in New York City in the late '20s and '30s than the story of Magistrates Court Judge Albert H. Vitale. In December 1929, after a midnight dinner for members of the Tippecanoe Democratic Club in honor of Judge Vitale—their honorary president for life—the judge was giving a speech to a group that included former Magistrate Michael Delagi, Police Detective Arthur Johnson, seven men with police records, and Ciro Terranova (the "Artichoke King" and one of the city's best-known racketeers), when six masked men entered the dining room, guns drawn, and ordered everyone to stand against the wall. The masked gunmen then proceeded to relieve the company of their money and jewelry, including three guns, one of which was given up by Detective Johnson. It was 2:00 A.M. when the holdup men left the club, and almost immediately after, Judge Vitale also left, presumably to go home. At 4:00 A.M. he returned to the club with the stolen money and jewelry, and personally handed Detective Johnson his stolen revolver. (When the incident became public knowledge, Johnson became an embarrassment to his superiors and was dismissed from the Police Department.)

Two months earlier, mayoral candidate Fiorello LaGuardia charged that Vitale, while on the bench, had "borrowed" $20,000 from notorious gambler and underworld figure Arnold Rothstein. The charge was investigated by the city Bar Association, sent on to the Appellate Division of the Supreme Court, and a unanimous court found cause for Vitale's removal. During the trial Vitale acknowledged that although his salary was only $12,000 a year, his total income during his four years as a judge was $165,000.[11]

Fiorello LaGuardia's accusation was, in one sense, as much against Mayor Jimmy Walker as it was against Vitale. LaGuardia was not a candidate for the Magistrates Court, he was a candidate for mayor of the City of New York. It was difficult for LaGuardia, a selfless, lifelong public servant, to understand why the people of New York would prefer a Tammany-supported Jimmy Walker to himself. He knew there were two sides to Mayor Walker, and he wished everyone did. The two sides of Walker are illustrated in the titles of two books: Gene Fowler's *Beau James* and William and John Northrup's *The Insolence of Office*. Fowler was not only Walker's principal biographer, but also his friend, and he shows us Walker at his best.

As a young man, Walker's ambition was to write popular songs, which may be the reason he came to prefer the company of show business people to those in the political arena. In his first interview in 1912 with Charles F. Murphy, a Tammany leader who was to help Walker become a state senator, Walker remembered Murphy saying to him, "You seem to have many friends on Broadway and in the sports world. I believe you are making us popular there."[12] Among those who would later become Walker's friends were Paul Whiteman, Vincent Lopez, George Jessel, John Barrymore, and an impressive throng of nightclub figures. His interest in sports was a matter of public record (as a state legislator he sponsored one bill to legalize boxing, another to permit baseball games on Sundays), and he knew fight promoter Tex Rickard, boxing champions Jack Dempsey and James J. Corbett, baseball magnate Jacob Ruppert, owner of the Yankees, and John McGraw of the New York Giants well enough to call them by their first names.

James J. Walker was born in June 1881 in New York's Greenwich Village. His Irish-born father was a lumber dealer with a strong interest in local politics. (Greenwich Village was important politically beyond its size; New York City was divided into assembly districts with a Democratic club located in each district. At the time, the Village included parts of four different assembly districts, thus entitling it to four Democratic clubs and four leaders.[13]) After attending school at St. Francis Xavier, young Walker spent three years at the New York Law School. Meanwhile, he had tried his hand at songwriting (his best-known effort: "Will You Love Me in December As You Do in May?") and various other occupations, including banking, before he was persuaded to go into politics. He was elected state assemblyman in 1909 and went to Albany, where he was taken in hand by State Senator Alfred E. Smith, who had been in the state capital since 1903. Al Smith, as everyone called him, had been a truckman's helper and a fish peddler, and never lost the stamp and speech of his early poverty-stricken surroundings on Manhattan's Lower East Side. Walker moved in another world; he dressed extravagantly, radiated confidence, orated easily, enjoyed nightlife, tipped lavishly, and was certainly getting by on something other than the fifteen hundred dollars paid to assemblymen—all of which impressed Al Smith no end.

For Walker, money *had* become a problem (and always would be), and in 1912, with his father's and fiancée's encouragement, he took the New York bar examination, passed it, and could now add to his income by practicing law. It was at this time, when Walker was thirty-one, that he had his interview with Tammany leader Murphy. A year-and-a-half later he was elected to the State Senate, where he held office for the next eleven years, during the last half of which he was Democratic floor leader. He had a quick wit, a sharp tongue for enemies, and seemed unafraid to speak his mind.

Fowler observed that "as a debater, conciliator, strategist, and political showman, his record in the red-carpeted hall of laws remains unsurpassed. In oratorical action, he fought with a rapier against barrel staves."[14] In his speech to the Senate when the ratification of the Eighteenth Amendment was being debated, Walker said, "This measure was born in hypocrisy, and there it will die. . . . In fact, even the Army and Navy of the United States are not large enough to enforce this unenforceable mockery."[15] Al Smith continued to admire Walker's rhetoric, if not his tastes. Smith's favor was crucial to Walker's future because Smith was now Governor Alfred E. Smith—an office he was to hold for four terms (1918–26); later, in 1928, Tammany Hall and Franklin D. Roosevelt would help Smith win the Democratic nomination for president (he was defeated by Herbert Hoover).

In 1925, with Mayor John. F. Hylan dangerously ill, the question of the succession to the mayor's office was not yet public, and when Walker was introduced at the Ringside, a new nightclub, as "the next mayor of the city of New York," his supporters thought it fitting. Shortly after, George Jessel, master of ceremonies at the opening of still another new nightclub, the Rue de la Paix, introduced Walker as "the man who will soon by mayor."[16] (If Walker had not already agreed to run in the Democratic primary against Mayor Hylan, these introductions may have made him feel obliged to do so.) And now the tempo of Walker's show business campaign picked up. Vincent Lopez and his band played "Will You Love Me in December?" at every opportunity, and Irving Berlin was moved to write a piece called "We'll Walk in with Walker." Mayor Hylan had been a judge for a dozen years before he was elected mayor; after eight years as mayor, during which he was frequently at odds with Tammany, he realized his time had come and so had Jimmy Walker's. He supported Walker. After the election in November, Walker showed his gratitude by appointing Hylan justice of the Children's Court.

During his first four years in office, Jimmy Walker was the very model of a perfect playboy mayor: debonair, a bit rakish, available for grand openings of public facilities and nightspots alike, best-known fan at prizefights, baseball games, and Broadway shows and, despite his marriage, full-time escort of actress Betty Compton. The voters of the City of New York enjoyed Walker's style, his wit, his confidence, and although there were rumors of graft and corruption in a number of municipal enterprises, including the Police Department, Walker himself appeared to be too busy fostering—even personifying—the spirit of New York to be concerned with the doings of minor officials. When he came up for reelection, LaGuardia's challenge to his second term as mayor was fended off easily.

The Wall Street crash in 1929 followed by the Great Depression with its long breadlines, thousands of jobless, and the sight of sad-faced men selling five-cent apples in the city's streets may have cast a shadow over Walker's spirit. His natural ebullience now seemed out of place and somewhat forced, and his political enemies recognized, and publicized, his weaknesses. His relationship with Betty Compton was being severely questioned, as was his glossing over of the apparent deep corruption in the city courts, Police Department, and various other agencies; in addition, he was not in the best of health—while his image was that of a young man on the move, he was approaching his fiftieth birthday. He tried nonetheless to carry on in the established Walker tradition: traveling, wearing good clothes, paying for expensive entertainment, maintaining two households, and providing newsmen with quotable remarks. (When he helped raise the mayor's annual salary from twenty-five to forty thousand dollars and Congressman LaGuardia questioned the timeliness and propriety of this increase in pay, Walker said, "That's cheap! Think what it would cost if I worked full time!"[17] Walker's enemies rejoiced at his ill-timed humor, and there was little laughter in New York streets.)

During the next two years, a series of disclosures by state legislators and the New York press showing evidence of corruption and wrongdoing in the city pressed Governor Franklin D. Roosevelt to initiate a series of investigations, conducted by

Samuel Seabury, a former justice of the State Court of Appeals. The last of three investigations would be of the mayor's office, which meant Walker himself. When Walker finally heard from Seabury in August 1931, who ordered him to produce all his financial papers and accounts, he did so; he then took official leave and sailed for Europe. Eight months later Walker appeared before the Seabury commission. After examining Walker and his accounts, including one for which he had put up no money and from which he had been paid $246,692 after taxes, Seabury sent the governor his report: fifteen charges of malfeasance, misfeasance, and nonfeasance against the mayor of the City of New York. Walker was called before the governor, and the question now was: Would Roosevelt remove Walker from office? Walker saved Roosevelt the necessity of making this difficult political decision: he resigned. Jimmy Walker died in November 1946.

What we have related to this point had been told, on the whole sympathetically, by Fowler. In contrast, we may note the work of the Northrups. William B. Northrup was assistant counsel in the Seabury investigations of the Magistrates Court and of District Attorney Crain, and associate counsel in the Walker investigation. John B. Northrup was a New York attorney. Although their stories of the "three separate though interlocking inquisitions" that Fowler called the Seabury investigations are not as interestingly told as Fowler's, their version of events during the Walker administration is based on the public record. Here, briefly, are some of the findings.

Investigation of the Magistrates Court: Besides Judge Vitale's connections with gambler Arnold Rothstein, it was revealed that the court had cooperated with gambling entrepreneurs running the Harlem numbers game by imposing light sentences on runners, collectors, and "bankers," since heavy prison sentences for the guilty might discourage gambling activities. Testimony from Joe Enrique Moro, a numbers "banker" who employed six collectors, led to the discovery of his bank accounts totaling $1,251,556.29, deposited between July 1927 and December 1930, during the

Walker administration; another numbers "banker," Wilfred Brunder, showed bank accounts with deposits between January 1925 and December 1930 of $1,753,342.33. Such operators regularly employed fixers who negotiated—with attorneys, judges, and officers of the court—light sentences for those convicted. As the Northrups put it, "This appointment of Magistrates by the Mayor—a political agency—is the central evil resident in these Courts."[18]

Investigation of the Mayor's Office: In addition to the account from which Walker, without putting up any money, drew over $246,000, Walker's personal accountant Russell T. Sherwood, opened an account with a broker with $100,000 in cash—money he stated was not his; five months later, without a single share of stock having been bought or sold, Sherwood closed the account and drew out, in cash, $261,000.

The Seabury investigations brought into the open the powerful connections between New York's politicians, police, judiciary, and underworld. We have already noted instances of Harlem's relation to downtown crime and corruption—gangster-controlled Harlem nightclubs, for one, and the connection between racketeers, the judiciary, and the numbers game, for another. Now we should explore further the general relation of downtown whites to uptown blacks before we focus on Harlem itself and its position in the history of New York jazz.

Harlem's leaders in the 1920s believed that Harlem was experiencing a cultural renaissance hampered only by the downtown whites' domination of blacks—a domination covering nearly all economic aspects of Harlem life, from the white-owned tenements and stores to the numbers game. Langston Hughes, arriving in Harlem when the renaissance was in full swing, wrote:

> I soon learned that it was seemingly impossible for black Harlem to live without white downtown. My youthful illusion that Harlem was a world unto itself did not last very long. It was not even an area unto itself. The famous night clubs were owned by whites, as were

the theatres. Almost all the stores were owned by whites. . . . The books of Harlem writers all had to be published downtown, if they were to be published at all. . . . Negroes could not even play their own numbers with their *own* people. And almost all the policemen in Harlem were white. Negroes couldn't even get graft from *themselves* for themselves by themselves.[19]

The distinguished black leader W. E. B. DuBois, commenting on amateur black actors appearing in adaptations of plays by white playwrights, told his black readers that Negro theater must be *about us, by us, for us,* and *near us.*[20] This principle of total independence from whites was easier to enunciate than accomplish. Furthermore, the cultural views of Harlem's intellectual leaders were not always the views or concerns of the man in the street. While the intellectuals envisioned a new black world of high culture—books, plays, symphonies by blacks—Roi Ottley, in his *New World A-Coming,* describes the Harlem of the '20s as seen and felt by some of its other black citizens:

For everywhere there seemed to be gaiety, good feeling, and the sound of jazz, ushering in an era of incredible doings. The rhythm of life seemed to beat to the clink of glasses and the thump of drums. From the windows of countless apartments, against a glow of dull red lights, silhouetted figures rocked and rolled to mellow music. Harlem was dancing to the syncopations of Fletcher Henderson's band and listening to the moanin' low of Bessie Smith. Urchins were happily tricking dance steps on the sidewalks. Laughter was easy, loud.[21]

For Harlem's cultural leaders in the '20s, social concerns— housing, employment, Having a Good Time—all were to be conquered under the banner of black cultural achievement. Serious black art, belles-lettres, ballet, and symphonies would show their white counterparts downtown (and perhaps whites in general) that black artists, and therefore blacks in general, were now to be taken seriously, to be listened to seriously, and to be recognized as a legitimate and powerful American cultural force. In their desire to equal what historian Nathan Irvin Huggins has called "the European-entranced white American," black cultural leaders wished to show that blacks were now civilized. He wrote:

It was commonly thought, in those decades around World War I, that culture (literature, art, music, etc.) was the true measure of civilization. Harlem intellectuals, sharing in that belief and seeing themselves as living out the moment of their race's rebirth, naturally marked off their achievement by such artistic production. Thus they promoted poetry, prose, painting, and music as if their lives depended on it.[22]

The situation had its irony. Jazz, while still relatively new to the white world in 1920, and a music which most whites would have been happy to acknowledge as exclusively black in origin and in spirit, was not generally considered by leaders of the Harlem Renaissance as worthy of inclusion in their list of serious achievements. Music, yes—but not the music of the fields, the primitive church, the streets, the dance halls, the sporting houses. One did not crash the invisible cultural barriers with field hollers, blues, rags, and stomps. Huggins comments on this irony: "While many Harlem intellectuals enjoyed the music of the cabarets, none were prepared to give someone like Jelly Roll Morton the serious attention he deserved. Jazz was infectious entertainment and not an ingredient of high civilization."[23] And so among promoters of the Harlem Renaissance—men like James Weldon Johnson, W. E. B. DuBois, E. Franklin Frazier, Arthur A. Schomberg, and Alain Locke, to name a few—performers like black tenor Roland Hayes, who stunned a Berlin audience in 1924 with his rendering of Schubert's "Du Bist die Ruh," were held up as models; as were Marian Anderson, who won first prize in a competition sponsored by the New York Philharmonic-Symphony; Paul Robeson, who gave a successful concert in New York's Town Hall; Jules Bledsoe, who sang with symphony orchestras Louis Gruenberg's symphonic setting of James Weldon Johnson's poem *The Creation*; and William Grant Still, whose composition for symphony orchestra,

Darker America, was performed in 1926 in New York's Aeolian Hall. (A year later, the Rodman Wanamaker Musical Composition Contest for blacks was set up, offering prizes for chamber music pieces and works for symphony orchestra.[24])

The "lower" forms of music, as we have seen, were not considered serious enough to serve as civilizing influences, and the true worth of such jazzmen as Duke Ellington, Fletcher Henderson, Don Redman, Louis Armstrong, Fats Waller, and James P. Johnson was overlooked. Also relatively neglected in Harlem's artistic circles was the 1921 all-black musical *Shuffle Along*, with book by Flournay Miller and Aubrey Lyles and music by Eubie Blake and Noble Sissle, in addition to a host of black musicals and revues from *Liza* in 1923 to *Hot Chocolates* in 1929, which produced Fats Waller's jazz standard "Ain't Misbehavin'." It appears that any sort of "serious" work, musical or otherwise, was in any case encouraged; quality was not always the prime consideration. Seriousness of purpose weighed heavily; if the work in question was serious, and also had merit, it was revered. Just the same, the Harlem Renaissance as a literary movement resulted in many works which turned out to be important social documents, significant cultural creations, or both. No discussion of the Harlem Renaissance would be complete without some mention of such leading writers and poets as Claude McKay, Langston Hughes, Countee Cullen, Jessie Fauset, Walter White, and, again, James Weldon Johnson.

Black cultural leaders saw the Harlem Renaissance as the first creative outburst of blacks who had been brought together from all parts of the world to the private and special world of Harlem. The magic of Harlem, the argument went, had brought all these forces together, and now, in the 1920s, the creativity was about to be released, and the white world would come to recognize that which they had tried to contain and suffocate. To understand the views of these leaders, we need the answers to two questions: Where were New York blacks before they were drawn to Harlem? and What was the special attraction of pre-black Harlem?

In New York, blacks lived as poorly as they did in other cities, and in the worst sections. Early in the nineteenth century they were concentrated in the Five Points area (what is now City Hall) in an environment of poverty, crime, drunkenness, and prostitution. By the 1830s they had started to move north and west into Greenwich Village, but they were eventually pushed out by Irish newcomers. At the turn of the twentieth century, of the city's black population of 60,666 (1.8 percent of the total population)[25] only about 2,000 were still living in Greenwich Village. The rest had moved uptown, between Twenty-third and Sixty-third Streets. Two sections of New York were now essentially black: the Tenderloin (an "old" Tenderloin went up to about Forty-second Street, and a "new" one to about Fifty-eighth Street), and San Juan Hill—Sixtieth Street to Sixty-fourth, between Tenth Avenue and the railroad tracks along Eleventh Avenue. The Tenderloin included New York's red-light district, and became the support of the city's crooked police and politicians. As the blacks moved into these neighborhoods, the whites gradually moved north toward Harlem. (On an island the shape of Manhattan, it was the only direction they could go.)

In 1658, Peter Stuyvesant had established the rural bottomland between what are now the Harlem River and Morningside Heights, in upper Manhattan, as Nieuw Haarlem. Between 1870 and the 1890s, the village of Harlem, with its marshes and meadows, became Manhattan's first suburb.[26] Earlier, it had been a collection of shanties and small farms; as Manhattan developed and the population grew, Harlem was annexed to the city in 1873, some of the marshes were filled in, houses were put up, and with the opening of an elevated railroad from downtown to Harlem, the building boom began in earnest. Apartment buildings were constructed in short order; many included elevators and servants' quarters, and were clearly intended to appeal to New York's upper classes. Appropriate stores, churches, restaurants, and theaters followed, including the Harlem Opera House on West 125th Street, built in 1889 by Oscar Hammerstein I,[27] and the rich and well-to-do moved into Harlem in the thousands.

But Harlem was not entirely deluxe apartments of powerful, music-loving residents with good taste. Marshy sections with garbage piled ten to twelve feet high[28] surrounded the community, and soon to settle near the marshes there came Italians from Rome and Naples and Sicily, who created a Little Italy between 110th and 125th Streets, east of Third Avenue to the East River; in addition, large numbers of blacks had also found their way to the same neighborhood. Two apartment houses, in fact, were exclusively black, and other tenements housing blacks were scattered throughout the area. Furthermore, new apartment houses and tenements in Harlem attracted many Lower East Side Jews who after years of economic struggle in their own ghetto could now afford to move into better quarters in better neighborhoods. The proximity of blacks, immigrant Italians, and Jews eventually resulted in an exodus of those old Harlemites who were affronted by the speech, manners, and tastes of their new neighbors. The luxurious apartment houses with their elevators and butlers' pantries and maids' rooms would now, temporarily at least, go begging.

Many blacks, particularly women, had found domestic employment in well-to-do neighborhoods around the city. At the turn of the century there were more black women in New York than black men; for every 1,000 women there were only 810 men. For the men, finding employment was a major concern. Gilbert Osofsky sums up the nature of the employment available to New York blacks of the time:

> Most of the Negro population in the 1890s worked at varieties of unskilled and low-paid jobs. The Negro middle class was quite small. The largest number, some 450, were clerks, followed, in descending order, by actors and actresses, musicians and music teachers, and small businessmen. A population of about 60,000 was serviced by only forty-two Negro physicians and twenty-six Negro lawyers. More than 90 percent of the community, male and female, were employed as menials or laborers: servants, porters, waiters, waitresses, teamsters, dressmakers, laundresses, janitors and "laborers not specified" (as the census-takers termed it).[29]

(Between 1720 and 1726, 800 slaves had been brought into New York to make up for a labor shortage, but after this period indentured servants and newly arrived Irish became the city's labor force, and slaves were used mainly as household servants.)[30]

Blacks migrated to New York mainly from Maryland, New Jersey, Pennsylvania, Virginia, and North and South Carolina for the same reason they migrated to Chicago and other large cities— greater opportunity. From the beginning of the century to World War I they came from the South in a series of relatively small migrations, the whole culminating in the Great Migration during the war itself. New York's black population went from 60,666 in 1900, to 91,709 in 1910, to 152,407 in 1920.[31] Born and raised in the traditional circumstances reserved for poor southern blacks, they brought their folkways to New York neighborhoods, and New Yorkers—black and white alike—looked upon the newcomers with distaste. Osofsky notes:

> The entire Negro community of New York City took on a southern flavor. Businesses expanded to service the wants of a growing population. . . . Negro restaurants, undertaking establishments, saloons, barbershops—the plethora of small businesses necessary to satisfy a community's needs—catered to the newcomers. Restaurants advertised special "southern-style" breakfasts and dinners. Negro grocers specialized in Virginia fruits, vegetables and chickens. Migrants asked friends to send them special southern delicacies.[32]

It was, in ironic fact, the migrants' desire to hold on to old ways that led to conflicts and antagonisms with those black New Yorkers who believed that the migrants, with their southern tastes, loudness, unsanitary habits, and illiteracy had compromised the position of *decent* New York blacks. White New Yorkers had similar feelings about the migrants, but for different reasons. Starting with a major race riot in 1900 in the Tenderloin and another in 1905 in the San Juan Hill district, evidence of the rise of less violent prejudice was to become abundantly clear in the treatment of black migrants by New York's white churches, fraternal organizations, hotels, restaurants, theaters, labor unions, and, inevitably, real estate operators. Racial discrimination in housing, as we have seen throughout this study, invariably leads to segregated communities; it finally led to the making of black Harlem.

The move uptown received added impetus when, around 1905, the speculations of Harlem real estate operators so inflated building values that the market collapsed. Black realtors—particularly the Afro-American Realty Company—stepped into the breach, and with a combination of leases, loans, and mortgages got together twenty-five buildings, mostly in Harlem and never previously available for rental to blacks. By 1911, in one three-by-five-block area alone—132nd to 137th Streets between Fifth and Eighth Avenues—lived an estimated 20,000 blacks.[33] Efforts by white property owners to keep blacks out failed because of lack of organization; since blacks would agree to pay higher rents than whites, some landlords opposed the white real estate associations and rented apartments to blacks.

By the time the United States entered the war in 1917, Harlem could offer "Refined Colored Tenants" such up-to-date amenities as steam heat, hot water, private tiled bathrooms, gas, and electricity in modern buildings in attractive neighborhoods. Overseas immigration was at a near standstill, industry was booming, and with immigrant competitors out of the game, employment opportunities seemed boundless. For New York blacks, the American dream of economic and racial independence seemed just around the corner. And before them lay Harlem, land of promise.

In the early 1920s a grandiose and romantic figure appeared in Harlem and promised those who would follow him still another land of promise—Africa—and a better life than Harlem could offer. Those who believed him were to be heartbreakingly disappointed. Marcus Garvey came to Harlem at age twenty-nine and established an organization to promote the idea of Africa as the parent nation of blacks everywhere, with himself as provisional president. He organized the Black Star Steamship Company, presumably to send American blacks to Africa, was convicted in 1925 of mail fraud by the federal government, served two years in prison, and was then deported to his native Jamaica. He died in London in 1940.

Still ahead for Harlem was the Great Depression, which for New York's 350,000 blacks would be, as Glazer and Moynihan noted, "a disaster that almost rivaled slavery."[34] They would become an impoverished people frightfully crowded together through natural increase and immigration, with no money, no mobility, and no place to turn to for comfort except, perhaps, Harlem's 160 black churches. The decline of Harlem was rapid. Neighborhoods were allowed to become dirty and run-down. Landlords spent little on maintenance, and tenants piled refuse in hallways and alleys. Rules of sanitation were ignored or unknown; venereal disease was rampant, as were tuberculosis, pneumonia, and death by violence.

Two items from the period point up the mixed intelligence coming out of Harlem in the late 1920s, as reported in two of the city's most respected newspapers. The first item, from the *New York Times*, appeared at a time when health authorities were exposing the section's terrible mortality rate of infants, children, and grownups. Under the heading "What Tempts Harlem's Palate?" John Walker Harrington asked, "If the Negro is to win New York to the fare he likes, as he has won the rest of the world to his jazz and his spirituals, what shall we be eating one of these days?" After a lengthy discussion of foods of Harlem, including "fruits which savor more of jungles than orchards," Harrington closed with the following romance:

> On Saturday afternoons and nights the broad sidewalks of Lenox Avenue become groves and gardens and broad fields. Out of huge barrels loom red sugar cane, six or eight feet high, which later, cut in short lengths, is eaten as a stick candy by children. Plantains and bananas in all shades of green and yellow and dark red are ranged in inviting "hands." Pyramids of banyans and eddoes loom; bushels of collards, and stacks of gigantic yellow and brown and reddish yams tempt the affluence of payday. One would go far before finding

anything more colorful and picturesque than this weekly food exposition which Harlem stages in the spirit of happy-go-lucky carnival.[35]

In the second item, headed "Population Rises Steadily: Illness
Takes Heavy Toll; Unemployment and Low Wages Result from
Race Prejudice," reporter Beverly Smith, in the *Herald Tribune*
discussed the viewpoint expressed commonly in the *Times* (if not in
the above story itself) as an introduction to the principal thrust of
his own piece. He wrote:

> The attitude of the average white New Yorker to Harlem is one of
> tolerant amusement. He thinks of it as a region of prosperous night
> clubs; of happy-go-lucky Negroes dancing all night to jazz music and
> living during the day by taking in each other's policy numbers; of
> Negro artists and intellectuals wealthy on the royalties of novels or
> salaries from the "talkies," and of a group of "high society" Negroes,
> most of them with foreign white servants, living high in the fashion
> of some of the characters of Carl Van Vechten's *Nigger Heaven*.
>
> The fact is that this community of 220,000 Negroes is the poorest,
> the unhealthiest, the unhappiest and the most crowded single large
> section of New York City.[36]

If there were blacks in Harlem who "danced all night to jazz
music," they were certainly something less than happy-go-lucky;
more likely they were indigent taxi dancers. On the other hand, to
call Harlem "a region of prosperous nightclubs" had its basis in
fact, and we now turn to the best known of these nightspots.

NEW YORK JAZZ: NIGHTLIFE, BIG BANDS, THE SPREAD

S eventh Avenue is Harlem's broadest street, with apartment houses, retail stores, restaurants, saloons, and nightspots; and Lenox Avenue—Harlem's "Main Street"—is a boulevard of trashy shops, pool halls, restaurants, saloons, and nightclubs. In the 1920s and '30s most well-known jazz spots were clustered on and around Seventh Avenue between 131st and 139th, and Lenox Avenue between 140th and 145th. A brief survey of these spots would include Connie's Inn, on 131st Street and Seventh Avenue, right next to the Lafayette Theater; Barron Wilkins's Inn, on 134th Street, where banjoist Elmer Snowden, who is supposed to have brought Duke Ellington to New York from Washington, played for six months; the Oriental Cafe, near Wilkins's, where Fats Waller played in banjoist Freddie Guy's band; Small's Paradise, on 135th Street (with an apostrophe-*s*, even though the owner's name was Ed Smalls), which opened in 1925 with space for fifteen hundred customers and where Charlie Johnson's orchestra later held forth, and which was called the Black Venus nightclub in Carl Van Vechten's fatuous and sentimental novel *Nigger Heaven*, a widely read curiosity of the '20s showing a white writer's "inside" view of Harlem; and two less pretentious and much less expensive nearby spots, the Yeah Man, on 136th Street and Seventh Avenue, and Herman's Inn, on 145th Street.

The stretch of 133rd Street between Seventh Avenue and Lenox was a tourist trap, for downtown slummers, called "Jungle Alley," and decoying activities along 133rd Street helped propagate the then-popular view of the black as "noble savage"—a point we will return to later in the chapter. The best-known spots in the immediate area included the Nest, a favorite with jazzmen looking for jam sessions; Mexico's, an after-hours club mainly for eating, drinking, and talking; Pod's and Jerry's (Mexico's competition); and Dickie Wells' club, named for the important jazz trombonist. Further uptown was the 101 Club on 139th Street, and the Capitol Palace on Lenox between 139th and 140th Streets, where pianist Willie ("The Lion") Smith worked, and where one could listen to Lloyd Scott's Syncopators, whose most distinguished sideman had been trombonist Dickie Wells. One of the best-known after-hours clubs on Lenox Avenue was the Lenox Club on 143rd Street. The club was open from eleven at night until seven in the morning, and offered dancing, a floor show, jam sessions, and a Monday morning breakfast dance one reporter described as "a five o'clock subway rush put to music."[1]

Just down the street from the Lenox Club was the Cotton Club, and when it closed at two, the men from Ellington's 1929 band would come to the Lenox to jam and give the house band— Cliff Jackson's Krazy Kats—a rest. The Cotton Club, along with Small's Paradise and Connie's Inn, made up Harlem's Big Three, and of these the Cotton Club was the most heavily advertised and thus easily the best known. The Cotton Club, at 142nd and Lenox, was opened by owner Bernard Levy in 1922 with black entertainers and musicians and a policy of white customers only, with guards on the door as enforcers; local pressures, however, soon forced Levy to admit blacks, but the club's high prices effectively enforced the club's original policy. Ellington opened at the Cotton Club in 1927, and when he left, after nearly five years, he was replaced by Cab Calloway and his Missourians, who were followed by Jimmie Lunceford's band.

Connie's Inn, run by Connie and George Immerman, was one of the highest-priced clubs in Harlem catering essentially to whites (in 1929 the cost per person for an evening at Connie's averaged twelve to fifteen dollars; by contrast, at Small's Paradise, the average was about four dollars). The club had a capacity of 250 people and offered them physical surroundings that may have been the ultimate in pretentiousness and bad taste. A reporter in 1929 describes one of the room's grotesqueries. "Walk down one flight of stairs and you are in this rendezvous, so low-ceilinged as to be cavelike. Around the dance floor is a three-foot barrier built in the semblance of a village, miniature bungalows and villas, and here and there a spired church, through the tiny windows of which comes the gleam of midget lights."[2] Connie's Inn gained the special attention of white Broadway audiences when in 1929 a Con-

nie's Inn revue, *Hot Chocolates,* moved into a Broadway theater
and enjoyed a run of six months. Leroy Smith and his band—
Connie's regular band on and off throughout the 1920s—was
moved downtown to accompany the revue, and Louis Armstrong,
leading Carroll Dickerson's band, moved in.

Connie's Inn, the Cotton Club, and Small's Paradise were not
representative Harlem nightclubs; they were simply the best
known to white "thrill seekers." While Harlem's middle-class
blacks looked upon white slummers visiting these clubs with open
disdain, Harlem's leaders were proud of these clubs and wished
there were more like them. In an interesting observation on Connie's, the Cotton Club, and Small's Paradise, James Weldon
Johnson, in his *Black Manhattan,* chided Harlem's self-righteous,
pious snobs for their attitude and then reminded them of the clubs'
economic importance to the community:

> To many, especially among coloured people, a Harlem night-club is
> a den of iniquity, where the Devil holds high revel. The fact is that
> the average night club is as orderly as many a Sunday-school picnic
> has been. These clubs are patronized by many quite respectable
> citizens. Anyone who visits them expecting to be shocked is likely to
> be disappointed. Generally night clubbers go simply to have a good
> time. They laugh and talk and they dance to the most exhilarating
> music. And they watch a first-rate revue. Certainly, there are infrac-
> tions of the Volstead Act; but they also take place in the best-
> regulated homes. . . .
> There are hundreds of musicians and hundreds of performers con-
> nected with the night-clubs of Harlem. The waiters, cooks, coat-
> room girls, doormen and others make up several more hundreds. It
> has been estimated that there are something like two thousand
> Negroes employed in these clubs.[3]

Among the clubs scattered throughout Harlem, two representative ones deserve special attention: the Sugar Cane Club, because it catered essentially to blacks; and the Rhythm Club, because black jazzmen considered it to be a club for jazzmen. The

,Sugar Cane, operated by Ed Smalls (of Small's Paradise), was a basement club at 135th Street and Fifth Avenue, somewhat removed from Harlem's main streets. It was a typical small club, which on occasion featured a young blues singer named Ethel Waters. Roi Ottley visited the Sugar Cane during the '20s and described the dancing there:

> At the bottom of a steep flight of stairs . . . was a damp, dimly lit cellar, with two-dozen-odd tables surrounding a tiny dance floor. From one side a five-piece band beat out rhythms, while each player in turn would "take a Boston"—that is, execute some unexpected riffs. (None of the musicians could read music, nor did the lack of knowledge seem important.) To such music, the patrons, mostly Negroes, would stand and shuffle their feet—dancing on a dime, it was called—while others did the aptly titled bump and mess-around.[4]

The Rhythm Club (formerly the Bandbox), was owned by a Bert Hale, and was a favorite gathering place for jazzmen, particularly on Monday afternoons when leaders paid sidemen for the weekend's gigs, after which there were jam sessions and "cutting" contests (to cut a musician was to outplay him, to show greater creativity, more originality). One Monday, Danny Barker visited the club for the first time. "A wild cutting contest was in progress," he recalled, "and sitting and standing around the piano were twenty or thirty musicians, all with their instruments out waiting for a signal to play choruses of Gershwin's *Liza*." The musicians gathered there represented a good cross-section of New York's black big-band jazzmen. Barker remembers:

> This day, at the Rhythm Club, most of the famous leaders, stars and sidemen were there; the big names I'd heard and read about: Benny Carter, Don Redman, Horace Henderson, Fess Williams, Claude Hopkins, Sonny Greer, John Kirby, Johnny Hodges, Freddie Jenkins, Bobby Stark, Chick Webb, Big Green and Charlie Johnson.[5]

(While the jam session was in progress, Fletcher Henderson played pool while King Oliver and Jelly Roll Morton watched.)

In addition to the clubs, Harlem had several theaters that provided work for jazzmen. The Lincoln Theater, at 58 West 135th Street, opened in 1915 with a seating capacity of about a thousand and specialized in stage acts, revues, and southern down-home entertainment; by 1928, however, the entertainment included jazz, and Ellington's band played there for a week as a replacement for Fletcher Henderson's Club Alabam Orchestra. The Lafayette Theater, on 131st Street and Seventh Avenue, had opened in 1912 as Harlem's legitimate theater, with two thousand seats; its programs later included vaudeville acts, stage shows, and revues, and in the '20s the theater finally advertised "A New Jazz Band Every Week."[6] The Apollo Theater, at 125th Street near Eighth Avenue, opened in 1914 as a burlesque house and eventually came to be called, facetiously, Harlem's "opera house." In 1934 it began to specialize in vaudeville acts including singers, dancers, comedians, and dance bands, offering new programs each week, and eventually succeeded in presenting virtually every major black dance band in the country.

Having a Good Time invariably included dancing, and black Harlem had its favorite dancing resorts. The Renaissance Casino (or Ballroom) on 137th Street and Seventh Avenue, known to its clientele as the Rennie, was in a brick building decorated inside and out with Middle Eastern motifs; Fletcher Henderson made his first appearance there in 1925, and a decade later the Rennie was still going strong, featuring Jimmie Lunceford and his orchestra. The Alhambra Ballroom, on 126th Street and Seventh Avenue, celebrated its opening in 1929 by hiring five bands: the Missourians, Zack Whyte and his Chocolate Beau Brummels, Lou Russell, Bennie Carter, and Johnson's Happy Pals; and as the poster advertising the grand opening had it, "17 Varieties of Spicy Entertainment."[7] In 1931, Cab Calloway and his band broke all attendance records there, playing for two thousand dancers.

The Savoy Ballroom, covering the entire block on Lenox Avenue between 140th and 141st Streets, with a capacity of fifteen hundred dancers, is Harlem's best-known dance hall. Although white customers were tolerated, the Savoy was a black ballroom, featuring black bands playing for black dancers, and was regularly advertised as "the home of happy feet." The notion that blacks are somehow born with rhythm in their souls (and, by extension, in their feet) dies hard. Black people dance, the myth has it, because they must. Even James Weldon Johnson perpetuated this myth. "An average group of Negroes," he wrote, "can in dancing to a good jazz band achieve a delightful state of intoxication that for others would require nothing short of a certain per capita imbibition of synthetic gin."[8] (While this may be true on occasion, it was not always true for dancers in the Savoy Ballroom. The writer has experienced a "delightful state of intoxication" at the Savoy, in the '30s, merely by walking slowly around the edges of the dance floor, breathing in the pungently heady aroma of marijuana cigarettes, or "reefers" as they were called.)

The Savoy opened in 1926 with the Savoy Bearcats (formerly the Charleston Bearcats), Fess Williams and his Royal Flush Orchestra, and Fletcher Henderson and his band. Admission was fifty cents on weekdays and seventy-five cents on Sundays and holidays. Dancers entered a spacious lobby, walked up a wide marble staircase, and entered a ballroom that seemed as long as a football field. At the far end one saw, through the red and blue lights, the moving silhouettes, and the haze of smoke, a long bar selling ten-cent beer and twenty-cent wine which one carried to a table at the edge of the dance floor. Along one wall was a bandstand long enough to hold the two featured big bands and their paraphernalia—a famous one, heavily advertised (the likes of Armstrong, Ellington, Calloway, or Henderson), and a "house band" that needed no advertising in Harlem (such as Teddy Hill's, the Savoy Sultans, or the Bearcats). Jazz writer Otis Ferguson, after attending a 1936 session at the Savoy, described a characteristic bandstand scene:

And when Teddy Hill's men begin swinging the last choruses of the specialty number "Christopher Colombo," with those driving brass figures and the reed section going down to give it body, the dancers forget dancing and flock around the stand ten deep, to register the time merely with their bones and muscles, standing there in one place with their heads back and letting it flow over them like water—invitation (and the waltz be damned) to blow the man down. The floor shakes and the place is a dynamo room, with the smoky air pushing up in steady waves, and swing it, men, get off, beat it out and in a word play that thing. It's a music deaf men could hear.[9]

Saturday-night gaiety at the Savoy Ballroom notwithstanding, the economic plight of black Harlem was an everyday reality. While one could stint on food, clothing, and entertainment, the rent *had* to be paid, and the combination of large black families, high unemployment, and high rents gave rise to what was called the "rent party." Just before the rent was due, the head of the household would hire a piano player for about a dollar-and-a-half for the night, print up tickets advertising the time and place of the party, then sell the tickets to friends, relatives, neighbors, and anyone else able to pay the fiteen- to twenty-five-cent admission charge. He had now a rent party in the making.

Nearly all Harlem people found the rent party attractive. For one thing, it took them, for a while, from their own mean, close quarters and gave them a cheap night out. Rent parties also provided a night's entertainment for black transients: railroad men, truck drivers, and blacks just visiting Harlem. Food and drink were sold at the party, with special emphasis on chitlins, pigs' feet, collard greens, and black-eyed peas. As for drinks, as one contemporary account put it, "the usual procedure is to sell a cheap brand of liquor at 25 cents a drink until either the rent is made up or the patrons pass out."[10] (The "cheap brand of liquor" was commonly a jug of corn, sold in portions called "shorties.") A successful rent party meant the host could put off moving for still another month, and by the mid-'20s Harlem rent parties had become so popular they were restricted only by the number of available piano players.

"Available" piano players meant those whose keyboard technique was based on the ragtime tradition and who were capable of playing all night long if necessary. Starting with such legendary pre-'20s figures as Charlie Cherry, Jack the Bear, and the Seminole, Harlem's party-piano men enjoyed varying degrees of local fame and adulation. Among the best known were: the Beetle, Eubie Blake, Russell Brooks, Fred Bryant, Willie Gant, Sam Gordon, Ernest Green, Fats Harris, James P. Johnson, Donald Lambert, Kid Lippy, Abba Labba McLean, Clarence Profit, Luckey Roberts, Alberta Simmons, Willie ("The Lion") Smith, Freddie Tonsil, Fats Waller, and Corky Williams.

If New York rent-party pianists in the '20s and '30s had a dean, it would have been James P. Johnson, whose playing was a curious combination of classical piano techniques and honky-tonk; it was as if Franz Liszt had discovered ragtime. Born in New Jersey in 1891, Johnson studied classical piano seriously as a youth and, later, building on his early foundation, developed a prodigious technical facility both as composer and performer. He apparently saw no conflict between such piano works of his as "Carolina Shout," "Mule Walk," and "Gut Stomp," on the one hand, and his four-movement *Harlem Symphony* for orchestra, on the other. His first love, however, was party piano. In an interview in the 1950s (he died in 1955) he said:

> About this time [1913] I played my first "Pigfoot Hop" at Phil Watkin's place on 61st Street. He was a very clever entertainer and he paid me $1.50 for a night's playing with all the gin and chitterlings that I could get down.
>
> This was my first "Chitterlin' Strut" or parlor social, but later in the depression I became famous at "Gumbo Suppers," "Fish Fries," "Egg Nog Parties," and "Rent Parties," I loved them all.[11]

Soon after, Johnson held forth at Barron Wilkins's place in Harlem, playing eight to ten hours nightly, developing and polishing his formidable technique. "I was playing a lot of piano then," he said, "traveling around and listening to every good player I could. I'd steal their breaks and style and practice them until I had them perfect." And, later, "Oh yes, I was getting around town and hearing everybody. If they had anything I didn't have, I listened and stole it." Johnson had a special admiration for Luckey Roberts, who is said to have founded the Harlem party-piano school, and may have been one of Johnson's teachers, but then, Johnson "studied" with almost everyone. "I was born with absolute pitch," he said, "and could catch a key that a player was using and copy it, even Luckey's."[12] His greatest admiration, however, was reserved for Jelly Roll Morton. In a discussion of piano players he had known, Johnson described Morton's suave approach to the keyboard: He'd remove his coat, lay it along the top of the piano, dust off the stool with a silk handkerchief, sit down and strike a chord and let it ring to gain everyone's attention, then he'd launch into a rag—"a spirited one to astound the audience." Other piano players would rattle off scales or arpeggios or a string of modulations as though nothing could be easier. A rousing opener would be followed by something moody or sentimental, after which the pianist would always "finish up with a hot rag and then stand up quickly, so that everybody in the place would be able to see who knocked it out."[13]

Such lessons in tactics were passed on by Johnson to his most apt pupil, Thomas ("Fats") Waller, who was born in New York City in 1904. Virtually self-taught, Waller at fourteen played organ accompaniments to silent movies at the Lincoln Theater (he no doubt had played organ earlier, since his father was a minister of the Abyssinian Baptist Church). At fifteen he won a piano contest in a local theater by playing Johnson's "Carolina Shout." Soon after, Waller's mother died and he went to live with Russell Brooks, a rent-party pianist who introduced young Waller to Johnson. Under Johnson's tutelage, Waller made rapid improvement, and when Johnson could not fulfill an engagement at Leroy's, a nightspot at 135th and Fifth, with an exclusively black clientele, Waller took his place. In short order Waller distinguished himself among his piano-playing peers. As Blesh put it,

"Negro jazz in New York begins almost simultaneously with groups which played with the Harlem party-piano players James P. Johnson and . . . 'Fats' Waller."[14]

The style of rent-party piano playing exemplified by Johnson, Waller, and others is sometimes called "stride" piano, and is characterized by a strong, steady, bouncing left-hand pattern in which a single note alternates with a chord (one-TWO-three-FOUR), while the right hand decorates the melody with runs, arabesquelike figures, scales, and arpeggios. Johnson was master of all these effects and their variations: shifting stride patterns in which, in the left hand, the single note does not always alternate with the chord (one-two-three-FOUR, or ONE-TWO-three-FOUR); "walking" basses, including walking tenths in the left hand; and, for the right hand, Lisztian filigrees of sound. What Johnson picked up from others he polished and made his own; he then added these musical ideas to the "tricks" (as he called them) he had developed on his own. "I did double glissandos straight and behind," he said, "glissandos in sixths and double tremolos." And, "I played rags very accurately and brilliantly—running chromatic octaves and glissandos up and down with both hands. It made a terrific effect."[15]

It may be of value to pause here to discuss another kind of New York party—the after-hours party, and the foremost after-hours pianist, Art Tatum. While rent parties were held at home, after-hours parties could be held anywhere—as long as an upright was there—and they were held most frequently in bars, clubs, and back rooms, after the legal closing time. People came expressly to hear the music and watch the "cutting," the competition between pianists seeking to prove, semipublicly at least, that they were as good as or better than the rest. "The world of after-hours jazz," Orrin Keepnews wrote, "was, by and large, a private world. . . . After hours a man played strictly as he pleased. . . . He played as long and as late as he pleased. . . . And he played primarily for friends and fellow musicians."[16] Art Tatum, who may have been the greatest of all after-hours pianists, came to New York from

Toledo in 1932, at age twenty-two, and a year later worked at the Onyx Club, on 52nd Street, where he attracted the attention of New York's jazzmen. By the mid-'30s he had proved that in the after-hours sessions at such Harlem places as the Hollywood Bar, the Chicken Shack, Reuben Harris's, and Leroy's, he was unrivaled. Tatum believed his strongest influence came from Fats Waller; Waller was taught by James P. Johnson, and Johnson said *his* playing came from cabaret and sporting house "ticklers," including Luckey Roberts.

Long before Johnson reached his peak as Harlem's premier solo pianist, he had worked with many small groups, and, toward the end of World War I, led a band from the Clef Club. The Clef Club was not a nightclub, but essentially a band-booking office, and was important both as a social phenomenon and as a part of the early history of the New York jazz scene. James Reese Europe—the Clef Club's best-known figure, its founder, and first president—was born in Mobile, Alabama, in 1881, was trained in Washington, D.C., and came to New York at the age of twenty-three to seek his musical fortune. A classically trained violinist and pianist with a penchant for conducting, Europe soon found employment with a large instrumental ensemble called the Memphis Sudents—a twenty-piece group made up of as unlikely a combination of instruments as one could imagine: banjos, mandolins, a violin, some brass and reed instruments, some percussion, and Will Dixon, a dancing conductor. The Memphis Students' first performance in 1905 was a popular success, and the group went on to tour Paris, London, and Berlin. Upon the group's return, Europe worked for several seasons as a musical director for the Cole-Johnson Company, which produced a variety of musical productions, sought all available dance jobs, and gave piano lessons. In 1910, frustrated with the difficulties black musicians had in finding employment, he organized a cooperative booking agency and clearing house through which the general public could hire black musical groups, opened an office and lounge on West 53rd Street, advertised their wares—bands from three to thirty men furnished at any time, day or night—and eventually brought to the membership more work and better pay than they had previously known.[17] By 1914, Europe's reputation was such that he was asked to organize and conduct an orchestra to accompany the world-famous ballroom dancers Irene and Vernon Castle; he accepted the position and they toured the country.

When the United States entered the First World War, black volunteers formed New York's Fifteenth Infantry Regiment, and Europe was given the job of organizing the regiment band. Once overseas, the regiment was attached to the French Army as the 369th Regiment when the American military there officially rejected the idea of black combat troops. The regiment distinguished itself nonetheless, being the first Allied unit to reach the Rhine. Upon its return home in February 1919, the 369th Regiment marched in a victory parade, from a victory arch at Twenty-fifth Street up Fifth Avenue and all the way through Harlem, led by Lieutenant James Europe and his Hell Fighters Band. Three months later, while the band was on tour, Europe was stabbed to death, by the band's drummer, in Boston. In evaluating Europe's contribution to the musical life of New York, Gunther Schuller wrote: "In summary, James Europe was the most important transitional figure in the pre-history of jazz on the East Coast."[18]

A year after the victory parade, twenty-two-year-old Fletcher Henderson—who was to become one of the most important figures in the history of jazz in New York—arrived from his home in Cuthbert, Georgia, not far from Atlanta University where he had just received his degree in mathematics and chemistry. As we mentioned in the previous chapter, apparently no one in New York in 1920 was especially interested in employing a black chemist, and he was reduced (if that is the word) to accepting a piano-playing job with W. C. Handy's company. Handy had moved to New York in 1918, where he started a music-publishing company with Harry Pace and, later, the Black Swan Record Company. Henderson had studied light classical music with his mother (she was a piano teacher), knew something about music theory, and read music fluently, a combination of abilities infrequent among the city's black pianists of the time and certainly unique in conjunction with a college degree.

After working for several years with small groups and as accompanist for a number of promotional tours with Black Swan blues singers, including Bessie Smith, Henderson assembled a group that opened in 1923 at the Club Alabam on West 44th Street. A rather shy, unassuming person both at the keyboard and away from it, Henderson surrounded himself with outward-going jazzmen, allowed them to express themselves, and carefully studied their ways. Henderson's band moved ahead rapidly, and in 1924 he bolstered the band's reputation by persuading Louis Armstrong to join them—an event that was to have considerable influence not only on the entire band but especially on the band's arranger, Don Redman, who in turn would influence Henderson's later arranging, which, in its turn, would influence a generation of big-band jazzmen.

In 1927 Henderson lost the man mainly responsible for the style of the band when Redman left to join McKinney's Cotton Pickers as co-leader. Redman's definition was a blow, and despite the musical growth of Coleman Hawkins, the addition of trombonist Jimmy Harrison, and Redman's replacement—Benny Carter—the band's morale and bookings went into a slump. Still, Henderson's 1928 band may have been his best. It included Russell Smith, Bobby Stark, and Rex Stewart on trumpet; Jimmy Harrison and Benny Morton on trombone; Buster Bailey on clarinet; Hawkins on tenor and Bennie Carter on alto saxophone; June Coles on bass; and Kaiser Marshall on drums.

In 1928 Henderson was in a serious automobile accident that broke his left collarbone, gashed his forehead, and left him weary and depressed. For the next several years the band extensively toured the West and Southwest, but its earlier spark, like Henderson's, seemed to be gone. The band personnel was constantly changing—not all jazzmen enjoy one-night stands—and finally Henderson returned to New York to begin a six-month stay at Connie's Inn. In 1932, bookings they had expected in theaters and nightclubs fell through, and it was a simple matter for sidemen to leave this gentle, easygoing man and seek steadier work elsewhere. About this time, Henderson began spending most of his time at serious arranging, and finally, in 1934, the band broke up. Here, in nontechnical language, jazz historian Barry Ulanov summarizes the Henderson style:

> Drive was the overwhelming point of Fletcher Henderson's music, and there was plenty of competition to establish the point, each soloist vying with the others in half-serious and sometimes dead earnest instrumental battles. Fletcher scored his arrangements to give the same quality to section choruses, so that brass and reed phrases sounded like spontaneous solo bursts. With this band, the exciting reiteration of two- and four-bar phrases, usually built on a blues pattern, became a basic big-band jazz formula. All of this drive and reiteration had become ordinary jazz currency by the time swing appeared, but none wrote it better than Fletcher, which is why Benny Goodman sent for him when the Goodman band was on its way to success.[19]

Before Henderson hit his stride as America's most influential arranger, his work for a time was an imitation of Don Redman's. Redman was a musician of exceptional ability and imagination, and his position in the history of jazz is not diminished because Henderson and others went on to explore, more successfully and more creatively, paths and directions Redman himself had found but did not follow. Don Redman was born in Piedmont, West Virginia, in 1900. A child prodigy, he played piano and cornet at eight, led his school band at fourteen, and soon after started arranging. After graduating from Storer College in Harper's Ferry, he joined Billy Paige's Broadway Syncopators, a popular Pittsburgh band, then came to New York where he teamed up with Henderson, first to make some recordings and later to open with a band at the Club Alabam. "We decided to make Fletcher the leader," Redman said, "because he was a college graduate and presented a nice appearance."[20] For three years nearly all the Henderson band's arrangements were by Redman; but Redman wished to be a leader.

McKinney's Cotton Pickers were based in Detroit, with the Greystone Ballroom as their headquarters. Bill McKinney was an ex-circus drummer cum business manager who had transformed an Ohio novelty group called the Synco Septet into the Cotton Pickers, and then, recognizing his inability to take them forward musically, hired Redman as musical director. Redman, anxious for the opportunity to shape a big band to his personal tastes, to work with a band over which he had creative control, a band he could *direct*, gave the Cotton Pickers four years of fire and polish. As Frank Driggs put it, "In 1927 he took an average Midwestern band, McKinney's Cotton Pickers, with vague qualities of musicianship and showmanship and little individuality, and made it one of the four top jazz orchestras for the duration of his four-year stay."[21] The other three "top jazz orchestras," according to Driggs, were the bands of Alphonso Trent, Fletcher Henderson, and Duke Ellington. Henderson's band was certainly close to the top by anyone's reckoning. Trent may have had the best band in Texas, but his fame was generally limited to the Southwest. There were other competitors—bands like Charlie Johnson's Paradise Band and Cab Calloway's Missourians—but their popularity was relatively short-lived. In New York in the late 1920s, Henderson had only one important and serious rival—Duke Ellington and his Cotton Club Orchestra—and they were showing unbelievable staying power.

Edward Kennedy ("Duke") Ellington is perhaps the most important figure in jazz history. Without distinguishing between one kind of musical composition and another, Gunther Schuller (who is himself one of America's significant composers) said, "Duke Ellington is one of America's great composers."[22] And Whitney Balliett, the noted jazz critic, reflecting the considered opinion of most of the world's jazz critics, wrote, in 1956, "the truth is that Ellington inescapably remains after almost thirty-five years as a professional the richest figure in jazz as well as one of the most inventive, original minds in American music."[23]

Ellington was born in Washington, D.C., in 1899. His middle-class parents started him on piano when he was seven, and by seventeen he was performing for money. He attended a manual training high school where he studied commercial art during the day; evenings he spent listening to and studying ragtime piano music. By the time he was twenty, he had played with many of Washington's best-known smaller dance bands, and he had also married. In 1922, Ellington, drummer Sonny Greer, and saxophonist Toby Hardwick left for a job with a band in New York, were not especially well received by the public, and returned to Washington disgruntled. A year later Ellington was again persuaded, this time by Fats Waller, to return to New York and try again.

After gigging around Harlem nightclubs, gathering little fame and less fortune, Ellington finally found a downtown job for a band at the Hollywood Cafe at 49th Street and Broadway (later called the Kentucky Club); he rounded up his friends and opened there as Duke Ellington and his Washingtonians—a job he was to hold for nearly five years, acquiring as he went along trumpeter Bubber Miley, trombonist Joe ("Tricky Sam") Nanton, baritone saxophonist Harry Carney, banjoist Freddie Guy, bassist Wellman Braud, and others. The most important break in Ellington's career came in December 1927, when his business associate, Irving Mills, arranged an engagement at the Cotton Club, an engagement that would last, on and off, until 1932; and with the addition of Barney Bigard on clarinet, Johnny Hodges on alto saxophone, Cootie Williams and Freddie Jenkins on trumpets, and Juan Tizol on trombone, Ellington's Cotton Club band became the best-known, most admired black band of its time.

Although Ellington's long and distinguished career encompassed a wide variety of stylistic innovations, his contributions arising out of his so-called jungle music have to be counted among his most significant. While it is true that in the 1920s and '30s other musicians were on the "jungle" bandwagon, so to speak (Chick Webb and his Jungle Band, for one), Ellington's work requires special notice. For others, jungle music was a vogue, a passing fancy, to be exploited while the climate was right. Musically, they contributed little or nothing to the style; they wished only to share in what appeared to be commercially sound. Further, perhaps the reasoning went, if it was good enough for Ellington, it ought to be good enough for any band. Ellington, however, was not following a style, he was making one; he was responsible for it. Ellington alone had the requisite talent to make jungle music palatable to the white audience at the Cotton Club; with great skill he succeeded in placing the listener at a safe remove from any hostility the music might express.

It is possible that Ellington and his men saw their jungle presentations as a private joke—corroborating the view of the Cotton Club's big spenders concerning the underlying primitiveness of blacks, and making money from it. Although the band's role in the lavish, jungle-oriented Cotton Club productions was as expert as Ellington and his band could make it, it is conceivable that there was considerable tongue-in-cheek, a high degree of put-on, during the creative process, rehearsal, and performance. However, the enormous success that followed, not only with Cotton Club customers but later with recordings, critics, and the general public, may have given Ellington and his men a different perception of the style, even if, indeed, they had not assigned much value to it at first. It seems likely that jungle music and its connotations could easily have been a passing fancy; but Ellington fashioned it into an established popular style, and his formidable imagination, stimulated and implemented by the men in his band, kept this curiously sultry music alive.

"The 'jungle' style," Schuller wrote in the best technical analysis of the Ellington style extant, "was the first really distinguishable trademark of the Ellington band."[24] What Cotton Club tourists wished to hear in Ellington's jungle music were sounds they could not predict, sounds that would seem to them strange, exotic, primitive, guttural. These expectations gave Ellington the license to try unusual chords, timbres, sonorities (unusual, that is, in the jazz of the time). Trumpeter Bubber Miley's use of the growl and the plunger and special mutes—devices modifying the traditional brass sound—made his instrument sound weird and eerie and somehow "African," as did Tricky Sam Nanton's bizarre, "wah-wah" muted trombone noises. Together, these men helped create what Cotton Club customers thought of as Ellington's jungle sound. Nanton's muted trombone seemed to "talk" to them in the same way African talking drums talked to natives. Later, this style, with its special sounds and effects, would influence the work of jazzmen everywhere.

To complement the "primitive" murals decorating the Cotton Club, Ellington and his band gave thrill seekers "Jungle Nights in Harlem," "Jungle Jamboree," "Jungle Blues," "Echoes of the Jungle" (Barry Ulanov, whose *Duke Ellington*, published in 1946, was the first full-length study of Ellington, entitled one of his chapters "Echoes of the Jungle"), and such tangential pieces as "Doin' the Voom Voom," "Eerie Moan," and "Shakin' the African." (A number of Ellington's Brunswick recordings of 1929 and 1930 are labeled simply "The Jungle Band.")

In searching out 1920s references to white "thrill seekers" traveling the arduous five miles from midtown Manhattan to the Cotton Club (a fifteen-minute ride by taxi), one notices the recurring use of "tourists," "safari," and, of course, "jungle" (West 133rd Street, we may recall, was known as Jungle Alley). Not all references to primitivism, natural states, and jungles, however, came from whites. In 1930, the *Amsterdam News*, a widely read Harlem newspaper, discussing Ellington and his Cotton Club Orchestra, said, "The success of Duke Ellington and his band has fulfilled . . . the Negro's rightful claim to the origination and evolution of jazz. . . . Ellington is the ace of rhythm jazz leaders, and his barbaric style of music is backed by a jungle atmosphere that has made this type of music a sensation."[25]

Ellington's "barbaric style of music," and the "jungle atmosphere" were created specifically for the nightly floor shows at the Cotton Club. Jazz historian Marshall Stearns visited the Cotton

Club one night to hear Ellington and his orchestra, and described the sort of floor show created for downtown voyeurs, to Ellington-inspired musical backgrounds:

> I recall one where a light-skinned and magnificently muscled Negro burst through a papier-mache jungle onto the dance floor, clad in an aviator's helmet, goggles, and shorts. He had obviously been "forced down in darkest Africa," and in the center of the floor he came upon a "white" goddess clad in long golden tresses and being worshipped by a circle of cringing "blacks." Producing a bull whip from heaven knows where, the aviator rescued the blonde and they did an erotic dance. In the background, Bubber Miley, Tricky Sam Nanton, and other members of the Ellington band growled, wheezed, and snorted obscenely.[26]

It is usual to attribute Harlem's great attraction, in the '20s, to simple voyeurism: curious whites traveled uptown where, with a minimum of time and effort, they could safely watch the primitives perform their rites in their native habitat, and by merely looking on they could revitalize their own sexually pale lives. But there may have been more to the Harlem experience than comfortable peeking at unfettered sex—although sex was certainly a part of it. Weighed down by the guilt imposed by civilizing forces, one theory goes, civilized whites are unable to be themselves, enjoy their passions, be natural. Uptown, however, life was lived more or less in the raw; only recently come to civilization, not yet fully civilized, Harlem blacks were unrestrained in their passions, their sex, and of course their music—that jungle music! To be free of restraining influences and conventions is to be innocent, and is not innocence the highest form of sophistication? To partake of this innocence, even vicariously, was to discover the meaning of one's own being before it was lost in the maze of the Protestant ethic and the conventional wisdom. Huggins describes in part what whites expected their journey to Harlem to bring them, and what they may have on occasion found:

In cabarets decorated with tropical and jungle motifs . . . they heard jazz, that almost forbidden music. It was not merely that jazz was exotic, but that it was instinctive and abandoned, yet laughingly light and immediate—melody skipping atop inexorable driving rhythm. The downtown spectator tried to encompass the looseness and freedom of dance. . . . In the darkness and closeness, the music, infectious and unrelenting, drove on. Into its vortex white ladies and gentlemen were pulled, to dance the jungle dance. Heads swayed, rolling, jerking; hair flying free and wild; arms and legs pumping, kicking, thrusting . . . bodies writhing and rolling with a drum and a beat as they might never with a woman or a man.[27]

The Harlem "experience" was, of course, a romantic illusion. Neither blacks nor whites really believed it, but in its time it seemed to be a necessary game for all. At the very least, the game enabled white men and women to feel a therapeutic naughtiness, and, as Huggins put it, "it brought downtown money uptown. What was looked for was found."[28] And Ellington flourished.

What was New York's white jazz scene? As we know, the word *jazz*, in print, was introduced to New York in 1917 by white musicians. Nick LaRocca's Original Dixieland Jazz Band came to New York from Chicago and opened in 1917 at the Paradise Ballroom as "The Jasz Band." A month later they opened at Reisenweber's Restaurant as the "Famous Original Dixieland Jazz Band."[29] The band then toured England, returned to New York, did a vaudeville tour, and again returned to New York, but their popularity was waning. By 1924, the ODJB had run its course, but not before their personal appearances and records had influenced many young white New York musicians, in much the same way the New Orleans Rhythm Kings had influenced the young Chicagoans.

The best survey of the New York white jazz scene immediately before and after World War I is found in Charters and Kunstadt's work. From them we learn that groups playing in New York or recording there included Earl Fuller's band at Rector's

Restaurant, with Ted Lewis on clarinet (Lewis became the leader a year later), Borbee's Jass Band, and the Frisco Jass Band—all white bands playing in 1917, and all heavily influenced by the style and financial success of the ODJB.[30] For purposes of tracing the growth of New York's white jazz scene, however, we need to emphasize the importance of the group called most frequently the Original Memphis Five, which flourished between 1920 and 1923 and included leader Phil Napoleon on trumpet, Miff Mole on trombone, Jimmy Lytell on clarinet, Frank Signorelli on piano, and Jack Roth on drums (Mole, Lytell, and Signorelli were native New Yorkers).

As we enumerate the changes in the group's personnel in the 1920s, we see the network of its influence and the development of the Chicagoans in New York. In 1924, recording as the Cotton Pickers, the group added saxophonist Frankie Trumbauer, who was later to be Bix Beiderbecke's closest friend and associate. A year later we find trumpeter Red Nichols and drummer Vic Berton in the band (Nichols came from Utah in 1923; Berton was a native New Yorker who had brought Beiderbecke and the Wolverines to New York in 1924). By 1928 the group was using Tommy Dorsey on trombone and brother Jimmy on clarinet. A year after that, the piano spot was taken over by Arthur Schutt, a Pennsylvanian who had met Philadelphia-born violinist Joe Venuti just before he, Schutt, had come to New York in 1921. Schutt had worked with Trumbauer, Beiderbecke, Nichols, and Philadelphia-born banjoist Eddie Lang, who as Salvatore Massaro had been a schoolmate of Venuti's, both having played in their school orchestra.

Between 1929 and 1930, Joe Venuti joined the group (now sometimes called Napoleon's Emperors, or the Charleston Chasers), as did clarinetist Fud Livingston—he replaced Jimmy Dorsey and was himself replaced by Benny Goodman, who had recently arrived in New York with former NORK drummer Benny Pollack and his band. In the summer of 1928, Goodman had recorded with the Whoopee Makers, including Jimmy McPartland on cornet, Jack Teagarden on trombone, and Chicagoan Gil Rodin, who had earlier played with Goodman in Pollack's band, on saxophone; the same summer Goodman also played with Irving Mills and His Hotsy Totsy Gang which, in addition to McPartland, Livingston, Eddie Lang, and Goodman's brother Harry on bass, had Ben Pollack on drums. It seemed to be the making of one big happy family.

The connections, however, were not yet complete. When Red Nichols left the Original Memphis Five in 1925, he did not leave his colleagues; he wished only to be a leader, to record under his *own* name whenever possible. In the mid-'20s the opportunities seemed limitless. Lanin's Red Heads in 1925 (starring red-headed Nichols and dark-haired Venuti) became the Red Heads (Nichols, Mole, Schutt, Jimmy Dorsey, Berton, and others) and, finally, in 1926, Red Nichols and His Five Pennies (Mole, Schutt, Jimmy Dorsey, Lang, and Berton). Between 1925 and 1932 the Five Pennies recorded about 130 sides, and again as many under such names as the Louisiana Rhythm Kings, the Six Hottentots, and the Midnight Airedales. The numbers in the band varied between six and ten, and leader Nichols showed strong preference for members of the "family," at least when they were available. At the peak of its popularity, a Red Nichols group might have Teagarden or Glenn Miller or Tommy Dorsey on trombone, Benny Goodman on clarinet, Livingston on tenor saxophone, and Gene Krupa or Davie Tough on drums. The game of musical chairs provided a goodly amount of recording-studio jobs for family members. Ben Pollack, of course, helped too; his 1929 orchestra included Jimmy McPartland, brother Dick on banjo, Teagarden, Gil Rodin, Goodman, and brother Harry on bass, with Ray Bauduc on drums.

Paul Whiteman also supported a small branch of the family. If there was only one name to be associated with white jazz in the 1920s, it would have to be Whiteman's. In the mind of the general public, both at home and abroad, Whiteman was the King of Jazz. He had styled himself so since the early '20s, and when he commissioned Gershwin's *Rhapsody in Blue* in 1924, his "jazz" image was reinforced; finally, when advertisements appeared for the 1930 motion picture *The King of Jazz*, the general public did not have to be told who the king was. Whiteman's "symphonic jazz" band was certainly the best-known band of the '20s, and at various times included Beiderbecke, Tommy and Jimmy Dorsey, Frank Trumbauer, Eddie Lang, Joe Venuti, Fud Livingston, and a host of other jazzmen who would become famous in the decades to follow.

It is somewhat surprising not to find Benny Goodman listed somewhere as having played with Whiteman's band; but even if some such reference should turn up, it would only prove the exception. Goodman, as we have seen earlier, stood on the fringe of the first-rank family of Chicagoans because they were aware that he was different—he did not need them. He proved this again in New York when he left Pollack's band to seek work on his own and think about becoming a leader. In the spring of 1928 he had had a taste of leadership with a record of Benny Goodman's Boys (the boys being mainly Irving Mills' Hotsy Totsy Gang), and with another by Goody and His Good Timers. But apparently his main chance had not yet come.[31] He continued to make records as a sideman with Red Nichols, Hoagy Carmichael, Ethel Waters, Lee Morse, Bix Beiderbecke, and a dozen others, and in 1931 he led a pit band for a Broadway revue that flopped. In 1933 he met the jazz entrepreneur John Hammond, who encouraged Goodman to assemble a band for a number of recordings to be made by two English companies; the result showed Goodman to have the necessary organizing ability. Early in 1934 he organized a band to audition for a job, at the new Billy Rose's Music Hall, that included five brass, four reeds, and four rhythm instruments—the essentially complete swing band. In September he won a spot on the National Broadcasting Company's weekly three-hour radio program, "Let's Dance," sharing it with Xavier Cugat's rhumba band and Kel Murray's society band. By the time Goodman—whose "hot" band had the last hour, 1:00 to 2:00 A.M.—had been heard on fifty-three NBC radio stations, coast to coast, week after week for twenty-six weeks, his success was assured, and the swing era had been ushered in.

In short order Benny Goodman became the King of Swing. With the help of big-band arrangements by Fletcher Henderson

(Goodman said, "Fletcher was the man who really made the band"[32]), the Goodman band became the model of success for all aspiring white swing bands, among the best known of which would later be Glen Gray, Tommy and Jimmy Dorsey, Woody Herman, Artie Shaw, Glenn Miller, and those who left Goodman's band, frequently with his financial backing, to lead their own bands: Gene Krupa, Harry James, Ziggy Elman, Teddy Wilson, and Lionel Hampton. We may also recall that it was through Goodman's efforts that Count Basie came from Kansas City to New York.

Basie, supported by John Hammond and agent Willard Alexander, arrived in New York in 1936 to open at the Roseland Ballroom. The Kansas City band's early public reception was less than enthusiastic. The band's sound may have been too raw, the ensemble too imprecise. The band Hammond had heard in Kansas City had nine pieces; for the Roseland debut five pieces were added. Basie's Kansas City specialty had been his band's "head" arrangements—ideas agreed upon during rehearsal, but not written down—full of provocative riffs behind exciting solo improvisations. Now with a library of arrangements on loan from Fletcher Henderson (with Goodman's blessing), written for six brass, four reeds, and four rhythm, Basie and his band were clearly out of their element. At the Roseland the band was frequently out of tune, the ensemble was ragged, and, most of all, they lacked bigband experience. Hammond and Alexander recognized the band's frustration and, when the Roseland job was finished, booked them into the Famous Door, a nightclub more suited to Basie's Kansas City style. Heavy advertising and promotion insured a standing-room-only opening-night audience, and the band, allowed to do what they did best, responded enthusiastically. Later, after several years of intensive rehearsals and experience Basie's band learned to handle big-band arrangements almost as well as their "head" arrangements and was one of the most famous and most admired black bands in the country. Basie said, "I wanted my fifteen-piece band to work together just like those nine pieces did."[33] Basie's band of 1939, which many believe was the best band he had, included Earl Warren on alto saxophone; Lester Young and Buddy Tate on tenor saxophones; Jack Washington on alto and baritone saxophones; Ed Lewis, Buck Clayton, Shad Collins, and Harry Edison on trumpets; Benny Morton, Dickie Wells, and Dan Minor on trombones; Jo Jones on drums; Walter Page on bass; Freddie Green on guitar; Jimmy Rushing on vocals; and Basie on piano. It is essential to note that of the sixteen men listed here, eight had been with Basie since the Kansas City days—Young, Washington, Lewis, Clayton, Minor, Jones, Page, and Rushing. And, of course, there was Basie himself.

The bands of Basie, Ellington, and Henderson were among the best bands in New York, black or white, and certainly among the best-known black bands. There was, of course, a profusion of competent minor black bands that contributed little to the development of jazz. Then there were others whose popularity was short-lived and who were not so well known to the white community as the major black bands, but who were historically important. The following are in that class, and their leaders are worthy of special mention: Cab Calloway came to Chicago from Baltimore as a young man, later took the Alabamians, a Chicago band, to New York in 1928, and then took over the Missourians; his principal fame, however, came in 1931 with his scat-vocal version of "Minnie the Moocher." Benny Carter, a native New Yorker, took over the direction of McKinney's Cotton Pickers when Don Redman left them; later, between 1932 and 1934, he led his own band. Andy Kirk, whose work we noted in Kansas City, appeared in New York quite regularly; between 1930 and 1931 he made successful appearances at the Savoy Ballroom and the Roseland Ballroom. Jimmy Lunceford was a jazzman on the move: born in Fulton, Missouri, he attended high school in Denver, played in New York while he was in his early twenties, moved to Memphis to become a high school music teacher, played in various bands in Ohio, returned to New York in 1933, and a year later opened at the Cotton Club. Chick Webb came to New York from Baltimore in 1925, at age sixteen, and two years later led a band at the Savoy Ballroom;

in 1935 he added Ella Fitzgerald to the band, and in 1937 successfully challenged Benny Goodman's band at the Savoy. Erskine Hawkins came to New York from Birmingham, Alabama, in 1936, and became well known in New York for his blues band; with his band's recording of "Tuxedo Junction" (the forerunner of Glenn Miller's version), Hawkins became a familiar name. Claude Hopkins was more popular with New York's black community than with the white. Born in Virginia and raised in Washington, D.C., he came to New York in 1924, toured Europe, and returned to New York in 1930, where for the next five years he appeared regularly at the Roseland Ballroom and at the Savoy. Fats Waller, a native New Yorker, played mostly with small groups—Fats Waller and His Rhythm; from time to time he would appear with a big band whose principal function was to provide background for Waller's engaging singing and stride piano. Luis Russell touched nearly all the jazz bases: He arrived in New Orleans in 1919, at age seventeen, from his home in Panama, went to Chicago in 1924, and moved to New York in 1927 to open at Harlem's Nest Club; during the next several years he played the Savoy Ballroom and Connie's Inn, and later led Louis Armstrong's backup band. Louis Armstrong, as we know, first came to New York to join Fletcher Henderson in 1924, and returned to Chicago about a year later. In the winter of 1929, Armstrong and Chicago band leader Carroll Dickerson, with whose band Armstrong had been playing, came to New York with Armstrong as the band's leader. Soon after their arrival they opened at Connie's Inn, after which Armstrong moved on to the *Hot Chocolates* Broadway revue, worked with Luis Russell's backup band, and went on to his spectacular and unprecedented popular success. Although Armstrong led a number of big bands, "Louis Armstrong and his Orchestra" generally meant Louis Armstrong, the world's foremost jazz trumpeter and jazz singer, and friends.

In 1933, a year before NBC introduced Goodman to late-night dancers, the Twenty-first Amendment to the Constitution was ratified, repealing the Eighteenth Amendment, and

Prohibition—except for local options—was over. Public drinking was easy now. It was no longer necessary to seek out speakeasies and "blind pigs"; liquor could now be served openly in public places, in glasses instead of teacups. Legitimate restaurants, hotels, nightclubs, and dance halls no longer had to compete with places selling liquor illegally, and the boom was on. Hotels could now provide guests with lodging, food, drink, dancing, and entertainment all under one roof. Major hotels created special "rooms," often exotically decked out, with such prepossessing names as the Persian Room, Madhattan Room, Gold Room, Empire Room, and Royal Box. Along with the new "rooms" and new bars, new dance floors were installed, and bands to play for dancing and floor shows became commonplace. The wage-scale for union musicians was relatively low, and musicians (still accustomed to Depression wages) were happy to find jobs opening up everywhere. For the hotels and nightspots, the cost of hiring a big band was not yet the major expense it would later become, and big bands—the first-rate, the mediocre, and the poor—grew in numbers beyond belief. The hotel and allied service industries were joined by the advertising, broadcasting, and recording industries to bring favored bands almost instantaneous fame and popularity and big money. Elsewhere, I wrote:

> Working almost as if by plan, the national broadcasters piped hotel music to hundreds of thousands of people who would then flock to dance halls and theaters to hear these same bands on tour, after which the broadcasters could sell the bands to sponsors who wished their products to be associated with these by now "name bands."[34]

As more and more band leaders and former sidemen entered the wide-open doors of the swing-band industry, the emphasis shifted from creativity in the music—the essence of jazz—to the talent and personality of the leader himself. There were, of course, attempts by band leaders, managers, and agents to distinguish one name band from another—the gurgling sound that introduced the "Rippling Rhythms" of Shep Fields, the "Ellington sound," the

"Glenn Miller sound," along with identifying "theme songs"—but on the whole, swing audiences bought Goodman and Shaw and Ellington and Miller in the same sense symphony audiences bought Stokowski and Koussevitsky—the identity of the orchestra was incidental.

What was not merely incidental (and made it impossible for the prevailing style, swing, to continue to flourish) was the lack of encouragement to jazzmen with the ability to create significant solo improvisations. While creative sidemen might be content to subordinate themselves to leaders who were themselves first-rate soloists, it soon became clear that there was little place for creative soloists in a group led by a non-performing personality, because the success of an individual band member could be an embarrassment to the leader. Everyone, it seemed, wished to be a star, and many sidemen sought to lead their own bands, to become stars in their own right. Stardom, however, was the province of those leaders most heavily promoted and advertised by the agencies. The most financially successful of the stars saw their sidemen as interchangeable parts—to be trusted only if they understood their obligation and responsibility to the leader, the acknowledged star. (Goodman, for one, had over 150 sidemen pass through his band.) As Charters and Kunstadt put it:

> The musicians moved from band to band, most of them losing any distinctive musical identity. Behind the elegant face that swing presented to the public was a nervous, tensely competitive entertainment industry that was exploiting the new style. If the music, despite its technical brilliance, often sounds shrilly empty, it is this, rather than the musicians, that is to blame.[35]

And it was the sameness of the music of the swing era that would eventually bring about its end. The formulas created by Don Redman and polished to a hard brilliance by Henderson were difficult to create, but easy to imitate. Swing-band arrangements—for six or seven brass, four or five reeds, and a rhythm section—were cobbled together and distributed in the thousands until, by the end of the '30s, what used to be a $37.50 Henderson-type arrangement became a stock arrangement that could be bought in any music store for a dollar or two.

The result of the proliferation of bands and big-band arrangements in which improvised solos (except sometimes for the leader's) were kept to the barest minimum, and which were usually arrangements of the popular songs of the day, full of the ubiquitous flaring "do-wahs" of the brass and the monotony of riffs grown old with repetition—all of it merchandised in the name of swing—created a general confusion in the public mind. What was all this to be called? Popular music was swing, the reasoning went, and swing was jazz; therefore, popular music was jazz. Besides, listening to "jazz" was much more sophisticated than listening to mere popular music. That the majority of bands were making fewer and fewer attempts to include solo improvisation in their performances meant little to the general public. In the industry itself it soon became evident that readers (nonimprovisers) were likely to be better paid and to work more regularly than nonreaders (improvisers)—simply corroborating what all jazzmen have known from earliest jazz times. Further, good improvisers were not to be trusted; like their solos, they were unpredictable and therefore (it was believed) unreliable, or even irresponsible. The swing industry was serious big business, with millions of dollars at stake, and there was little reward for jazzmen whose work and lives were unpredictable, unreliable, and irresponsible—adjectives previously associated with the "jazz life" best personified by such jazzmen as Bix Beiderbecke, Mezz Mezzrow, and the young Chicagoans.

The New Orleans style, as it came to Chicago and that city's aspiring young jazzmen, eventually became as old-fashioned as pride, adolescent loyalty, hard work, and playing for the love of it. While many musicians still have these qualities, or the capacity to develop these qualities within them (what we might think of as Ellington's "right" product), there may no longer be another "right" time or "right" place. Richard Hadlock, writing in 1965, discusses this interesting question, perhaps a bit nostalgically:

> There can never be another group like the Chicagoans, for they represent the coming together of two provincial forces—the New Orleans musical fraternity and the Chicago jazz gang—and the sturdy music that resulted from this meeting. . . . As the swing era, during which each of the Chicagoans reached the apex of his creative powers, came to a close, members of the old gang either withdrew from the competitive arena or huddled together for protection again—this time against the shift to modern jazz. . . . So the music of the Chicagoans came and went. Their records tell us how good it was—while it lasted.[36]

The Chicagoans were not alone in their bewilderment. The coming together in New York of jazzmen from everywhere continued the cross-fertilization of the 1920s and '30s that began when outside jazzmen visited New Orleans before World War I and New Orleans jazzmen went to Chicago and other points during and after the war. We have seen the frustration of the Kansas City jazzmen immediately after their arrival in New York, their early attempt and failure to do what everyone else in New York was doing, and their subsequent (but still temporary) reversion to their own style. Historically speaking, their initial failure was a blessing in disguise. Hsio points out that the coming of Basie and southwestern jazzmen to New York "revitalized big-band jazz"—implying, of course, that without this infusion of new life, big-band jazz would have withered away even sooner than it did. Emphasizing this point, Hsio notes what happened later, when new infusions were no longer forthcoming and cross-fertilization was contained—the restraining agent being the ever-growing popularity and style (and sameness) of the Henderson big-band arrangements:

> The increasing popularity of swing arrangements on the Henderson model led to a general similarity of style in all the big bands, Negro

and white. Goodman, Shaw, the Dorseys, Barnet, Hines, Calloway, Teddy Hill, Webb were all approaching the same standards of proficiency. . . . By the early 1940s the gradual elimination of stylistic variations had killed big-band jazz. It was a death by entropy.[37]

Jazz, of course, would go on. New ideas would be added to old styles, and new styles would emerge. But there would be no "new" jazz cities (although some, like Boston, would make creditable attempts to be one); and the old jazz cities would lose their former spirit and cachet. New Orleans would never again regain its position as a jazz center, except as a tourist oddity; Chicago would lose its position as a center of traditional jazz to San Francisco; Kansas City would go on to produce Charlie Parker, and then withdraw as a major jazz center, concerned mainly with the physical restoration of early nightspots; and New York would have to share much of its earlier attraction with Los Angeles. The effect of the Second World War on mobility, and the creation of new employment centers, new transport cities; the effects of urban development—the razing of old jazz neighborhoods followed by the construction of housing projects, high-rise buildings, and freeways; the effect of union wages on jobs for jazzmen and the desire of jazzmen to live ordinary, consumer-oriented lives—all would contribute to the decentralization of jazz. The music itself, however, would continue to burgeon, to flourish, and on occasion be declared dead, only once again to turn up, fully resurrected.

NOTES

CHAPTER 1

1. Charles L. Dufour, "The People of New Orleans," in *The Past as Prelude*, edited by Hodding Carter (New Orleans: Pelican Publishing House, 1968), pp. 26–27.

2. Ibid., p. 29.

3. Hodding Carter, *Lower Mississippi* (New York: Farrar and Rinehart, 1942), p. 40.

4. W. J. Cash, *The Mind of the South* (New York: Vintage Books, 1941), p. 5.

5. Herbert Asbury, *The French Quarter* (New York: Garden City Publishing Co., 1938), p. 36.

6. James Marston Fitch, "Creole Architecture, 1718–1860: The Rise and Fall of a Great Tradition," in Carter, *The Past as Prelude*, pp. 74–75.

7. Ibid., p. 79.

8. Carter, *Lower Mississippi*, p. 302.

9. John Hope Franklin, *From Slavery to Freedom*, 3rd ed. (New York: Alfred A. Knopf, 1967), p. 57.

10. Ibid., p. 59.

11. George W. Cable, *The Negro Question*, edited by Arlin Turner (New York: W. W. Norton, 1958), p. 54.

12. Franklin, *From Slavery to Freedom*, p. 30.

13. Ibid., p. 35.

14. Robert C. Reinders, *End of an Era: New Orleans, 1850–1860* (New Orleans: Pelican Publishing Co., 1964), p. 28.

15. Melville J. Herskovits, *The American Negro*, originally published by Alfred A. Knopf, 1928 (Bloomington: Indiana University Press, 1964), p. 3.

16. Mark Twain, *Life on the Mississippi* (New York: Harper and Brothers, 1901), p. 310.

17. Cash, *The Mind of the South*, p. 147.

18. Joy J. Jackson, *New Orleans in the Gilded Age* (Baton Rouge: Louisiana State University Press, 1969), p. 303.

19. Ibid., p. 285.

20. Grace King, *Creole Families of New Orleans* (New York: Macmillan, 1921), p. 3.

21. Ibid., p. 230.

22. M. A. Roussève, *The Negro in Louisiana* (New Orleans: Xavier University Press, 1937), pp. 23–26.

23. Reinders, *End of an Era*, p. 25.

24. Henry Kmen, *Music in New Orleans: The Formative Years, 1791–1841* (Baton Rouge: Louisiana State University Press, 1967), pp. 47–48.

25. Ibid., p. 49.

26. George W. Cable, *Old Creole Days* (New York: Charles Scribner's Sons, 1900), p. 7.

27. Phil Johnson, "Good Time Town," in Carter, *The Past as Prelude*, p. 237.

28. Reinders, *End of an Era*, p. 66.

29. Roger W. Shugg, *Origins of Class Struggle in Louisiana* (Baton Rouge: Louisiana State University Press, 1939), p. 58.

30. Ibid., p. 85.

31. Reinders, *End of an Era*, p. 5.

CHAPTER 2

1. Arthur Scully, Jr., *James Dakin, Architect* (Baton Rouge: Louisiana State University Press, 1973), p. 39.

2. Gerald M. Capers, *Occupied City: New Orleans Under the Federals, 1862–1865* (Lexington: University of Kentucky Press, 1965), p. 10.

3. Roger W. Shugg, *Origins of Class Struggle in Louisiana* (Baton Rouge: Louisiana State University Press, 1939), p. 54.

4. Joy J. Jackson, *New Orleans in the Gilded Age* (Baton Rouge: Louisiana State University Press, 1969), p. 188.

5. Robert C. Reinders, *End of an Era: New Orleans, 1850–1860* (New Orleans: Pelican Publishing Co., 1964), p. 168.

6. Henry Kmen, *Music in New Orleans: The Formative Years, 1791–1841* (Baton Rouge: Louisiana State University, 1967), p. 203.

7. John W. Blassingame, *Black New Orleans, 1860–1880* (Chicago: University of Chicago Press, 1973), p. 3.

8. Capers, *Occupied City*, p. 67.

9. Ibid., p. 204.

10. W. J. Cash, *The Mind of the South* (New York: Vintage Books, 1941), pp. 116–17.

11. Blassingame, *Black New Orleans*, p. 156.

12. Lee Collins, *Oh, Didn't He Ramble: The Life Story of Lee Collins,* as told to

Mary Collins, edited by Frank J. Gillis and John W. Miner (Urbana: University of Illinois Press, 1974), p. 45.

13. Ibid., p. 44.

14. Pops Foster, *The Autobiography of a New Orleans Jazzman*, as told to Tom Stoddard (Berkeley: University of California Press, 1971), p. 65.

15. Ibid., pp. 61–62.

16. Samuel B. Charters, *Jazz: New Orleans, 1885–1957*, rev. ed. (New York: Oak Publications, 1963), p. 45.

17. Ibid., p. 3.

18. Herbert Asbury, *The French Quarter* (New York: Garden City Publishing Co., 1938), pp. 233, 387.

19. Al Rose, *Storyville, New Orleans* (University:University of Alabama Press, 1974), p. 216.

20. Ibid., p. 3.

21. Quoted in Nat Shapiro and Nat Hentoff, eds., *Hear Me Talkin' to Ya* (New York: Rinehart and Co., 1955), p. 11.

22. Sidney Bechet, *Treat It Gentle* (New York: Hill and Wang, 1960), p. 53.

23. Quoted in Shapiro and Hentoff, *Hear Me Talkin' to Ya*, p. 7.

24. Quoted in ibid., p. 12.

25. Foster, *Autobiography*, p. 30.

26. Rose, *Storyville, New Orleans*, p. 124.

27. Collins, *Oh, Didn't He Ramble*, p. 44.

28. Foster, *Autobiography*, p. 16.

29. William Russell and Stephen Smith, "New Orleans Music," in *Jazzmen*, edited by Frederic Ramsey, Jr. and Charles Edward Smith (New York: Harcourt, Brace and Co., 1939), p. 35.

30. Asbury, *The French Quarter*, p. 437.

31. Rudi Blesh, *Shining Trumpets: A History of Jazz*, rev. ed. (New York: Alfred A. Knopf, 1958), p. 201.

32. Bechet, *Treat It Gentle*, p. 48.

CHAPTER 3

1. John Smith Kendall, "The French Quarter Sixty Years Ago," *Louisiana Historical Quarterly* 24 (April 1951): 91.

2. Ibid., p. 92.

3. Ibid., pp. 91–102.

4. Joy J. Jackson, *New Orleans in the Gilded Age* (Baton Rouge: Louisiana State University Press, 1969), p. 63.

5. Ibid., p. 64.

6. Ibid., p. 234.

7. Irving Sablosky, *American Music* (Chicago: University of Chicago Press, 1969), p. 62.

8. Ibid.

9. Sidney Bechet, *Treat It Gentle* (New York: Hill and Wang, 1960), p. 215.

10. Louis Armstrong, *Satchmo* (New York: New American Library, 1955), p. 73.

11. Martin Williams, *Jazz Masters of New Orleans* (New York: Macmillan, 1967), p. 181.

12. Lee Collins, *Oh, Didn't He Ramble: The Life Story of Lee Collins*, as told to Mary Collins, edited by Frank J. Gillis and John W. Miner (Urbana: University of Illinois Press, 1974), p. 20.

13. Samuel B. Charters, *Jazz: New Orleans, 1885–1957*, rev. ed. (New York: Oak Publications, 1963), p. 19.

14. See A. M. Jones, *Studies in African Music*, 2 vols. (London: Oxford University Press, 1959).

15. Edward Larocque Tinker, "Gombo: The Creole Dialect of Louisiana," *Proceedings of the American Antiquarian Society* 45, no. 1 (1935): 116.

16. Quoted in Bernard Katz, *The Social Implications of Early Negro Music in the United States* (New York: Arno Press, 1969), pp. 41–42.

17. Quoted in ibid., p. 35.

18. Quoted in ibid., p. xix.

19. Quoted in ibid., p. xviii.

20. Sablosky, *American Music*, p. 45.

21. Nathan Irvin Huggins, *Harlem Renaissance* (New York: Oxford University Press, 1971), p. 273.

22. Rudi Blesh, *Shining Trumpets: A History of Jazz*, rev. ed. (New York: Alfred A. Knopf, 1958), p. 168.

23. Quoted in Jack V. Buerkle and Danny Barker, *Bourbon Street Black* (New York: Oxford University Press, 1973), p. 60.

24. Charters, *Jazz: New Orleans*, pp. 2, 14.

25. Ibid., p. 8.

26. Eileen Southern, *The Music of Black Americans: A History* (New York: W. W. Norton, 1971), p. 142.

27. Bechet, *Treat It Gentle*, pp. 69, 95.

28. Quoted in Nat Shapiro and Nat Hentoff, eds., *Hear Me Talkin' to Ya* (New York: Rinehart and Co., 1955), p. 19.

29. Armstrong, *Satchmo*, pp. 77–78.

30. Collins, *Oh Didn't He Ramble*, p. 14.

31. H. O. Brunn, *The Story of the Original Dixieland Jazz Band* (Baton Rouge: Louisiana State University Press, 1960), p. 2.

32. Al Rose and E. Souchon, *New Orleans Jazz: A Family Album* (Baton Rouge: Louisiana University Press, 1967), p. 130.

33. Quoted in Blesh, *Shining Trumpets*, pp. 156–57.

34. William J. Schafer and Johannes Riedel, *The Art of Ragtime* (Baton Rouge: Louisiana State University Press, 1973), p. 5.

35. Ibid., p. xii.

36. Gunther Schuller, *Early Jazz: Its Roots and Musical Development* (New York: Oxford University Press, 1968), p. 139.

37. Pops Foster, *The Autobiography of a New Orleans Jazzman*, as told to Tom Stoddard (Berkeley: University of California Press, 1971), p. 41.

38. Collins, *Oh, Didn't He Ramble*, p. 5.

39. Rudi Blesh and Harriet Janis, *They All Played Ragtime* (New York: Oak Publications, 1966), p. 23.

40. Blesh, *Shining Trumpets*, p. 208.

41. Schuller, *Early Jazz*, p. 71.

42. Ibid., pp. 55, 62.

43. Leroy Ostransky, *The Anatomy of Jazz* (Seattle: University of Washington Press, 1960), pp. 157–58.

44. Southern, *The Music of Black Americans*, p. 359.

45. Charters, *Jazz: New Orleans*, p. 20.

46. Blesh and Janis, *They All Played Ragtime*, p. 17.

47. Quoted in Al Rose, *Storyville, New Orleans* (University: University of Alabama Press, 1974), p. 167.

CHAPTER 4

1. Marshall Stearns, *The Story of Jazz* (New York: Oxford University Press, 1956), p. 118.

2. John Steiner, "Chicago," in *Jazz*, edited by Nat Hentoff and Albert McCarthy (New York: Rinehart and Co., 1959), p. 141.

3. Pops Foster, *The Autobiography of a New Orleans Jazzman*, as told to Tom Stoddard (Berkeley: University of California Press, 1971), p. 37.

4. Eileen Southern, *The Music of Black Americans* (New York: W. W. Norton, 1971), p. 337.

5. Steiner, "Chicago," p. 145.

6. Ibid., p. 145.

7. Sidney Bechet, *Treat It Gentle* (New York: Hill and Wang, 1960), p. 116.

8. Al Rose, *Storyville, New Orleans* (University: University of Alabama Press, 1974), p. 69.

9. Frederic Ramsey, Jr., and Charles Edward Smith, eds., *Jazzmen* (New York: Harcourt, Brace, 1939), p. 95.

10. Quoted in Nat Shapiro and Nat Hentoff, eds., *Hear Me Talkin' to Ya* (New York: Rinehart and Co., 1955), p. 90.

11. Mezz Mezzrow and Bernard Wolfe, *Really the Blues* (New York: Random House, 1946), p. 23.

12. H. O. Brunn, *The Story of the Original Dixieland Jazz Band* (Baton Rouge: Louisiana State University Press, 1960), p. 26.

13. Gunther Schuller, *Early Jazz: Its Roots and Musical Development* (New York: Oxford University Press, 1968), p. 178.

14. Al Rose and E. Souchon, *New Orleans Jazz: A Family Album* (Baton Rouge: Louisiana State University Press, 1967), p. 21.

15. Brunn, *Original Dixieland Jazz Band*, pp. 27–28.

16. Quoted in Shapiro and Hentoff, *Hear Me Talkin' to Ya*, p. 83.

17. Steiner, "Chicago," p. 149.

18. John Sirjamaki, *The Sociology of Cities* (New York: Random House, 1964), p. 19.

19. Bessie Louise Pierce, *A History of Chicago* (New York: Alfred A. Knopf, 1937), 1: 12.

20. Ibid., 1: 14.

21. Ibid., 1: 413.

22. Edith Abbott, *The Tenements of Chicago, 1908–1935* (Chicago: University of Chicago Press, 1936), p. 1.

23. Ibid., p. 14.

24. St. Clair Drake and Horace R. Cayton, *Black Metropolis* (New York: Harcourt, Brace, 1945), p. 20.

25. Carl W. Condit, *The Chicago School of Architecture* (Chicago: University of Chicago Press, 1964), p. 15.

26. Ibid., p. 18.

27. Pierce, *History of Chicago*, 1: 478.

28. Harold F. Gosnell, *Negro Politicians* (Chicago: University of Chicago Press, 1967), p. 13.

29. Lincoln Steffens, *The Shame of the Cities* (New York: Peter Smith, 1948 [first published 1904]), p. 243.

30. Quoted in Jack P. Kornfeld, ed., *A Study of Organized Crime in Illinois* (Chicago: Illinois Law Enforcement Commission, 1972), p. 113.

31. Archibald Byrne, "Walter L. Newberry's Chicago," *Newberry Library Bulletin* 3 (August 1955): 262–63, quoted in Condit, *Chicago School of Architecture* p. 18.

32. John M. Allswang, *A House for All Peoples* (Lexington: University Press of Kentucky, 1971), p. 16.

33. Pierce, *History of Chicago*, 2: 482.

34. Quoted in Richard T. Ely, ed., *Hull-House Maps and Papers* (New York: Thomas Y. Crowell, 1895), p. 3.

35. Quoted in ibid., p. 17.

36. Quoted in ibid., p. 22

37. Pierce, *History of Chicago*, 2: 431.

38. Ibid., 2: 435.

39. Lloyd Wendt and Herman Kogan, *Big Bill of Chicago* (New York: Bobbs-Merrill Co., 1953), p. 34.

40. Ibid., p. 37.

41. Ibid., p. 35.

42. Walter C. Reckless, *Vice in Chicago* (Chicago: University of Chicago Press, 1933), p. 101.

43. Ibid., p. 102.

44. Kornfeld, *Organized Crime in Illinois*, p. 117.

45. Reckless, *Vice in Chicago*, p. 70.

46. Ibid., p. 83.

47. Wendt, *Big Bill of Chicago*, p. 139.

48. Gosnell, *Negro Politicians*, p. 127.

49. Ibid., p. 131.

50. Chicago Commission on Race Relations, *The Negro in Chicago* (Chicago: University of Chicago Press, 1922), p. 622.

51. Reckless, *Vice in Chicago*, p. 22.

CHAPTER 5

1. Otis Dudley Duncan and Beverly Duncan, *The Negro Population of Chicago* (Chicago: University of Chicago Press, 1957), p. 21.
2. Chicago Commission on Race Relations, *The Negro in Chicago* (Chicago: University of Chicago Press, 1922), p. 139.
3. Edith Abbott, *The Tenements of Chicago, 1908–1935* (Chicago: University of Chicago Press, 1936), p. 318.
4. Chicago Commission, *The Negro in Chicago*, p. 140.
5. Allan H. Spear, *Black Chicago* (Chicago: University of Chicago Press, 1967), p. 126.
6. Duncan and Duncan, *The Negro Population*, p. 34.
7. Chicago Commission, *The Negro in Chicago*, p. 87.
8. U.S., Bureau of the Census, *Fourteenth U.S. Census, 1920* (Washington, D.C.: Government Printing Office).
9. Chicago Commission, *The Negro in Chicago*, p. 93.
10. Quoted in Spear, *Black Chicago*, p. 25.
11. Abbott, *Tenements of Chicago*, pp. 69–70.
12. Chicago Commission, *The Negro in Chicago*, p. 153.
13. Abbott, *Tenements of Chicago*, p. 319.
14. St. Clair Drake and Horace R. Cayton, *Black Metropolis* (New York: Harcourt, Brace, 1945), p. 178.
15. Spear, *Black Chicago*, p. 29.
16. U.S., Bureau of the Census, *Twelfth U.S. Census, 1900,* and *Thirteenth U.S. Census, 1910.*
17. Drake and Cayton, *Black Metropolis*, p. 220.
18. Alma Herbst, *The Negro in the Slaughtering and Meat-Packing Industry in Chicago* (New York: Houghton Mifflin, 1932), p. xxii.
19. Spear, *Black Chicago*, p. 168.
20. Drake and Cayton, *Black Metropolis*, p. 525.
21. Ibid., pp. 388–89.
22. Ibid., p. 609.
23. Ibid., p. 610.
24. Harold F. Gosnell, *Negro Politicians* (Chicago: University of Chicago Press), p. 115.
25. Lloyd Wendt and Herman Kogan, *Big Bill of Chicago* (New York: Bobbs-Merrill, 1953), pp. 95–104.

26. Ibid., p. 121.

27. Gosnell, *Negro Politicians*, pp. 40–41.

28. John M. Allswang, *A House for all Peoples* (Lexington: University Press of Kentucky, 1971), p. 161.

29. Quoted in Gosnell, *Negro Politicians*, p. 41.

30. Ibid., p. 55.

31. Ibid., p. 62.

32. Quoted in Wendt and Kogan, *Big Bill of Chicago*, p. 156.

33. Quoted in ibid., p. 192.

34. Ibid., p. 204.

35. Jack B. Kornfeld, ed., *A Study of Organized Crime in Illinois* (Chicago: Illinois Law Enforcement Commission, 1972), p. 122.

36. Wendt and Kogan, *Big Bill of Chicago*, p. 276.

CHAPTER 6

1. Walter C. Reckless, *Vice in Chicago* (Chicago: University of Chicago Press, 1933), p. 161.

2. Ibid., p. 113.

3. Ibid., p. 122.

4. Quoted in Whitney Balliett, *The New Yorker*, August 18, 1975, pp. 36–37.

5. Eddie Condon, *We Called It Music*, as told to Thomas Sugrue (New York: Henry Holt and Co., 1947), p. 135.

6. Quoted in Nat Shapiro and Nat Hentoff, eds., *Hear Me Talkin' to Ya* (New York: Rinehart and Co., 1955), p. 130.

7. Benny Goodman and Irving Kolodin, *The Kingdom of Swing* (Harrisburg, Pa.: Stackpole and Co., 1939), p. 73.

8. Ibid., p. 79.

9. Condon, *We Called It Music*, p. 123.

10. Ibid., p. 112.

11. Quoted in Shapiro and Hentoff, *Hear Me Talkin' to Ya*, p. 107.

12. Reckless, *Vice in Chicago*, p. 133.

13. Quoted in ibid., p. 87.

14. Quoted in Dave Dexter, Jr., *The Jazz Story* (Englewood Cliffs, N.J.: Prentice-Hall, 1964), p. 39.

15. Frederic Ramsey, Jr., and Charles Edward Smith, eds., *Jazzmen* (New York: Harcourt, Brace, 1939), p. 96.

16. Quoted in Shapiro and Hentoff, *Hear Me Talkin' to Ya*, pp. 86–88.

17. Albert McCarthy, *Big Band Jazz* (New York: G. P. Putnam's Sons, 1974), p. 20.

18. Ramsey and Smith, *Jazzmen*, p. 70.

19. Edmond Souchon, "King Oliver: A Very Personal Memoir," in *Jazz Panorama*, edited by Martin Williams (New York: Crowell-Collier, 1962), pp. 28–30.

20. Sidney Finkelstein, *Jazz: A People's Music* (New York: Citadel Press, 1948), p. 24.

21. Richard Hadlock, *Jazz Masters of the Twenties* (New York: Macmillan, 1965), p. 14.

22. Quoted in ibid.

23. Ibid., p. 24.

24. Shapiro and Hentoff, *Hear Me Talkin' to Ya*, p. 81.

25. Ibid., pp. 119–21.

26. Hadlock, *Jazz Masters of the Twenties*, p. 106.

27. Dexter, *Jazz Story*, p. 36.

28. Neil Leonard, *Jazz and the White Americans* (Chicago: University of Chicago Press, 1962), p. 66.

29. R. M. Sudhalter and P. R. Evans, with William Dean-Myatt, *Bix: Man and Legend* (New York: Arlington House, 1974), p. 343.

30. Béla Bartók, *Hungarian Folk Music* (New York: Oxford University Press, 1931), pp. 2–3.

31. Quoted in Shapiro and Hentoff, *Hear Me Talkin' to Ya*, p. 139.

32. Condon, *We Called It Music*, p. 148.

33. Hadlock, *Jazz Masters of the Twenties*, p. 110.

34. Goodman and Kolodin, *Kingdom of Swing*, p. 75.

35. Quoted in Shapiro and Hentoff, *Hear Me Talkin' to Ya*, pp. 77–78.

36. Mezz Mezzrow and Bernard Wolfe, *Really the Blues* (New York: Random House, 1946), p. 104.

37. Barry Ulanov, *A History of Jazz in America* (New York: Viking Press, 1952), pp. 125–26.

38. Hadlock, *Jazz Masters of the Twenties*, p. 23.

CHAPTER 7

1. *Missouri: An Exhibition in the Library of Congress* (Washington, D.C.: Library of Congress, 1971), p. 17.
2. H. C. McDougal, "Historical Sketch of Kansas City from the Beginning to 1909," *Missouri Historical Review* 4, no. 1 (October 1909): 1–17.
3. Darrell Garwood, *Crossroads of America: The Story of Kansas City* (New York: W. W. Norton and Co., 1948), p. 14.
4. *Where These Rocky Bluffs Meet* (Kansas City, Mo.: Chamber of Commerce, c. 1938), p. 16.
5. Garwood, *Crossroads of America*, p. 32.
6. A. Theodore Brown, *Frontier Community: Kansas City to 1870* (Columbia: University of Missouri Press, 1963), p. 130.
7. Quoted in Henry J. Haskell, "Houn' Dog vs. Art," in *The Taming of the Frontier*, edited by Duncan Aikman (New York: Minton, Balch and Co., 1925), p. 207.
8. Garwood, *Crossroads of America*, p. 321.
9. Ibid., p. 36.
10. *Missouri: An Exhibition*, p. 52
11. Edwin C. McReynolds, *Missouri: A History of the Crossroads State* (Norman: University of Oklahoma Press, 1962), pp. 248–49.
12. *Missouri: An Exhibition*, p. 57.
13. Garwood, *Crossroads of America*, pp. 90–91.
14. Arthur M. Schlesinger, *The Rise of the City, 1878–1898* (New York: Macmillan, 1933), p. 38.
15. Quoted in *Missouri: An Exhibition*, p. 45.
16. Brown, *Frontier Community*, p. 266.
17. Quoted in Garwood, *Crossroads of America*, p. 81.
18. Robert A. Olson, *Kansas City Power and Light Company: The First Ninety Years* (Princeton, N.J.: Princeton University Press, 1972), p. 9.
19. William M. Reddig, *Tom's Town* (New York: J. B. Lippincott, 1947), p. 24.
20. Lyle W. Dorsett, *The Pendergast Machine* (New York: Oxford University Press, 1968), p. 4.
21. Ibid., p. 5.
22. William Allen White, *The Autobiography of William Allen White* (New York: Macmillan, 1946), p. 205.

23. Ibid., p. 209.

24. Dorsett, *The Pendergast Machine*, p. 21.

25. Ibid., pp. 32–33.

26. Garwood, *Crossroads of America*, p. 179.

27. Quoted in Dorsett, *The Pendergast Machine*, p. 48.

28. Ibid., p. 45.

29. Reddig, *Tom's Town*, p. 123.

30. Dorsett, *The Pendergast Machine*, p. 87.

31. Reddig, *Tom's Town*, p. 145.

32. Maurice M. Milligan, *The Inside Story of the Pendergast Machine by the Man Who Smashed It* (New York: Charles Scribner's Sons, 1948), p. 105.

33. Ibid., p. 10.

34. Reddig, *Tom's Town*, p. 250.

35. John Otey Walker, "Fiction Is a Police Curse: What Are the Facts," *American City*, August 1929, pp. 85–88.

36. Milligan, *The Inside Story*, pp. 11–12.

37. Ibid., p. 18.

38. Ibid., p. 84

39. Ibid.

40. Ross Russell, *Bird Lives! The High Life and Hard Times of Charlie (Yardbird) Parker* (New York: Charterhouse, 1973), p. 50.

41. Garwood, *Crossroads of America*, p. 300.

42. Reddig, *Tom's Town*, p. 321.

43. Ibid., p. 277.

44. Ibid., p. 277–78.

CHAPTER 8

1. Quoted in Gordon Stevenson, "A Brief History of Jazz in Kansas City" (manuscript collection, Missouri Valley Room, Kansas City [Mo.] Public Library, 1965).

2. Henry J. Haskell, "Houn' Dog vs. Art," in *The Taming of the Frontier*, edited by Duncan Aikman (New York: Minton, Balch and Co., 1925) p. 229.

3. Quoted in Rudi Blesh and Harriet Janis, *They All Played Ragtime* (New York: Oak Publications, 1966), p. 20.

4. H. W. Schwartz, *Bands of America* (New York: Doubleday, 1957), p. 130.

5. William Allen White, *The Autobiography of William Allen White* (New York: Macmillan, 1946), p. 211.

6. Ibid., p. 253.

7. Stevenson, "Brief History of Jazz," pp. 1–8.

8. Schwartz, *Bands of America*, p. 287.

9. Ibid., pp. 225–26.

10. Dave Dexter, *The Jazz Story* (Englewood Cliffs, N.J.: Prentice-Hall, 1964), p. 76.

11. William M. Reddig, *Tom's Town* (New York: J. B. Lippincott, 1947), p. 176.

12. Ibid., p. 88.

13. Ibid., p. 27.

14. Shifra Stein, "Renewal Effort at 18th and Vine," *Kansas City Star*, January 6, 1977, section C.

15. Quoted in Jess Ritter, "Goin Out," *Kansas City Times*, January 2, 1976, p. 8D.

16. Ross Russell, *Jazz Style in Kansas City and the Southwest* (Berkeley: University of California Press, 1971), p. 19.

17. Ibid., p. 16.

18. Quoted in Nat Hentoff, "Jazz in the Twenties: Garvin Bushell," in *Jazz Panorama*, edited by Martin Williams (New York: Crowell-Collier, 1962), pp. 71–90.

19. *New York Times*, February 12, 1922, p. 1.

20. Franklin S. Driggs, "Kansas City and the Southwest," in *Jazz*, edited by Nat Hentoff and Albert J. McCarthy (New York: Rinehart and Co., 1959), p. 193.

21. Ibid., p. 194.

22. Ibid., p. 206.

23. Stanley Dance, "Kansas City Perspective," *Saturday Review*, July 31, 1965, p. 607.

24. Raymond Horricks, *Count Basie and His Orchestra* (London: Victor Gollancz, 1957), p. 43.

25. Quoted in Frank Driggs, "Andy Kirk's Story," in Williams, *Jazz Panorama*, pp. 124–25.

26. Quoted in Nat Shapiro and Nat Hentoff, eds., *Hear Me Talkin' to Ya* (New York: Rinehart and Co., 1955), p. 298.

27. Driggs, "Kansas City and the Southwest"; Dexter, *The Jazz Story*; Russell, *Jazz Style*; Gunther Schuller, *Early Jazz: Its Roots and Musical Development* (New York: Oxford University Press, 1968); Horricks, *Count Basie*.

28. Leroy Ostransky, *The Anatomy of Jazz* (Seattle: University of Washington Press, 1960), p. 205.

29. Russell, *Jazz Style*, p. 50.

30. Schuller, *Early Jazz*, p. 284.

31. Hsio Wen Shih, "The Spread of Jazz and the Big Bands," in Hentoff and McCarthy, *Jazz*, pp. 173–87.

32. Schuller, *Early Jazz*, p. 271.

33. Russell, *Jazz Style*, p. 212.

CHAPTER 9

1. Stanley Walker, *The Night Club Era* (New York: Blue Ribbon Books, 1933), pp. 68–69.

2. Ibid., p. 88.

3. Benny Goodman and Irving Kolodin, *The Kingdom of Swing* (Harrisburg, Pa.: Stackpole and Co., 1939), p. 101.

4. Walker, *The Night Club Era*, p. 201.

5. Ibid., pp. 158–59.

6. Albert McCarthy, *Big Band Jazz* (New York: G. P. Putnam's Sons, 1974), p. 40.

7. "Barron D. Wilkins Slain," *New York Times*, May 25, 1924.

8. Denis Tilden Lynch, *"Boss" Tweed* (New York: Boni & Liveright, 1927), p. 15.

9. James F. Richardson, "To Control the City: The New York Police in Historical Perspective," in *Cities in American History*, edited by Kenneth T. Jackson and Stanley K. Schultz (New York: Alfred A. Knopf, 1972), p. 282.

10. Herbert Asbury, *The Gangs of New York* (New York: Alfred A. Knopf, 1929), p. 186.

11. William B. Northrup and John B. Northrup, *The Insolence of Office* (New York: G. P. Putnam's Sons, 1932), pp. 3–4.

12. Quoted in Gene Fowler, *Beau James* (New York: Viking Press, 1949), p. 72.

13. Carolyn F. Ware, *Greenwich Village, 1920–1930* (Boston: Houghton Mifflin Co., 1935), p. 269.

14. Fowler, *Beau James*, p. 74.

15. Ibid., p. 92.

16. Ibid., p. 137.

17. Ibid., p. 230.

18. Northrup and Northrup, *The Insolence of Office*, p. 102.

19. Langston Hughes, "My Early Days in Harlem," in *Harlem: A Community in Transition*, edited by John Henrik Clarke (New York: Citadel Press, 1964), p. 63.

20. Quoted in Nathan Irvin Huggins, *Harlem Renaissance* (New York: Oxford University Press, 1971), p. 292.

21. Roi Ottley, *New World A-Coming* (Boston: Houghton Mifflin Co., 1943), p. 59.

22. Huggins, *Harlem Renaissance*, p. 9.

23. Ibid., p. 64.

24. Eileen Southern, *The Music of Black Americans* (W.W. Norton, 1971), pp. 412–46.

25. Ira Rosenwaike, *Population History of New York City* (Syracuse, N.Y.: Syracuse University Press, 1972), p. 76.

26. Gilbert Osofsky, *The Making of a Ghetto* (New York: Harper & Row, 1966), p. 71.

27. Ibid., p. 78.

28. Ibid., p. 81.

29. Ibid., p. 4.

30. Rosenwaike, *Population History*, p. 77.

31. Seth M. Scheiner, *Negro Mecca* (New York: New York University Press, 1965), p. 221.

32. Osofsky, *The Making of a Ghetto*, p. 32.

33. Scheiner, *Negro Mecca*, p. 20.

34. Nathan Glazer and Daniel P. Moynihan, *Beyond the Melting Pot* (Cambridge: MIT Press and Harvard University Press, 1963), p. 28.

35. John Walker Harrington, "What Tempts Harlem's Palate?" *New York Times*, July 15, 1928.

36. Beverly Smith, "Population Rises Steadily . . .," *New York Herald Tribune*, February 10, 1930.

CHAPTER 10

1. Frank Dolan, "Harlem Breakfast Caps Gotham Night," *New York Daily News*, October 31, 1929.

2. Frank Dolan, "Socialites Mix in Harlem Orb," *New York Daily News*, November 1, 1929.

3. James Weldon Johnson, *Black Manhattan* (New York: Arno Press, 1968), pp. 179–80.

4. Roi Ottley, *New World A-Coming* (Boston: Houghton Mifflin Co., 1943), p. 62.

5. Danny Barker, "Jelly Roll Morton in New York," in *Jazz Panorama*, edited by Martin Williams (New York: Crowell-Collier, 1962), p. 14.

6. Samuel B. Charters and Leonard Kunstadt, *Jazz: A History of the New York Scene* (New York: Doubleday, 1962), p. 198.

7. Quoted in ibid., p. 201.

8. Johnson, *Black Manhattan*, p. 162.

9. Otis Ferguson, "Breakfast Dance in Harlem," *New Republic*, February 12, 1936, p. 15.

10. Frank Dolan, "Speaks Whoop after Clubs Pipe Down," *New York Sunday News*, November 3, 1929.

11. Quoted in Tom Davin, "Conversation with James P. Johnson," in Williams, *Jazz Panorama*, p. 51.

12. Quoted in ibid., p. 52.

13. Quoted in ibid., pp. 60–61.

14. Rudi Blesh, *Shining Trumpets: A History of Jazz* (New York: Alfred A. Knopf, 1958), p. 274.

15. Quoted in Davin, "Conversation with James P. Johnson," p. 52.

16. Orrin Keepnews, "Art Tatum," in *The Jazz Makers*, edited by Nat Shapiro and Nat Hentoff (New York: Rinehart and Co., 1957), pp. 151–53.

17. Charters and Kunstadt, *Jazz: The New York Scene*, pp. 24–26.

18. Gunther Schuller, *Early Jazz: Its Roots and Early Development* (New York: Oxford University Press, 1968), p. 249.

19. Barry Ulanov, *A History of Jazz in America* (New York: Viking Press, 1952), p. 148.

20. Frank Driggs, "Don Redman, Jazz Composer-Arranger," in Williams, *Jazz Panorama*, p. 95.

21. Ibid., p. 92.

22. Schuller, *Early Jazz*, p. 318.

23. Whitney Balliett, "Celebration for the Duke," *Saturday Review*, May 12, 1956, p. 30.

24. Schuller, *Early Jazz*, p. 332.

25. "Duke's Music for Amos 'n' Andy," *Amsterdam News*, July 9, 1930.

26. Marshall Stearns, *The Story of Jazz* (New York: Oxford University Press, 1958), p. 133.

27. Nathan Irvin Huggins, *Harlem Renaissance* (New York: Oxford University Press, 1971), pp. 89–90.

28. Ibid., p. 90.

29. H. O. Brunn, *The Story of the Original Dixieland Jazz Band* (Baton Rouge: Louisiana State University Press, 1960), pp. 52, 57.

30. Charters and Kunstadt, *Jazz: The New York Scene*, pp. 76–77.

31. Donald Russell Connor, *B. G.—Off the Record* (Fairless Hills, Pa.: Gaildonna Publishers, 1958), p. 11.

32. Quoted in Eddie Condon and Richard Gehman, eds., *Eddie Condon's Treasury of Jazz* (New York: Dial Press, 1956), p. 263.

33. Quoted in Nat Shapiro and Nat Hentoff, eds., *Hear Me Talkin' to Ya* (New York: Rinehart and Co., 1955), p. 304.

34. Leroy Ostransky, *The Anatomy of Jazz* (Seattle, University of Washington Press, 1960), p. 224.

35. Charters and Kunstadt, *Jazz: The New York Scene*, p. 242.

36. Richard Hadlock, *Jazz Masters of the Twenties* (New York: Macmillan, 1965), p. 152.

37. Hsio Wen Shih, "The Spread of Jazz and the Big Bands," in *Jazz*, edited by Nat Hentoff and Albert McCarthy (New York: Rinehart and Co., 1959), pp. 186–87.

A
SELECTED
BIBLIOGRAPHY

NEW ORLEANS

APTHEKER, HERBERT. *A Documentary History of the Negro People in the United States.* New York: Citadel Press, vol. 1, 1949; vol. 2, 1973.

ASBURY, HERBERT. *The French Quarter.* New York: Garden City Publishing Co., 1938.

BLASSINGAME, JOHN W. *Black New Orleans, 1860–1880.* Chicago: University of Chicago Press, 1973.

CABLE, GEORGE W. *The Negro Question.* New York: W. W. Norton, 1958.

———. *Old Creole Days.* New York: Charles Scribner's Sons, 1900.

CAPERS, GERALD M. *Occupied City: New Orleans Under the Federals, 1862–1865.* Lexington: University of Kentucky Press, 1965.

CARTER, HODDING. *Lower Mississippi.* New York: Farrar and Rinehart, 1942.

———, ed. *The Past as Prelude.* New Orleans: Pelican Publishing House, 1968.

CASH, W. J. *The Mind of the South.* New York: Vintage Books, 1941.

EATON, CLEMENT. *Freedom of Thought in the Old South.* New York: Peter Smith, 1951.

FRANKLIN, JOHN HOPE. *From Slavery to Freedom.* 3rd ed. New York: Alfred A. Knopf, 1967.

GAYARRÉ, CHARLES E. A. *History of Louisiana*, 3rd ed. 4 vols. New York: AMS Press, 1972.

HERSKOVITS, MELVILLE J. *The American Negro.* Bloomington: Indiana University Press, 1964.

JACKSON, JOY J. *New Orleans in the Gilded Age.* Baton Rouge: Louisiana State University Press, 1969.

KING, GRACE. *Creole Families of New Orleans.* New York: Macmillan, 1921.

REINDERS, ROBERT C. *End of an Era: New Orleans, 1850–1860.* New Orleans: Pelican Publishing Company, 1964.

ROUSSÈVE, M. A. *The Negro in Louisiana.* New Orleans: Xavier University Press, 1937.

SCULLY, ARTHUR JR. *James Dakin, Architect.* Baton Rouge: Louisiana State University Press, 1973.

SHUGG, ROGER W. *Origins of Class Struggle in Louisiana.* Baton Rouge: Louisiana State University Press, 1939.

TWAIN, MARK. *Life on the Mississippi.* New York: Harper and Brothers, 1901.

CHICAGO

ABBOTT, EDITH. *The Tenements of Chicago, 1908–1935*. Chicago: University of Chicago Press, 1936.

ALLSWANG, JOHN M. *A House for All Peoples*. Lexington: University of Kentucky Press, 1971.

CHICAGO COMMISSION ON RACE RELATIONS. *The Negro in Chicago*. Chicago: University of Chicago Press, 1922.

CONDIT, CARL W. *The Chicago School of Architecture*. Chicago: University of Chicago Press, 1964.

DRAKE, ST. CLAIR, AND HORACE R. CAYTON. *Black Metropolis*. New York: Harcourt, Brace and Co., 1945.

DUNCAN, OTIS DUDLEY, AND BEVERLY DUNCAN. *The Negro Population of Chicago*. Chicago: University of Chicago Press, 1957.

ELY, RICHARD T., ed. *Hull-House Maps and Papers*. New York: Thomas Y. Crowell, 1895.

FEDERAL WRITERS PROJECT. *Illinois*. Chicago: A. C. McClurg and Co., 1939.

GOSNELL, HAROLD F. *Negro Politicians*. Chicago: University of Chicago Press, 1935; with new introduction, 1967.

HERBST, ALMA. *The Negro in the Slaughtering and Meat-Packing Industry in Chicago*. New York: Houghton Mifflin Co., 1932.

JACKSON, KENNETH T., AND S. K. SCHULTZ, eds. *Cities in American History*. New York: Alfred A. Knopf, 1972.

KORNFELD, JACK P., ed. *A Study of Organized Crime in Illinois*. Illinois Law Enforcement Commission, 1972.

PIERCE, BESSIE LOUISE. *A History of Chicago*. 3 vols. New York: Alfred A. Knopf, 1937.

RECKLESS, WALTER C. *Vice in Chicago*. Chicago: University of Chicago Press, 1933.

SIRJAMAKI, JOHN. *The Sociology of Cities*. New York: Random House, 1964.

SPEAR, ALLAN H. *Black Chicago*. Chicago: University of Chicago Press, 1967.

STEFFENS, LINCOLN. *The Shame of the Cities*. New York: McClure, Phillips and Co., 1904.

WENDT, LLOYD, AND HERMAN KOGAN. *Big Bill of Chicago*. New York: Bobbs-Merrill, 1953.

KANSAS CITY

AIKMAN, DUNCAN, ed. *The Taming of the Frontier.* New York: Minton, Balch and Co., 1925.

BROWN, A. THEODORE. *Frontier Community: Kansas City to 1870.* Columbia: University of Missouri Press, 1963.

DORSETT, LYLE W. *The Pendergast Machine.* New York: Oxford University Press, 1968.

GARWOOD, DARRELL. *Crossroads of America: The Story of Kansas City.* New York: W. W. Norton, 1948.

KANSAS CITY CHAMBER OF COMMERCE. *Where These Rocky Bluffs Meet.* Kansas City, Mo.: Chamber of Commerce, c. 1938.

OLSON, ROBERT A. *Kansas City Power and Light Company: The First Ninety Years.* Princeton, N. J.: Princeton Universtiy Press, 1972.

MC REYNOLDS, EDWIN C. *A History of the Crossroads State.* Norman: University of Oklahoma Press, 1962.

MILLIGAN, MAURICE M. *The Inside Story of the Pendergast Machine by the Man Who Smashed It.* New York: Charles Scribner's Sons, 1948.

Missouri: An Exhibition in the Library of Congress. Washington, D.C.: Library of Congress, 1971.

REDDIG, WILLIAM M. *Tom's Town.* New York: J. B. Lippincott Co., 1947.

SCHLESINGER, ARTHUR MEIER. *The Rise of the City, 1878–1898.* New York: Macmillan, c. 1933.

THOMAS, TRACY, AND WALT BODINE. *Right Here in River City.* New York: Doubleday and Co., 1976.

TREXLER, HARRISON ANTHONY. *Slavery in Missouri, 1804–1865.* Johns Hopkins University Studies. Baltimore: Johns Hopkins Press, 1914.

WHITE, WILLIAM ALLEN. *The Autobiography of William Allen White.* New York: Macmillan, 1946.

NEW YORK CITY

ASBURY, HERBERT. *The Gangs of New York.* New York: Alfred A. Knopf, 1929.

CLARKE, JOHN HENRIK. *Harlem: A Community in Transition.* New York: Citadel Press, 1964.

FEDERAL WRITERS PROJECT. *New York City Guide.* New York: Random House, 1939.

FOWLER, GENE. *Beau James.* New York: Viking Press, 1949.

GAYLE, ADDISON JR., ed. *The Black Aesthetic.* New York: Doubleday, 1971.

GLAZER, NATHAN, AND DANIEL P. MOYNIHAN. *Beyond the Melting Pot.* Cambridge: MIT Press and Harvard University Press, 1963.

HUGGINS, NATHAN IRVIN. *Harlem Renaissance.* New York: Oxford University Press, 1971.

JACKSON, KENNETH T., AND S. K. SCHULTZ, eds. *Cities in American History.* New York: Alfred A. Knopf, 1972.

JOHNSON, JAMES WELDON. *Black Manhattan.* New York: Arno Press, 1968 (originally published 1930).

LYNCH, DENIS TILDEN. *"Boss" Tweed.* New York: Boni & Liveright, 1927.

NORTHRUP, WILLIAM B., AND JOHN B. NORTHRUP. *The Insolence of Office.* New York: G. P. Putnam's Sons, 1932.

OSOFSKY, GILBERT. *Harlem: The Making of a Ghetto.* New York: Harper & Row, 1966.

OTTLEY, ROI. *New World A-Coming.* Boston: Houghton Mifflin Co., 1943.

ROSENWAIKE, IRA. *Population History of New York City.* Syracuse, N.Y.: Syracuse University Press, 1972.

SCHEINER, SETH M. *Negro Mecca.* New York: New York University Press, 1965.

SCHLESINGER, ARTHUR MEIER. *The Rise of the City, 1878–1898.* New York: Macmillan, 1933.

SCHOENER, ALLON, ed. *Harlem on My Mind.* New York: Random House, 1968.

WALKER, STANLEY. *The Night Club Era.* New York: Blue Ribbon Books, 1933.

WARE, CAROLYN F. *Greenwich Village, 1920–30.* Boston: Houghton Mifflin Co., 1935.

WHITE, E. B. *Here Is New York.* New York: Harper and Brothers, 1949.

THE MUSIC

ARMSTRONG, LOUIS. *Satchmo.* New York: New American Library, 1955.

BARTÓK, BÉLA. *Hungarian Folk Music.* New York: Oxford University Press, 1931.

BECHET, SIDNEY. *Treat It Gentle.* New York: Hill and Wang, 1960.

BLESH, RUDI. *Shining Trumpets.* Rev. ed. New York: Alfred A. Knopf, 1958.

——, AND HARRIET JANIS. *They All Played Ragtime.* New York: Oak Publications, 1966.

BRUNN, H. O. *The Story of the Original Dixieland Jazz Band.* Baton Rouge: Louisiana State University Press, 1960.

BUERKLE, JACK V., AND DANNY BARKER. *Bourbon Street Black.* New York: Oxford University Press, 1973.

CHARTERS, SAMUEL B. *Jazz: New Orleans, 1885–1957.* Belleville, N.J.: Walter C. Allen, 1958. Rev. ed.—New York: Oak Publications, 1963.

—— AND LEONARD KUNSTADT. *Jazz: A History of the New York Scene.* New York: Doubleday, 1962.

COLLINS, LEE. *Oh, Didn't He Ramble: The Life Story of Lee Collins.* As told to Mary Collins. Edited by Frank J. Gillis and John W. Miner. Urbana: University of Illinois Press, 1974.

CONDON, A. E., AND H. O'NEAL. *The Eddie Condon Scrapbook of Jazz.* New York: St. Martin's Press, 1973.

CONDON, EDDIE. *We Called It Music.* As told to Thomas Sugrue. New York: Henry Holt and Co., 1947.

——, AND RICHARD GEHMAN, eds. *Eddie Condon's Treasury of Jazz.* New York: Dial Press, 1956.

CONNOR, DONALD RUSSELL. *B.G.—Off the Record.* Fairless Hills, Pa.: Gaildonna Publishers, 1958.

DEXTER, DAVE. *The Jazz Story.* Englewood Cliffs, N.J.: Prentice-Hall, Inc., 1964.

DODDS, WARREN. *The Baby Dodds Story.* As told to Larry Gara. Los Angeles: Contemporary Press, 1959.

FINKELSTEIN, SIDNEY. *Jazz: A People's Music.* New York: Citadel Press, 1948.

FOSTER, POPS. *The Autobiography of a New Orleans Jazzman.* As told to Tom Stoddard. Berkeley: University of California Press, 1971.

GITLER, IRA. *Jazz Masters of the Forties.* New York: Macmillan, 1966.

GOODMAN, BENNY, AND IRVING KOLODIN. *The Kingdom of Swing.* Harrisburg, Pa.: Stackpole and Co., 1939.

HADLOCK, RICHARD. *Jazz Masters of the Twenties.* New York: Macmillan, 1965.

HANDY, WILLIAM C. *Father of the Blues: An Autobiography.* New York: Macmillan, 1941.

HENTOFF, NAT, AND ALBERT MC CARTHY, eds. *Jazz.* New York: Rinehart and Co., 1959.

HORRICKS, RAYMOND. *Count Basie and His Orchestra.* New York: Citadel Press, 1958.

HUGGINS, NATHAN IRVIN. *Harlem Renaissance.* New York: Oxford University Press, 1971.

JONES, A. M. *Studies in African Music.* 2 vols. London: Oxford University Press, 1959.

KATZ, BERNARD, ed. *The Social Implications of Early Negro Music in the United States.* New York: Arno Press, 1969.

KEEPNEWS, ORRIN, AND BILL GRAUER. *A Pictorial History of Jazz.* New York: Crown Publishers, 1955.

KENNINGTON, D. *The Literature of Jazz.* American Library Assoc., 1971.

KMEN, HENRY. *Music in New Orleans: The Formative Years, 1791–1841.* Baton Rouge: Louisiana State University Press, 1967.

LEONARD, NEAL. *Jazz and the White Americans.* Chicago: University of Chicago Press, 1962.

LOMAX, ALAN. *Mister Jelly Roll.* New York: Duell, Sloan and Pearce, 1950.

MC CARTHY, ALBERT. *Big Band Jazz.* New York: G. P. Putnam's Sons, 1974.

MELLERS, W. *Music in a New Found Land.* London: Barrie and Rockliff, 1964.

MERRIAM, ALAN P., WITH ROBERT J. BANFORD. *A Bibliography of Jazz.* Philadelphia: American Folklore Society, 1954.

MEZZROW, MEZZ, AND BERNARD WOLFE. *Really the Blues.* New York: Random House, 1946.

OSTRANSKY, LEROY. *The Anatomy of Jazz.* Seattle: University of Washington Press, 1960; reprinted—Westport, Conn.: Greenwood Press, 1973.

RAMSEY, F. *Been Here and Gone.* New Brunswick, N.J.: Rutgers University Press, 1960.

RAMSEY, FREDERIC, JR., AND CHARLES EDWARD SMITH, eds. *Jazzmen.* New York: Harcourt, Brace and Co., 1939.

ROSE, AL. *Storyville, New Orleans.* University: University of Alabama Press, 1974.

——, AND EDMOND SOUCHON. *New Orleans Jazz: A Family Album.* Baton Rouge: Louisiana State University Press, 1967.

RUSSELL, ROSS. *Bird Lives! The High Life and Hard Times of Charlie (Yardbird) Parker.* New York: Charterhouse, 1973.

——, *Jazz Style in Kansas City and the Southwest.* Berkeley: University of California Press, 1971.

SABLOSKY, IRVING. *American Music.* Chicago: University of Chicago Press, 1969.

SCHAFER, WILLIAM J., AND JOHANNES RIEDEL. *The Art of Ragtime.* Baton Rouge, Louisiana State University Press, 1973.

SCHULLER, GUNTHER. *Early Jazz: Its Roots and Early Development.* New York: Oxford University Press, 1968.

SCHWARTZ, H. W. *Bands of America.* New York: Doubleday, 1957.

SHAPIRO, NAT, AND NAT HENTOFF, eds. *Hear Me Talkin' to Ya.* New York: Rinehart and Co., 1955.

————, eds. *The Jazz Makers.* New York: Rinehart and Co., 1957.

SHAW, ARTIE. *The Trouble with Cinderella.* New York: Farrar, Straus and Young, 1952.

SIMON, GEORGE T. *The Big Bands.* New York: Macmillan, 1967.

SMITH, WILLIE, AND G. HOEFFER. *Music on My Mind: The Memoirs of an American Pianist.* New York: Doubleday, 1964.

SOUTHERN, EILEEN. *The Music of Black Americans: A History.* New York: W. W. Norton, 1971.

STEARNS, MARSHALL. *The Story of Jazz.* New York: Oxford University Press, 1958.

STEVENSON, GORDON. "A Brief History of Jazz in Kansas City." Manuscript collection, Missouri Valley Room, Kansas City (Mo.) Public Library, 1965.

STEWART, REX. *Jazz Masters of the Thirties.* New York: Macmillan, 1971.

SUDHALTER, RICHARD M., AND PHILIP R. EVANS, WITH WILLIAM DEAN-MYATT. *Bix: Man and Legend.* New Rochelle, N.Y.: Arlington House, 1974.

ULANOV, BARRY. *Duke Ellington.* New York: Creative Age, 1946.

————, *A History of Jazz in America.* New York: Viking Press, 1952.

WAREING, CHARLES H., AND GEORGE BARLICK. *Bugles for Beiderbecke.* London: Sidgwick and Jackson, 1958.

WILLIAMS, MARTIN. *Jazz Masters of New Orleans.* New York: Macmillan, 1967.

————, ed. *Jazz Panorama.* New York: Crowell-Collier, 1962.

A
SELECTIVE
DISCOGRAPHY

One of the basic requirements of our selection is that the titles shown be in print and readily available. The records listed below, therefore, are not a collector's list; with one or two exceptions, the records shown are all easily available as of this writing. Two collections are not available in retail stores: records from the Smithsonian Collection and from New World Records. Their mail-order addresses are: Smithsonian Institution, P.O. Box 1641, Washington, D.C. 20013; and New World Records, 3 East 54th Street, New York, N.Y. 10022.

NEW ORLEANS

African and Voodoo

African Ju Ju Witchcraft, Request 5030
Ceremonial and Folk Music, Nonesuch 72063
Drum, Chant, and Instrumental Music, Nonesuch 72073
Ritual Drums of Haiti: Voodoo Trance Music, Lyricord 7279
Ti Roro and Voodoo Drums, Request 733
Tribal, Ritual, and Love Songs, Request 5033

American Background

American Skiffle Bands, Folkways 2610
Birth of Jazz (Music of New Orleans, vol. 4), Folkways 2464
The Blues (Jazz, vol. 2), Folkways 2802
Blues Roots/Mississippi, Folkways RF 14
Traditional Cajun Fiddle, Folkways FM 8361
Cajun Songs, Folkways 4438
Chain Gang, vols. 1 and 2, Stinson 7
Dance Halls (Music of New Orleans, vol. 3), Folkways 2463
The Gospel Ship: Baptist Hymns and White Spirituals from the Southern Mountains, New World Records
Minstrel Days, Golden Crest 3065

Negro Prison Songs, Tradition 1020
John Philip Sousa Conducts Own Marches, Everest 3260E
Jazz, vol. 1: *The South*, Folkways 2801

The Bands

Louis Armstrong, *Genius*, vol. 1: *1923–33*, Columbia CG 30416
Papa Celestin, *Ragtime Band*, Jazzology JCE-21
Dixieland of New Orleans, Golden Crest 3021
Johnny Dodds with Tommy Ladnier, 1923–28, Biograph 12024
Bunk Johnson, *Superior Jazz Band*, Good Time Jazz 12048
Freddie Keppard, 1926, Herwin 101
Jelly Roll Morton, 1923–24, Milestone 47108
Jimmy Noone/Bunk Johnson, *Kings of New Orleans*, Trip 2
King Oliver's Jazz Band, 1923, Smithsonian R 001
Jim Robinson and His New Orleans Band, Biograph CEN-8

Ragtime

Black and White Ragtime, Biograph 12047
Music of Joplin, RCA CRL5-1106
Scott Joplin, *Piano Rolls*, Biograph 1013-14
Wally Rose, *Ragtime Classics*, Good Time Jazz 10034

Anthology

The Smithsonian Collection of Classic Jazz, Smithsonian

CHICAGO

Background

Blues Roots: Chicago, Folkways RF 16
Ma Rainey, Milestone 47021

The Bands (black)

Louis Armstrong, *Genius*, vol. 1: *1923–33*, Columbia CG 30416
Louis Armstrong and Earl Hines, 1928, Smithsonian R 002
New York Jazz Repertory Company, *Music of Armstrong*, Atlantic 1671
Chicago #1 (black) (Jazz, vol. 5), Folkways 2805
Johnny Dodds with Tommy Ladnier, 1923–28, Biograph 12024
Freddie Keppard, 1926, Herwin 101
King Oliver's Jazz Band, 1923, Smithsonian R 001
Jabbo Smith: Trumpet Ace of the 20s, Melodyland 7326-7

The Bands (white)

Bix Beiderbecke, *The Chicago Cornets (1924)*, Milestone 47019
Bix Beiderbecke Story, vols. 1 and 2, Columbia CL-844–45
Chicago #2 (white) (Jazz, vol. 6), Folkways 2806
Best of Eddie Condon, MCA 4071E
Jimmy McPartland/Bobby Hackett, *Shades of Bix*, MCA 4110
Miff Mole: Immortal, Jazzology 5
New Orleans Rhythm Kings, 1922–23, Milestone 47020
Muggsy Spanier, Jazzology 33

Piano

Boogie Woogie Rarities, 1927–43, Milestone 2009
Meade Lux Lewis, *Barrelhouse Piano*, Archive of Folk and Jazz 268E

Anthologies

Chicago Jazz, 1925–29, Biograph 12043
Jive at Five: The Style-Makers of Jazz, 1920s–1940s, New World Records
Original Dixieland Jazz Band and others, *Best of Dixieland*, RCA ANL1-1431E
The Smithsonian Collection of Classic Jazz, Smithsonian

KANSAS CITY

Bands

The Best of Basie, MCA 4050E
Count Basie, *Good Morning Blues (1937–39),* MCA 4108
Count Basie, *Kansas City Seven,* Impulse S-15
Buck Clayton/Buddy Tate, *K.C. Nights,* Prestige 24040
Coleman Hawkins, Archive of Folk and Jazz 252
The Best of Andy Kirk and Clouds of Joy, MCA 4105
Lester Young with Kansas City Seven, *Prez Leaps Again,* Soul P5015

Piano

Barrelhouse Piano, 1921–36, Yazoo 1028E
Boogie Woogie, Jump, and Kansas City (Jazz, vol. 10), Folkways 2810
Music of Scott Joplin, RCA CRL5-1106
Wally Rose, *Ragtime Classics,* Good Time Jazz 10034

Territory Bands

Jammin' for the Jackpot: Big Bands and Territory Bands of the 30s (includes Moten, Zack Whyte, Boots and His Buddies), New World Records
Sweet and Low Blues: Big Bands and Territory Bands of the 20s (includes Jesse Stone, Troy Floyd, Page's Blue Devils, Alphonso Trent, and others), New World Records
Jack Teagarden, *King of the Blues Trombone,* Columbia Special Products JSN 6044

Anthologies

Count Basie, *From Spirituals to Swing,* Vanguard 47-48
Jimmy Rushing, *The Finest of the Folk Bluesmen,* Bethlehem BCP 6024

The Smithsonian Collection of Classic Jazz, Smithsonian
The Tenor Sax, Atlantic 2-307

NEW YORK CITY

Bands

New York Jazz Repertory Company, *Music of Armstrong,* Atlantic 1671

Young Louis Armstrong, 1932–33, Bluebird AXM2-5519

The Best of Basie, MCA 405OE

Count Basie, *Savoy Ballroom, 1937,* Archive of Folk and Jazz 318

The Bix Beiderbecke Story, vol. 3 (with Paul Whiteman), Columbia CL 846

Willie Bryant—Jimmy Lunceford, Bluebird AXM2-5502

Cab Calloway, *The Hi De Ho Man,* Columbia CG 32593E

Benny Carter, 1933, Prestige 7643E

The Best of Eddie Condon, MCA 4071E

The Best of Jimmy Dorsey, MCA 4073E

The Best of Tommy Dorsey, RCA ANL1-1087E

Duke Ellington, 1938, Smithsonian P2-13367

Duke Ellington at the Cotton Club (not easily available), RCA Camden 459

The Ellington Era, vol. 1, Columbia C3L-27

Gunther Schuller and Jazz Repertory Orchestra, *Music of Ellington,* Golden
    Crest 31041

The Complete Benny Goodman, vols. 1–4, Bluebird AMX2-5505, 5515, 5532,
    5537

Benny Goodman Presents Fletcher Henderson Arrangements, Columbia Special
    Products JGL 524

Benny Goodman Radio Broadcasts, Mark 56736

Erskine Hawkins, *After Hours,* RCA LPM 2227

The Complete Fletcher Henderson, RCA AXM2-5507

Fletcher Henderson: Developing an American Orchestra, 1932–37, Smithsonian
    Collection

Fletcher Henderson, 1923–27, Biograph 12039

The Best of Andy Kirk and Clouds of Joy, Mainstream 299

Eddie Lang and Joe Venuti, *Stringing the Blues* (not easily available), Columbia C2L 24

Jimmie Lunceford, *Lunceford Special*, Columbia CS 9515E

Jimmy McPartland/Bobby Hackett, *Shades of Bix*, MCA 4110

The Immortal Miff Mole, Jazzology 5

Red Nichols and His Five Pennies, Hall 619; Mark 56 612

Original Memphis Five, Folkways RBF-26

The Complete Artie Shaw, vol. 1, RCA AXM2 5517

Muggsy Spanier, Jazzology 33

Jack Teagarden, *In Concert*, Sounds S1203

Joe Venuti Plays Gershwin, Golden Crest 3100

The Best of Chick Webb, MCA 4107

Ben Webster and Coleman Hawkins, *Giants of the Tenor Saxophone*, Columbia PG 32774

The Lester Young Story, vol. 1, Columbia CG 33502

Piano

Eighty-six Years of Eubie Blake, Columbia C2S 847

James P. Johnson, *Father of Stride*, Columbia CL 1780

James P. Johnson, *New York Jazz*, Stinson 21

James P. Johnson, *Johnson Plays Waller*, MCA 4112

The Immortal Jelly Roll Morton, Milestone 2003

Jelly Roll Morton, Archive of Folk and Jazz 267E

Luckey Roberts and Willie Smith, Good Time Jazz 10035

Willie ("The Lion") Smith, *Live at Blues Alley*, Chiarascura 104

Art Tatum, *Rarest Solos*, CMS/Saga 6915

Art Tatum, *Solo Masterpieces*, vols. 4–7, Pablo 2310789–92

Fats Waller Piano Solos (1939–41), Bluebird AXM2-5518

Anthologies

Big Bands before 1935 (Jazz, vol. 8) (Moten, Pollack, and others), Folkways 2808

Big Bands' Greatest Hits, vol. 2, Columbia CG 31213

This Is the Big Band Era (Moten, Tommy Dorsey, and others), RCA VPM 6043

Black and White Ragtime (Morton, James P. Johnson, and others), Biograph 12047

History of Jazz: New York Scene, 1914–45 (James Europe, Charlie Johnson, and others), Folkways RF3

The Music Goes Round and Around: The Golden Years of Tin Pan Alley, 1930–39 (Pha Terrell with Andy Kirk, Ella Fitzgerald with Chick Webb, and others), New World Records

New York, 1922–34 (*Jazz*, vol. 7) (McKinney's Cotton Pickers and others), Folkways 2807

The Original Sound of the Twenties (Whiteman and others), Columbia C3L 35

Parlor Piano (Luckey Roberts and others), Biograph 1001Q

Piano Roll Hall of Fame (Morton, Waller, and others), Sounds S 1202

Sound of Harlem (*Jazz Odyssey*, vol. 3) (James P. Johnson, Bessie Smith, others), Columbia C3L-33

Stars of the Apollo (Buck and Bubbles, Claude Hopkins, Pearl Bailey, and others), Columbia CG 31788

Steppin' on the Gas: Rags to Jazz, 1913–1927 (James Europe, New Orleans Rhythm Kings, and others), New World Records

The Smithsonian Collection of Classic Jazz, Smithsonian

The World of Swing, Columbia PG 32945

Yes Sir, That's My Baby: The Golden Years of Tin Pan Alley, 1920–1929 (Armstrong's "Ain't Misbehavin' " and others), New World Records

INDEX